D0945350

Pushing the Faith

Stanley M. Wagner, General Editor

EDITORIAL COMMITTEE

PUSHING THE FAITH

——— ◆ ———

Proselytism and Civility in a Pluralistic World

Edited by Martin E. Marty
and Frederick E. Greenspahn

CROSSROAD • NEW YORK

1988

The Crossroad Publishing Company
370 Lexington Avenue, New York, N.Y. 10017

Copyright © 1988 by University of Denver (Colorado Seminary)

Printed in the United States of America

Library of Congress Cataloging-in-Publication Data

Pushing the faith : proselytism and civility in a pluralistic world /
edited by Martin E. Marty and Frederick E. Greenspahn.
   p.   cm.
   Papers from a symposium sponsored by the University of Denver
Center for Judaic Studies and made possible by funding from the
Phillips Foundation.
   Contents: Religions, worlds, and order / Charles H. Long —
Modernity and pluralism / Benton Johnson — The place of other
religions in ancient Jewish thought, with particular reference to
early rabbinic Judaism / Robert Goldberg—Joining the Jewish
people from Biblical to modern times / Robert M. Seltzer —
Proselytism and exclusivity in early Christianity / John G. Gager —
Christianity, culture, and complications / William R. Hutchison —
Changes in Roman Catholic attitudes toward proselytism and mission /
Robert J. Schreiter — Fundamentalists proselytizing Jews / Nancy T.
Ammerman — The psychology of proselytism / H. Newton Malony —
Proselytizing processes of the new religions / James T. Richardson.
   ISBN 0-8245-0871-8
   1. Proselytes and proselyting, Jewish—Congresses. 2. Missions-
-Congresses. I. Marty, Martin E., 1928– . II. Greenspahn,
Frederick E., 1946– . III. University of Denver. Center for
Judaic Studies. IV. Phillips Foundation of Minneapolis (Minn.)
BM729.P7P6   1988
291.7—dc19   88-3719
                                                                CIP

Contents

Foreword

This volume is the fifth on "Jewish and Christian Traditions" to emerge out of the Phillips Symposia sponsored by the University of Denver's Center for Judaic Studies. These works make available the scholarship and insights of those who have focused their research on the interrelationship between the Christian and Jewish heritages. We are grateful both to Frederick Greenspahn and the editorial committee working with him for organizing these outstanding symposia and, with Martin Marty, editing these works.

The subject of "Proselytism and Civility in a Pluralistic World" has a special fascination in our age, with its openness and acceptance on the one hand and missionary, salvationist zeal on the other. The Western democratic tradition, which encourages pluralism and self-assertion, affirmation and tolerance, makes the contemporary scene so very different from the historic relationship between Christendom and the Jewish people. The erudite scholars who have contributed to this collection have both delicately and impressively enriched us intellectually in a field of inquiry in which, often, more heat is generated than light.

We especially wish to express our indebtedness to Dr. Paula Bernstein and the Phillips Foundation for funding our original symposium and to the University of Denver for its perennial encouragement and support.

Before exploring the scholarly treasure of this volume, we might ponder these poet's words:

> At the muezzin's call for prayer,
> The kneeling faithful thronged the square,
> And on Pushkara's lofty height
> The dark priest chanted Brahma's might.
> Amid a monastery's weeds
> An old Franciscan told his beads;
> While to the Synagogue there came
> A Jew to praise Jehovah's name.
> The one great God looked down and smiled

And counted each His loving child;
For Turk and Brahmin, monk and Jew
Had reached Him through the gods they knew.

(Harry Romaine: *Ad Coelum*)

Stanley M. Wagner, Director
Center for Judaic Studies
University of Denver

Introduction

Many Christians, Muslims, and Jews view monotheism as both a truer and a higher form of religion than other beliefs. Such people regard it as not just quantitatively different, but qualitatively better than other faiths; indeed, they often think of monotheism as *the* critical distinction between advanced (Western) religion and primitive paganism.

The roots of Western monotheism reach back to the Hebrew Bible, where Israel's God is identified as the Creator of the world. As such, He controlled not only the fate of this one people, but also of her neighbors and her enemies. The prophets taught that God used other nations to work His will on Israel, whether to punish her sins or to deliver her from suffering. Isaiah described Assyria as the "rod of God's anger," just as a later generation saw the Persian Emperor Cyrus as His anointed one.[1]

To ascribe the activities of other people to God's will meant that they were subject to Him, too. Thus the prophets did not hesitate to pass judgment on the nations and even looked forward to a time when they would all recognize Israel's God and say, "Come, let us go up to the Lord's mountain, to the house of Jacob's God, so that He may instruct us in His ways and we may walk in His paths."[2]

Such views leave no room for other gods. Theological universalism is thus intimately bound up with monotheism. Related to this is the conclusion that other religions' deities are either impotent or illusory. In the prophet's words, "Thus says the Lord . . . 'I am the first and I am the last, and there is no god but Me.'"[3]

Israel's religion did not earn the success that its proponents felt it deserved; instead, the Jews spent the better part of their history living alongside people who were unimpressed by their one God. This incongruity between theological universalism and an all too particularistic reality no doubt strengthened their conviction. The belief in a universal God, joined with Israel's need to define and justify her distinctiveness, thereby played a significant role in forming the exclusivism so familiar in both Judaism and Christianity.

The ancient rabbi who taught that "non-Jews have no portion in the world to come" would have had little difficulty understanding the bishop who asserted, "There is no salvation outside of the church" *(salus extra Ecclesiam non est).*[4] Such statements are a source of reassurance for the communities in which they are made, reminding adherents that being different has its compensations as well as its price. The resulting sense of superiority strengthens the members of that community, enabling them to endure persecution and even martyrdom. However, it can also encourage less passive behavior, such as idol-smashing,[5] and has often stimulated proselytizing activities. Jesus is reported to have said that some Jews traveled "over sea and land to make a single convert," which is evidently similar to what he commanded his own apostles: "Go and make disciples of all the nations, baptizing them in the name of the Father and the Son and the Holy Spirit."[6]

Judaism spread widely through the Mediterranean basin as its adherents bore witness to their monotheistic conviction. Christianity's missionary impulse resulted in a similar expansion, until it became the official faith of the Roman Empire in the fourth century, its triune God replacing the multiplicity of pagan deities.

The sixteenth-century exploration and colonization opened up new worlds, vibrant with many religions. This challenged the Church to a vast missionary effort through which, it was hoped, the entire world would be both civilized and Christianized. But the dream was only partially realized. Not only did the world's major religions resist evangelization, they renewed themselves and expanded their own influence.[7]

Within Europe and the West, the Enlightenment posed a different challenge to exclusivistic claims. Religious uniformity was no longer seen as necessary to national unity; so the nation-state's concern with religion was significantly altered. Each tradition was to be ensured equal treatment, but none officially endorsed. In Rousseau's words, "There are, and can be, no longer any exclusive national religions, [therefore] we should tolerate all creeds which show tolerance to others."[8]

Institutionalizing pluralism was more difficult than articulating it. Exclusivistic doctrines did not simply disappear in order to conform with the newly expected public toleration. The result was a kind of ideological schizophrenia. "Inwardly, to their communicants, [religions] continue to assert that they possess the only complete version of the truth. But outwardly, in their civic relation with other churches and with the civil power, they preach and practice toleration."[9]

This situation was complicated by the very nature of a pluralistic society, in which religious privacy is structurally impossible. The inevitable interaction of religious communities makes even limited claims of superiority problematic. Beliefs that "we alone are saved" are not heard by believers alone, but also those outside the community. Originally self-justifying statements thus become something of an embarrassment, at the very least. Translated into action, even such benign rubrics as "witnessing" are inevitably perceived as threatening and judged to have breached the etiquette of pluralism.[10] Conviction and civility are now at odds.

Various communities have tried different ways of alleviating the tension between the apparent demands of their theological rhetoric and the convention of social pluralism. Most modern countries have seen fit to tolerate proselytizing activities that are not socially disruptive. Following logically from the high value accorded freedom of expression, this is no doubt facilitated by the view that religion is part of a person's private life and therefore not properly subject to government interference. Nations in which such behavior is prohibited or closely regulated—Israel and Greece come most readily to mind, along with many Muslim and Communist countries—are also those in which religion (or totalistic ideologies) are integral parts of the community's self-understanding and not, therefore, a purely private affair. Such laws may be understood as efforts to limit competition, turning back the clock, as it were, on modernity so as to avoid the stresses that are an inevitable by-product of the interaction of diverse groups in an open society.

Religious communities, too, have had to find ways of accommodating this tension. Some continue to follow the imperative of religious universalism, proselytizing in accordance with what they understand to be long precedent. Using tactics that can range from physical or psychological coercion to rational persuasion, they see the integrity of their own belief system as enhanced whenever it "defeats" competing religions, a reaction that inevitably makes one wonder whether proselytes' salvation is their only goal.

Other groups seek to accommodate social demands for politeness with less obvious forms of evangelism, spreading the message without actively encouraging others to change their affiliation. Possibly seeking to salve consciences guilty from the activities of earlier periods, some have substituted dialogue—with or without evangelistic intentions—for proselytism. Still others claim that, in some mysterious way, the adherents of different religious traditions are "anonymous Christians," a concept with its own subtle imperialism.[11]

Then there are those who reject proselytizing outright and with it anything that looks like evangelism. This attitude is not always benign. Pseudoindifference ("You may believe that, but I certainly don't") entails a sense of superiority, avoiding conflict by raising oneself above all real contact. Tolerant pluralism ("Live and let live") may be equally condescending if its underlying intention is to permit others to persist in their error.

Not all religions proselytize. While some, such as Islam, have engaged in far-reaching missionary activity, others, such as Shinto, do not seem to share that impulse. Nor are individual traditions entirely uniform in their practice. For example, the Hare Krishna movement, which does seek converts, evolved out of Hinduism, which generally does not. Conversely, there are Christian denominations that do not actively proselytize, despite that tradition's deeply rooted evangelical impulse. Indeed, most communities that are old enough and large enough have and have not proselytized at different times or in different places. American Methodists were very much involved in such activities during the eighteenth and nineteenth centuries, although many of their contemporary heirs eschew this practice. Similarly, Jews, who have generally refrained from such efforts, were active proselytizers two thousand years ago, an approach that has attracted increasing interest in recent years.[12]

Although not limited to any one tradition, or even those of a specific region, proselytism is particularly characteristic of certain groups.[13] Traditions which emphasize salvation, however that may be conceived, have strong reasons to spread their message, just as those that make claims as to the exclusive nature of their truth are surely more inclined to evangelism than those who understand their beliefs to be but one of several possible truths. The Christian emphasis on "catholicity" thus stands in radical contrast to what sociologists call "folk" religions, which understand themselves as belonging only to a particular people.[14] This contrast is well illustrated by the seventeenth-century confrontation between American Indians and French Jesuits. As one of the latter reported, "when we preach to them of one God, Creator of Heaven and earth, and of all things, and even when we talk to them of Hell and Paradise and of our other mysteries, the headstrong savages reply that this is good for our Country and not for theirs; that every Country has its own fashions."[15]

A similar cultural gap exists between contemporary Christians and Jews. For Christianity, which "exists by mission, just as a fire exists by burning," the Jewish lack of interest in their message can appear confusing and even elitist.[16] On the other hand, Judaism is not without its own missionary impulse, most vividly manifest in the activities of the Lubavitcher Chassidim. These efforts are, however, directed solely at assimilated Jews, who are to be brought "back to Israel," a goal with which many non-Chassidic groups are fundamentally sympathetic.

This clash of perspectives is sharply reflected in the warning of an Orthodox Jewish organization that "Thousands of Russian Jewish immigrants have escaped the raging flames of Soviet persecution . . . only to be endangered in this country by the raging flames of soul-snatching Christian missionaries. . . . Free clothing, gifts, summer camps and social gatherings are springboards to brainwashing and baptism."[17] The authors of these words proceed to request contributions, explaining their plan to use free educational and social programs to "show these Jewish souls the splendor of our Holy Torah."

For any religious community, identifying the appropriate targets of proselytization is an exercise in self-definition. If "the true church can tolerate no strange church,"[18] then one must decide which churches are strange, an enterprise affected in no small measure by how broad one's own church is understood to be. Should Catholics proselytize Protestants? Or one denomination, members of another? Determining who stands outside the community of the saved forces believers to consider who stands within.

Some have seen cultural advancement as so closely related to Christianity that it must be made a significant part of the missionary enterprise, which is, therefore, to be directed toward "primitive" societies. For those holding this view, religion has served as a wedge, bringing the saving power of "advanced civilization" to cultures whose needs are not purely theological. Similar goals may explain some contemporary groups' interest in the "unchurched," a qualification perhaps also intended to avoid charges of "sheep-stealing" lest their own flock be attacked.[19]

The continuing Christian interest in proselytizing Jews adds yet another dimension to this issue. The fact that Jews are frequently singled out confirms Christendom's obsession with its roots, reflecting the ambivalence of this two-thousand-year parent-child relationship[20] as much as Jews' fear of proselytization betrays their own theological insecurity.[21]

Sociological factors can be as important as theology in determining a group's position on proselytism. Some try to conform to legal or social norms; others intentionally flout such standards. Recruitment may also be critical for institutional survival, particularly in new communities or those without other means of maintaining their numbers. The celibate Shakers are an obvious example, as were their Essene predecessors some two millennia ago.[22] Proselytization also strengthens the commitment of those already in a group, its psychological effects on the missionary being at least as important as the number of new members it generates.

For many of us, children of the Enlightenment and citizens of the modern world, the obtrusiveness of proselytization violates a very deep sense of propriety. Early in this century a leading rabbi, speaking of Judaism's expressed mission to spread ethical monotheism, asked, "Where are its apostles? Mere protestations and assertion do not make an inspired evangelist. We cannot help but ask ourselves if missionaries can flourish in the soil that produces department-store and factory owners, corporation lawyers, labor leaders, itinerant professional propagandists and high-salaried rabbis?"[23] Such observations betray the discrepancy between theological rhetoric and social reality. Our religious commitments may not be based on convictions as deep as we (politely) profess.

These issues cut close to the heart of interfaith relations in contemporary America, where civility sometimes seems in short supply.[24] Whether or not religious communities should proselytize, something no analysis of their motives is likely to affect, exploring these questions can help us understand our own attitudes and behavior, whether as proselytizers, whose activities some find offensive, or as non-proselytizers, whose passivity makes protestations of religious conviction suspect. Bridging these two positions is itself a worthwhile undertaking. "In a world where the religiously committed are not very civil and the religiously civil do not often seem very committed, we look for a new style of consciousness that combines civility and commitment."[25]

Editorial Committee

Part One

Universalism and Pluralism

1

Religions, Worlds, and Order: The Search for Utopian Unities

CHARLES H. LONG

Religious Orientations in Time and Space

Throughout human history, religion has been the most decisive way of defining a cosmos or a world. All meaningful forms of being, structures of human and nonhuman existence, rhythms, actualities, and possibilities are included in this meaning, which refers to the ordered form of the situation that defines the human mode of being. Human identity is recognized and known within this context, the sacrality of which renders a reality and absoluteness of the human mode of being and to those structures that sustain and embody it. Religion, or the sacred, and the identity of a people are thus correlative, forming a relationship of dependency.

This is the reason that the cosmogonic myth or those narratives and modes of behavior that express cosmogonic meaning possess an exemplary prestige in most religious orders, including those which predate the beginnings of urbanization as well as those which stem from city traditions. The myth of the world's beginning has a foundational meaning and provides the basis for a people's creation; the creation of a world and the coming into being of a people are coincidental. Furthermore, the cosmogonic myth centers a people within a particular world and gives them a sense that they have an appropriate and necessary role as a people within that world.

In many so-called tribal societies, the tribe's name means simply "the people" or "the human beings." It states that "we are the people created

3

in this particular world." As in the case of the West African Yoruba, this identification is equally the name given to their language, their gods, their rituals, and the like. It describes the landscape in which they live and the forms of their common life. To speak of "the religion of the Yoruba" is, therefore, redundant and tautological. The meaning of the world and their identification with it fashion the mode of their identity, which *is* their religion.

For the greater part of human history, the basis for a people's identity was religious, revealing a world or cosmos for their habitation. Along with the gods and any other superhuman realities, the world and the meaning of religion defined a geographical locus that enabled them to inhabit their specific space and time. It was within the context of that space that people were who they were. This is what it means to say that religion is a people's ultimate orientation in time and space.

Even in religions of this kind, the meaning of the sacred has a basis that implies a transregional context, though it is not often fully actualized. In the religious sense, this possibility is related to the presence and revelation of a "high god," a Supreme Being who made that particular culture's world and is thus capable of creating all other actual or possible worlds.

With the beginnings of city traditions in the ancient Near East, another meaning of the sacred and order may be discerned.[1] All city traditions presuppose a ceremonial center as their basis. This center is the appearance of a hierophany within the landscape. In itself this is not unique, for such hierophanies existed prior to the beginnings of cities. In precity traditions, however, the hierophanies took on the modality of the forms in which they appeared—such as trees, stones, or water. The symbol of orientational order among Australian Arunta was a sacred pole that they took with them during their peregrinations over the landscape, erecting it wherever they chose to dwell and uprooting it when they moved to another location.

City traditions, which came into being during the Neolithic Age, opened the possibility for the human community to become sedentary, defining themselves as beings who are centered and gain their orientation from living in *one* place. Early cities were built on the sites of ceremonial centers or acknowledged particular ceremonial centers as their origin. The sacrality of city traditions' ceremonial center was revealed not simply in and through objects, but primarily and more importantly in the way in which the sacrality of a particular space was revealed as absolute and effective. The ceremonial center is the revelation of space as sacred and capable of domestication, thus making space itself a category of human habitation. The city form is itself, therefore, the macrosymbol of sedentariness, of which the enclosed shelter of the house and the domestication of plants and animals around the house-holder are microsymbols.

Though the city was located in a specific space and defined by a ceremonial center, it exerted its power and significance over the surrounding territory. Power radiated to wider and wider areas, bringing them under the sovereignty and "domestication" of the city-as-center. Besides the city's religious power being deployed over adjacent spaces, there is also a reverse movement, for while power moves from the center, it equally returns the power of the peripheries back to the center. This centripetal/centrifugal rhythm describes the fundamental motions of the city's religious power. The city's military, economic, and technological activities simulate the same rhythms.

The religion of the city as ceremonial center thus extends itself beyond its region of origin and stabilization. The official cult is defined on the basis of the sacred center, and from here its meanings and rituals are extended to wider areas. The local religions and the gods of adjacent spaces are amalgamated to the interpretive, symbolic, and coercive powers of the ceremonial center in one form or another; in other cases, these religions form a residuum, maintaining the possibility for a more concrete pole of religious experience and expression, even though the region's official religion is defined in terms of the city as imperium. This structure can be seen in the old city traditions of Asia, Africa, and the ancient Near East.

The civilizational religions of ancient cities memorialize the hierophany of their founding in the ceremonial centers by establishing the city as the sedentary meaning of human existence and by extending the meaning of this hierophany to wider, extraregional geographical space. In so doing, localized religions and cults are subordinated to the power and hegemony of the center. Regional loyalties must now be interpreted and screened through the center's hegemonic rituals and belief structures. The modes of relationship through kinship, marriage, and various sorts of exchanges may remain intact, but they are reinterpreted in light of the city-center's officialdom. From one point of view, the civilizational form of religion "domesticates" or amalgamates to itself various and sundry local religious orientations through the actual and empirical realities of trade or conquest. On the symbolic level this can be seen in the extension of familial kinship symbolism through the sharing of common religious symbols and rituals. The unity achieved in the amalgamation of several peoples and spaces into an ordered whole, presided over through the power of the city-center, can be seen as an attempt to bring the multiplicity and pluralities of peoples and spaces into an ordered meaning of the "world" under the hierarchical structures of kinship symbolism. This form of civilizational religion, which expresses itself in the spatial radiation of sacral power, extended the possibility of sacralizing all space, becoming one of the dominant ways in which religious authority was extended over several societies and cultures. In so doing, coercion, rather than persuasion, dominated.

The Religious Community
as Extraregional Hierophany

In the religion that stems from the acts and teachings of the Buddha, the religious community is based on a sacred meaning of extraregional belonging. This is achieved through persuasion rather than coercion or conquest. It is through the *preaching* of the Buddhist monks and their expressions of the monastic order that one becomes a follower of the Buddha. In Buddhism a new religious community, the *sangha,* comes into being, and in the Buddhist notion of *anatta* (no-self) religion's normal structures and symbolisms as part and parcel of kinship ties that are bound to geographical locations and castes are undercut.

The Buddhist notion of "no-self" has deep religious and philosophical implications, but on the practical level it expressed a critical stance toward a meaning of religion that was centered around and located in familial orders and relationships, all of which had been sacralized in Hinduism. From this point of view, the Buddhist notion of "no-self" enunciates religious meaning as a lack, expressed in terms of the loss of the centeredness of the human mode of being which is defined by that centralized meaning called "the self." This critique of the loss of human order implies another critique of the public and geographical meanings of centeredness as a religious principle, thus opening up the meaning of Buddhism as a religion that cannot be defined by a specific ethnic group or geographical location.

This is an ideal meaning of Buddhism. In point of fact, specific local and regional modes of religious life were legitimated as Buddhism spread through Asia and was accepted as the manner in which one held on to local specificity while still participating in an ecumenical order of the world.

A similar situation occurred in Christianity. The Christian story expresses the same sort of religious loss or lack in relationship to its own heritage within the religious traditions of the Hebrews. The symbolism of this is found in the crucifixion of Jesus and his resurrection as Jesus the Christ. The Christian's faith is in the resurrected Lord, who is now in heaven and sits on the right hand of God, the Father. The resurrected body is the body that has died to the older traditions of the Hebrews, their ethnicity, and sacred geography. This body has shed those meanings of religious orientation that would tie it to regional and ethnic specificity.

The Christian admonition, "Go therefore make disciples of all nations" (Matt. 28:19) is similar to the Buddhist notion of preaching to all sentient beings. These teachings undercut those religious traditions out of which Gautama and Jesus arose. How can there be a single religious message of salvation for everyone? The very enunciation of these messages evokes changes and new orientations regarding the nature of the human mode of being and how this mode is situated within a world.

The enunciation of a religious message of salvation for all human beings does not eliminate former religious specificities, but subordinates them. They appear under and through the new universal message in those areas that have accepted this message. Lionel Rothkrug has recently shown how the ethnic specificities of Western Europe were incorporated into Christianity through the cult of relics and the veneration of saints.[2] In this manner European Christianity retained its specificity, producing not "Christianity-in-general," but Gallic Christianity, English Christianity, and German Christianity.

Calvinism creates a different kind of problem. As a reforming movement, Calvinism did not rely on the basic substratum of ethnic and regional belonging. In his critique and restatement of Max Weber's thesis regarding the relationship of Calvinism to capitalism, Benjamin Nelson points out that the Calvinist treatment of the problem of usury destroys the notion of an original or primary community as the basis for religious intimacy.[3] Everyone, whether within or outside of an ethnic or religious community, is an "other." Usury thus becomes a universal principle. In one sense this parallels the meaning of preaching the Gospel to all persons. All are in need of salvation; and if this is so, former ties of ethnic or regional belonging do not constitute an authentic community in the face of the Gospel.

Immigrations, Toleration, and the Religions of No-Place

This has a great deal to do with the nature of human community from a religious point of view. How is this identity made, and what happens to this identity when a religious message is addressed to all human beings? Does one really proselytize everyone, or are some communities exempt?

Within the post-Reformation national communities of Northern Europe, Protestant church groups felt that by and large all groups and persons outside their community were fair prospects for proselytization. It was only those nations that defined the national community through the form of a national church that arrested rampant proselytization within the national community. Such definitions, however, did not deter proselytization altogether; often they led to divisions of such depth that for many groups emigration to new lands seemed the only solution.

The principle of religious toleration was one response to the fragmentation occasioned by the divisions of Protestant Christendom. It expressed a secularized type of universalism that parallels the much older meaning of the city-as-ceremonial-center in which the cultures of Western Europe may be seen as a center. The civilizational meanings are expressed by principles of manners that are appropriate to cosmopolitanism.[4] These manners, which are embedded in the newer conceptions of political order as republicanism and democracy, defined religion as one of an individual's private preferences. Within the civilizational and democratically oriented societies, one's religious preferences were to be respected in the same manner as one's privacy. The most radical form of this is embedded in the American Republic, where it is referred to as the principle of the separation of Church and State. This does not prevent proselytization, but it separates the meaning of religious belonging from the meaning of the national community. To the extent that proselytism was justified within the structure of manners and polite behavior of cosmopolitan and civilizational orders, it was always those who fell outside the meaning of the civilization's manners and morals that were most open to justifiable proselytization.

This complex relationship between the meaning of civilization on the one hand and religious national communities on the other led to some equally complex situations. Roman Catholic and Protestant groups alike felt that all those who fell outside civilizational structures ought to be proselytized, including all cultures outside the Western world. To the extent that various Christian groups defined the general meaning of civilization from a Christian perspective, Jews who lived within the cosmopolitan civilizational orders were also to be proselytized. John Cuddihy points out that the very notions of manners, morals, and politeness emerged from a specifically Christian understanding of the secular, so that Jews were often considered not so much un-Christian as uncivilized within the Christianized, secularized Western culture of the post-Reformation periods.[5] Catherine Albanese has observed that the very formula "Protestant-Catholic-Jew," which expresses the secularized religious identity of the American national community, is in fact the enunciation of a Protestant meaning of toleration and identity.[6]

This raises some peculiar issues regarding religion in America. Unlike Europeans, Americans have mostly rejected the meaning involved in having an aboriginal order in their religious orientation. By this I mean that outside of their political identity as citizens there does not exist another and prior meaning in their identity. Europeans are aware that they possessed an identity as a people prior to their Christianization; conversion to Christianity among the European people only enhanced the meaning of this prior aboriginality. But those Europeans who came to North America did not relate their religious orientations to those of the aborigines as did the Spanish who came to Mexico, for instance. In this country there is no self-conscious resolution of continuity with aboriginal traditions.

From a constitutional point of view, religious bodies in the United States are considered to be voluntary associations, referred to as "denominations." In the United States such bodies are always seen and understood in their plurality; there are several, not one. It is therefore impossible to perceive or understand the manner in which a meaning of the sacred or the gods defines an identifiable group in this space. American religion thus becomes a highly ambivalent phenomenon. Americans pride themselves on their separation from Europe on the one hand and refer to their beginnings as Europeans as their aboriginal meaning on the other. This leaves the meaning of *homo religiosus Americanus* unresolved. The issue of proselytism within the United States becomes, on one level, that of adjudicating the several religious bodies in this country with one another. To the extent that a specific meaning of America is presumed or understood in either theological or secular terms as merely Christian, it tends to limit the religious realities presented within the geographical boundaries of the United States.

Another religious meaning of America might come to the fore if we defined this country through a structure of its meaning as an Aboriginal-Euro-African culture. This affords a way of raising a discourse about what really happened in this time and space we identify as America, and it would allow different and new issues to arise regarding the meaning of the American national community and thus pose other kinds of issues regarding proselytism.[7]

2

Modernity and Pluralism

BENTON JOHNSON

The term "modernity" refers to the civilization that originated in Western Europe several centuries ago and has now influenced in one way or other virtually every section of the globe. Although modernity has certain features that have so far proved stable, its most striking characteristic, especially in comparison to previous civilizations, is its capacity for dynamic change. In fact, it was the rapid acceleration of social change in the late eighteenth and nineteenth centuries that brought social science as we know it into being. All the major founders of sociology and political economy generated theories to explain this pattern of change and discern its implications for the future. It is this dynamic character of our civilization that leads many of today's theorists to prefer the term "modernization," which highlights the processual aspects of modernity. But a warning is in order here: The term "modernization," like the term "modernity" itself, is suspect in some quarters. Accounts of the history and destiny of our civilization differ in important ways. An old-line Marxist would regard most of modernization theory as just so much ideological prattle. And, as we shall see, even those who speak of modernization have serious disagreements on basic issues.

Modernization as an Evolutionary Process

What is modernization? Those who write about it would all agree that it involves the great growth of science and technology, the industrialization of economic production, and the adoption of bureaucratic forms of large-scale organization. Some, like Peter Berger, would identify the very core of modernization as the complex of bureaucracy and technology-driven economic production.[1] Others would include the system of universalistic legal norms, the erosion of the power and influence of traditional religion, and the breakdown of primordial solidarities based on family and community. In my opinion, the most fruitful scheme for thinking about modernization is Talcott Parsons's paradigm of evolutionary change.[2] It is true that his theories have been so severely criticized that many sociologists consider them wrong-headed and obsolete. But it has recently become clear that much of the criticism was itself wrong-headed for the simple reason that it was misinformed. It read Parsons badly and only in part. In any event, a critical reappropriation of Parsons's work is now under way both here and in Europe. Most important for our purposes is the fact that two of the most influential contemporary theorists of modernization, namely Jürgen Habermas and Niklas Luhmann, conceptualize it in evolutionary terms and have drawn heavily, though in rather different ways, on Parsons.[3]

Before developing Parsons's paradigm let me clarify the sense in which I use the term "evolutionary" change. Regarding biological evolution, it is no longer possible to speak of a basic process that leads inevitably to the generation and dominance of higher, more complex forms over lower and simpler ones. To be sure, the simpler forms came first historically, but many complex forms have become extinct and many of the simplest have proved remarkably persistent. Biological evolution is no longer thought of as a ladder but simply as a set of mechanisms governing the development and fate of biological variations. These mechanisms are mutation and genetic recombination, by which variations are generated; natural selection, which screens out certain variations and encourages others; and stabilization, which distributes successful variations within breeding populations. Sociocultural evolution may be analyzed in roughly similar terms, but unlike biological evolution, it involves at least the possibility of assuming a direction. In sociocultural evolution the equivalent of mutation is the exercise of human imagination, and the equivalent of the winnowing process of natural selection tends to favor those exercises of imagination we call inventions and discoveries, exercises that enlarge the autonomy of individuals and groups within their environments. Because inventions and discoveries can be preserved and diffused as part of a cultural tradition, they can accumulate over time, which means that the horizon of human possibilities can in principle be progressively extended. I believe Habermas is right to assume that certain sociocultural innovations cannot easily be forgotten.[4] When the cultural tradition itself actively encourages further innovations, and stabilizing mechanisms for putting them into practice are readily available, the horizon of possibilities can be extended in fact. If one wishes to pronounce this developmental trend a desirable one, then it is possible to speak of a ladder of sociocultural evolution. It is, however, a ladder with no known top.

With these points in mind, let me now present Parsons's paradigm of evolutionary change as a convenient framework for conceptualizing the main processes involved in modernization. The first process is what Parsons calls *differentiation*. It is a key concept—perhaps *the* key concept—in theories of modernization. Differentiation involves the separating of two or more formerly linked elements of a sociocultural tradition and the reorganization of each of them along new and distinct lines. Differentiation occurs at every level of the human enterprise. One of its most familiar and easily understood examples is the relatively recent separation of economic production from family life. Both activities are now organized according to very different principles. In the Christian West, Church and State have been distinct organizations for centuries, and in some nations the state is now thought of as completely secularized. In the West, law has become differentiated from morality, art has become differentiated from religion, fact has become differentiated from value, and people's identities and sense of self-worth have become differentiated from the various roles they occupy. The list is endless.

According to Parsons's paradigm, differentiation must be accompanied by three other processes before it constitutes an evolutionary change. The first of these three is *adaptive upgrading*, which refers to the improved capacity of at least one of the newly differentiated pairs to accomplish its "work," that is, to yield something of value in greater abundance and without undue cost. In the field of economic production we may credit Adam Smith and Charles Babbage with first clearly perceiving the benefits of a division of labor, which is itself, of course, a form of differentiation. Smith saw that productivity would increase if machines were introduced and workers were kept at single tasks, and Babbage proved that costs would decrease if workers did not perform tasks below the level of their highest skills.[5] Regardless of one's moral judgment of the capitalist system, virtually all observers, including Karl Marx, agreed that it resulted in an enormous increase in economic productivity. Moreover, so far as I know, no really successful large-scale industry has fully abandoned Smith's and Babbage's principles. To take another example of adaptive upgrading from an entirely different realm, I think it can be said that the recent differentiation between fact and value has resulted in a more precise, and therefore more serviceable, conception of the meaning of truth.

Parsons's third evolutionary process is *inclusion* of the newly differentiated and upgraded elements in the larger system in which they are imbedded. Essentially this is a process of integrating these elements with others so that they can all operate as effectively and harmoniously as possible. As we will see later, it is often not possible to accomplish this task completely or without friction, but if evolutionary changes are to be stabilized, some degree of inclusion is essential. Adam Smith pointed out, for example, that the benefits of modern production methods could not be achieved unless people were free to start businesses, take up trades, develop markets, and go where the jobs are; in other words, unless they were freed from traditional restrictions on economic activities. The process of opening up access to economic opportunities is still going on and is a classic example of the evolutionary process of inclusion. According to Luhmann, one of the most important stabilizing mechanisms of our highly differentiated society is the principle of equal treatment in terms of the operating rules of each of its major sectors.[6] The great sociologist Emile Durkheim pointed out long ago that social integration—he called it solidarity—could actually be enhanced by a very high degree of the differentiation of tasks because no one could possibly be proficient in all of them and everyone would therefore be dependent on others for most of the services vital to their well-being.[7]

The last of Parsons's evolutionary processes is *value generalization*. Like many sociological theorists, Parsons believed that shared values play a key role in social life. First, they define the desirable type of society, thereby providing a sort of gyroscope that can keep a society on course over time by allowing its institutional structure to be periodically evaluated. And second, when they are embodied in concrete theologies or ideologies, values can mobilize the mass commitment needed for preserving a threatened social order or changing an existing one. The great ideologies of recent times, e.g., Marxism and the millennial theology of the American civil religion, have functioned in just this way. Sociocultural innovations, whether of evolutionary significance or not, must be legitimized if they are to be stabilized. It is not enough that they have adaptive significance or that they fit well with other elements in society; they must also be thought of as morally acceptable. But as society becomes increasingly differentiated and therefore increasingly complex, traditional ideological and theological formulations of its value system are simply too narrow and concrete to legitimize all innovations having evolutionary significance. Hence, as Parsons puts it, a condition of their acceptance is the formulation of more generalized versions of this value system. An example of value generalization from American history is the progression from the notion that "this is a white man's country"—an expression prevalent not so long ago—to a much broader conception of citizenship and human rights.

Before moving on to the subject of pluralism, I should point out that Parsons's paradigm has nothing to say about what triggers evolutionary innovations or whether all societies are destined to climb the ladder of modernization. Perhaps no general statement can be made about how evolutionary innovations are triggered. As Luhmann might put it, such innovations are, like genetic mutations, statistically improbable events. There are many, however, including Parsons himself, who believe that the basic world view—the cognitive and moral codes if you will—that made modernization possible has deep roots in the ancient religious and secular cultures of the West. These codes did not determine the content of particular evolutionary developments, but they may have enhanced the probability that they would occur and, having occurred, that they would be stabilized. As for the future, it seems likely that further modernization will occur, at least for a while, but the costs and dangers of this process are so great that it could easily stall or be reversed, with truly catastrophic consequences. I will have more to say about the costs of modernization later on.

Modernity and Pluralism

Pluralism is a necessary consequence of the process of differentiation. Pluralism comes with modernity for the simple reason that differentiation increases the diversity of social life. And increasing diversity leads in turn to greater degrees of *individuation* of the units of society and to *decentralization* of decision-making.

Let me illustrate these two phenomena with examples from personal life. We are indebted to Durkheim for showing that the modern notion of human individuality itself is a social product, and in fact a product of our own civilization.[8] For most of human history the mass of people have been locked into a small number of roles ascribed to them on the basis of circumstances over which they had little or no control. People were who they were because of their age, their sex, and the kinship, community, and class networks into which they were born. Their very identities were inseparable from these basic roles. Of course, even then life involved some choices, but it did not involve the luxury of asking, "What shall I do with my life?" The conception of the individual person as a unique and autonomous entity with its own values and aspirations is relatively modern, and is closely linked with the processes that vastly increased the number of different roles available and decentralized the mechanisms for allocating people to them. In this case decentralization took the form of transferring most of the decision-making from the custom-encrusted rules of kinship and other primordial bodies to the individuals themselves. The process is far from complete, but in the Western world it has gone a very long way.

Just as most of us no longer define our identity completely in terms of our sex or our family background, we are less willing than our parents or grandparents to let *one* of our key roles determine for us what the others will be. This makes for a much greater variety of role combinations, which in turn accelerates the process of individuation. Not so long ago if you were a faculty member at an American college or university you were expected to receive and be received socially by your department head and other coworkers, you were strongly encouraged to find a "church home" and perhaps even to join Rotary or some other service club. Moreover, your life was an open book. Your marital status was duly recorded in the campus directory. If you enjoyed certain kinds of amusements or were seen in the wrong places with the wrong people, your career could suffer. You could even be fired. Nowadays, what faculty members do off duty is widely regarded as their own business. This has resulted in an increasing amount of personal privacy.

The individuation that pluralism creates is also evident in group life. In the economic sector, the proliferation of occupational specialties has generated numerous subcultures with their own expertise and "shop talk." A similar development has occurred in government, in education, in medicine, in psychotherapy, in entertainment, in publishing, in research, and in the arts. If we add to all these the great variety of lifestyle options, of consumer products, of religious and spiritual perspectives and regimens, of political causes and political subcultures, then pluralism and individuation can be seen as pervading every sphere of life in the Western world.

Decentralization is also a prominent feature of economic and political organization. At first glance this may not seem to be the case. The United States, for example, has changed in little more than 150 years from a nation of small farms and small government to a nation of giant corporations and public agencies. But growth in the scale of organizations and the resources they command does not in itself imply that these organizations are tightly controlled from some center. Despite numerous interconnections and interdependencies, economic decisions, ranging all the way from consumer choices to board-room policy-making, are highly decentralized, and the economic power of virtually all businesses is subject to change without notice as a result of market forces. Analogous observations can be made about government. The original checks and balances of the American federal system are intact, and elections still turn politicians out of office. Americans are protected from complete government control in the economic realm by the institution of private property just as they are protected in the political realm by the institution of civil rights. In tracing the effects of modernization on business and government, the relevant comparison is not with the United States as it is now and the United States as it was in 1840, for the process of modernization in these spheres was already far advanced in this country by that date. The relevant comparison is with the precapitalist, predemocratic societies of Europe, with their restricted, custom-bound economies and their far more controlling systems of political power. The range, scale, and resources of business and government have increased since then, but no control center has emerged that makes all their decisions in detail.

It can be argued, in fact, as Luhmann does, that the modernized societies of the West have no single "center" of any sort in the traditional sense, except perhaps during great national crises when sheer survival requires a high degree of coordinated control.[9] The absolute monarchies, the feudal ruling classes, and the monolithic ecclesiastical establishments are all institutions of the past. The effective operation of highly differentiated societies seems to require a very large degree of *de*centering if only for the reason that no overall control system can possibly keep abreast of everything it needs to know to make workable decisions.

If modernized societies are so pluralistic and decentralized, what keeps them operating as smoothly as they sometimes do? If control centers and common values no longer serve as social regulators, what keeps these societies from flying apart at the seams? We have already noted Durkheim's partial answer to that question, namely the fact that all of us nowadays are completely dependent on exchanges with other individuals and organizations to maintain our way of life. These exchanges are mediated and facilitated by a host of mechanisms and conventions that give social interaction whatever coherence it has. One of the main mechanisms is money, which does very heavy duty in modern societies. Aside from being a measure and a store of value, money is one of the principal exchange mechanisms of modern life. Another mechanism is authority, which makes binding decisions in cases of actual or potential conflicts. Underlying money, authority, and many other interactions and exchanges is the law, which has increasingly become the major regulatory backbone of society. An important feature of the modern monetary, administrative, and legal systems is their flexibility in responding to changing circumstances. Prices respond to market influences, rules and regulations are altered when new needs arise, and law itself is continuously interpreted and modified. The element of fixity and rigidity that regulated interactions in premodern societies recedes in modern times. More and more matters are treated as changeable and negotiable rather than as unalterable matters of custom or morality.

John Murray Cuddihy has called attention to another class of mechanisms that help forestall conflict at the level of interpersonal relations. These mechanisms are our customs of civility and "niceness." They make it possible to jostle someone by mistake in the elevator and avoid a flare-up. They enable customers and clerks, diners and waiters, clients and attorneys to conclude transactions with each other quickly and with a minimum of friction. As Cuddihy puts it, civility allows us "to live with unknown others without transforming them into either brothers or enemies."[10] Michael Novak has pointed to a related set of mechanisms that make interaction easier. Americans in particular, he argues, have cultivated a friendly, equalitarian style that gets new relationships started in an atmosphere of trust and good will and that takes the rough edges off the exercise of authority and the voicing of differences that are involved in all organizational life.[11]

The pluralism of the political and religious spheres poses especially difficult problems for the integration of modern societies because it permits a diversity of views and activities that affect the vital interests of organized groups. Democracy, which is the institutionalized form of pluralism in the political sphere, appears to be stabilized in the Western world, but this is a relatively recent achievement and in most nations democracy is either nonexistent or highly precarious. Religious pluralism is somewhat more common, but its development in the modern West is a major break with the traditional Christian policy of religious uniformity protected by the state. And we must not forget the severe restrictions on religious diversity, and even on religion itself, that are imposed by many modern states. In the Anglo-American legal and cultural tradition, the process of enlarging the range of tolerated religious and political diversity went hand in hand, with the first major breakthrough being the open organization of political parties and the official recognition of religious dissent in the last decade of the seventeenth century. The political party or interest group is the analogue of the religious sect or denomination. But to this day the boundary line between permissible and impermissible political and religious activity has never been clearly defined. In the past decade and a half many issues have arisen that test this boundary line. Should the state harass and restrict new religious movements like the Unification Church while exempting old-line Christian and Jewish bodies from similar treatment? In publicly supported universities, is Marxist proselytizing to be permitted in the classroom but Christian or Hindu proselytizing, no matter how "soft sell," to be prohibited? Is "secular humanism" a religion, and if it is, should it be the only one taught in the public schools? For that matter what, legally speaking, *is* religion?

On the whole, political and religious pluralism has proved compatible with a high degree of social integration. In the first place, most people strongly endorse it, at least in principle. A set of arrangements that originated in an uneasy compromise has not only been greatly extended, it is also seen as a positive good, indeed as the very foundation of our freedoms. In the second place, a number of practices have evolved that help forestall polarization along religious or political lines. One of these is the custom of simply avoiding partisan conversations in mixed company. A related practice is the avoiding of controversial issues in large public forums. Even network television dramas that are supposed to be "true to life" steer clear of political and religious topics. We know whom J. R. Ewing is sleeping with, but we don't know anything about his religion. No doubt J. R. is a gentile, but is he an atheist or just a lapsed Baptist? Is Miss Ellie an Episcopalian? One could watch hour upon hour of network television in the United States and never gain an inkling that this is the most religious of all the major industrialized nations. We do know a little more about J. R.'s politics. He is cynical and interest-driven, but we don't know whether he is a new Texas Republican or an old oil Democrat. When Bobby Ewing was in the legislature a few years ago, we heard talk of "the party," but we were never told what party.

In the sphere of religion another practice that minimizes confrontations is the abandonment of proselytizing. Of course, the right to proselytize is a fundamental one in our system and it is vigorously exercised by a large number of religious groups ranging all the way from the Mormons to the Jews for Jesus, but some groups have given it up. Although Congregationalists and Presbyterians could use a few new members, they are reluctant to go after them in an aggressive way, and they would be quite averse to targeting Catholics and Jews as potential converts. In a widening circle of religious bodies civility takes the form of not encroaching on each other's constituencies. I might add that in this respect evangelicals and fundamentalists are inadvertently civil themselves. They seek members far and wide, but apparently they mainly manage to bring in their own lost sheep.[12] There is no evidence that they are growing at a rate faster than the population as a whole.

Finally, there are important structural facts of American life that mitigate the potentially polarizing effect of religious and political diversity. As Parsons and others have pointed out, Americans tend to have memberships in a variety of different groups none of whose members see eye-to-eye with each other on everything.[13] Members of the county Republican committee, for example, may all have supported Reagan, but some of them will lean toward libertarianism, others will emphasize a strong military posture, and still others will be chiefly concerned with school prayer and abortion. The local bar association will contain some Methodists, Jews, and freethinkers. It might even have one or two liberals. In short, the phenomenon of cross-cutting solidarities widens our exposure to people with whom we do not entirely agree, and makes it unlikely that all our important membership groups will become mobilized around a "package" of issues on which all are united. In addition to putting some issues on the back burner, we tend to fight out others one at a time.

The Costs and Risks of Modernization

So far I have confined myself almost entirely to the "sunny side" of modernity and pluralism. I have done so in order to highlight the evolutionary processes involved in modernization and some prime examples from Western societies of their stabilized results. I have deliberately obscured the costs and the risks of modernization. But modernization is not a smoothly unfolding process that produces only benefits and provokes no resistance. It does incur costs and risks, and it is to these that we must now turn.

Even in biological evolution the development of organic structures that enhance the survivability of a species often entails a sacrifice of other capacities. For example, bisexual reproduction confers many advantages on a species, but only at the cost of the certain death of all its individual members. In the human species, the enormous expansion of cranial capacity was achieved at a cost of greatly weakened jaws and hence a diminished ability to chew. Although everyone who has written about modernization has been aware that it sometimes produces unwanted side effects, its major theorists have tended, in Cuddihy's graphic phrase, to write "from within the eye of the hurricane,"[14] that is, from a perspective sheltered from the storminess that modernization can produce. But there is a major literature about that storminess. Conservatives write of the winds of change that have swept away the foundations of tribe and community and have destroyed systems of morality and meaning. They view the present with despair and the past with nostalgia. Marxism, too, is about the stormy side effects of modernization. To Marxists, capitalism is the author of all the added misery and exploitation of modernity, and its eradication is essential if life is to be harmonious and free. They view the present with anger and the future with hope. Moreover, many who have some sympathy with modernization have called attention to its dangers. From Peter Berger on the Right to Jürgen Habermas on the Left, they have identified its unredeemed losses and its undelivered promises.[15]

I find it convenient to use Parsons's own conceptual framework to identify a few of the problematic side effects of modernization that have special relevance for individuation and pluralism. Let us begin by recalling the evolutionary process of differentiation, whereby one element in a system of action is divided into two. Let us also begin with the illustration of which Parsons was fondest, the separation of economic production from family activities. Now in discussing adaptive upgrading, which must take place if the differentiation is to have evolutionary significance, Parsons says that "economic production is typically more efficient in factories than in households," but he does not say that what families do is also upgraded. All he says is that the household "may well perform its other functions better."[16] On the other hand, of course, it may not. Differentiation affects both elements that are split off, but adaptive upgrading very often applies only to one of them. The one to which it does not apply is like a jilted lover whose partner has gone off to greater things. It is left in a weakened state, much like an orphan abandoned by its parents.

The family became a kind of orphan when it no longer worked together as a team to produce its own livelihood, or when it no longer controlled a business enterprise. The force of custom and the continuing subordination of women kept the family system from collapsing immediately, but for those with economic prospects the temptation not to marry, or not to stay married, or not to be bothered with children, or not to be bothered with how they are brought up, must have surfaced fairly soon. There were innumerable attempts to provide new forms for the family, new tasks for it, and new motivations for participating in it, but most of these have proved transitory and unstable, with the result that in the Western world the family system now seems on its last legs, with no workable substitutes for its functions on the horizon. At the level of intimate relations we are now approaching a state of individuation so extreme that long-term liaisons and commitments are very difficult to achieve.

Let us now consider the differentiation between matters of fact and matters of value. This relatively recent development came about as a result of rigorous philosophical reflections on what it means to say that a statement is true. In the process it became clear that only certain kinds of statements have the capacity to be true, with the result that the older unity between the true and the good was shattered. This differentiation did upgrade, or tighten up, the criteria for assessing truth or falsity, but at the same time it weakened the grounds for justifying assertions about values, because it deprived values of the possibility of being true. Values must be justified in some other way, as Max Weber so clearly saw, and to this date no consensus has emerged among those who work on this problem concerning how they might be justified. In the meantime, there is a strong tendency—and not just among academicians—to justify them subjectively by recourse to feelings or to merely arbitrary choices. Like the family, the realm of values, and by implication of morality as well, is an orphaned victim of the process of differentiation.

Let us consider a third, and final, case of differentiation, namely the process whereby religions have suffered a series of losses of their traditional functions. In the spheres of education, welfare, and cosmology religion has been obliged to surrender its monopoly to independent agencies and perspectives claiming greater competence. In the process, the compulsory character of religion that has united communities as small as the *shtetls* of Poland and as large as the whole Spanish nation has given way to a legally guaranteed pluralism and individuation of religious choice. This process, whether it is called secularization or something else, has proceeded unevenly and has provoked a variety of responses and adjustments, but almost everywhere in the Western world it has destroyed the possibility of widespread consensus on a theologically elaborated world view with binding consequences for the organization of collective and personal life. This is just as true of the United States, where 40 percent of the population attends religious services weekly, as it is of Sweden, where virtually no one does. It may be true, as a host of social theorists insist, that the core functions of religion have not been usurped by differentiation, but these theorists do not agree on what those functions are or which new religious developments might hold out some promise of performing them in keeping with the upgraded requirements of modernity. Religion, too, is something of an orphan in the modern world.

Of course, not everyone experiences these results of differentiation as troublesome. In the United States even the religious Right does not propose to repeal the First Amendment or prohibit birth control or bring back strict divorce laws. The authors of *Habits of the Heart* found that the collapse of a language of commitment and moral obligation did not prevent their well-educated respondents from living reasonably virtuous lives.[17] Great numbers of Americans manage to cope with the uncertainties of their work and intimacy by empowering themselves in various ways, e.g., by jogging, or meditating, or taking personal-growth seminars. And we must not forget that millions of people have experienced the erosion of old norms and institutions as liberations. Who wants to be stuck in a miserable marriage or to be disfranchised for one's faith or to live in fear of mortal sin?

But history shows there are circumstances in which large numbers of people do feel threatened by the loss of institutions and traditions that are undermined by modernization processes. They feel the very foundations of their life, and hence the very basis of their identities, cut out from under them by alien forces. As Cuddihy puts it, modernization "slices through ancient primordial ties and identities, leaving crisis and 'wholeness-hunger' in its wake."[18] When rallied by leaders who define the situation in a simple but dramatic way, people can react with extraordinary zeal to defend their primordial ties and the moral and religious systems embedded in them. In mobilizing themselves they purify their ranks of alien elements and reintegrate the whole of society around a collective purpose. The result is a *de*differentiation and *de*-pluralization of society that often entails the brutal treatment of dissenters and an early recourse to violence and open warfare. More than forty years ago, in an essay on fascism, Parsons identified such reactionary movements as defensive reactions against what he would later call modernization. He labeled them *fundamentalist* reactions, a term he obviously borrowed from the American movement of that name.[19] Happily, the American movement, including its recent politically mobilized descendant, is moderate and civil in comparison to the Nazi movement or to the varieties of Islamic fundamentalism and militant nationalisms that have sprouted like mushrooms in recent decades as the modernization process has touched more areas of the globe.[20]

Reactions to modernization that involve dedifferentiation and de-pluralization are often not simply reactionary and defensive but embody an attempt to achieve the benefits of modernization while avoiding its unpleasant side effects. The most prominent examples in our times are the various Marxist-inspired socialist movements. They are forward-looking, hope-inspired efforts to construct a new social order that is superior to any in the past. Marxism promises to cull the living flowers of modernity while breaking the chains with which modernity has allegedly enslaved the better part of humanity. The flowers to be culled are equality, justice, abundance, and happiness for everyone. The chains to be thrown off are the profit system, the bourgeois state and its legal apparatus, and the fragmentation of community and personal life. What is dedifferentiating and depluralizing about hard-line Marxisms, from Stalin to Mao to Castro to Pol Pot, is their insistence on the total integration of all aspects of life in the interest of building the new order. All of social existence must be organized according to the requirements of a compulsory political morality. Those identified as dissidents or parasites await the same fate as free-thinkers and cosmopolitans in reactionary regimes. If modernization theorists are correct, hard-line Marxisms will not deliver on their promises because they cannot permit the degree of individuation and autonomy among major system elements that is needed to redeem them. Moreover, these Marxisms produce distressing side effects of their own, including an implacable hostility toward bourgeois regimes, which in turn have reacted in a militantly defensive way, the result being the arms race and the threat of nuclear war. The dreadful irony of our century is that the search for prosperity and happiness has greatly increased the likelihood of their total negation.

Meanwhile, back in the heartland of capitalist democracy, theorists of modernity ponder the question of how serious the side effects of modernization really are in their own societies and whether a major change of course is needed to correct them. At the risk of oversimplifying a complex and hotly debated set of issues, I think it can be said that the core of the discussion involves the nature of the relationship between values, beliefs, and morality on the one hand, and the large-scale organizations and processes in the economic, political, and legal realms on the other. At bottom is the question of how what I have called these orphaned elements are integrated with the subsystems that operate in terms of money and power. One position in this debate is represented by Luhmann, who minimizes the role of shared values and moral codes in the large-scale structures and processes of modern life.[21] He argues that as value generalization proceeds, values become formulated at too high a level of abstraction to have clear-cut, unarguable implications for particular programs or policies. Moreover, it becomes increasingly difficult for people to agree how to prioritize the values they do share. As for moral codes, they are too inflexible to respond easily to the rapidly changing requirements of business or government. Markets, contracts, legislation, court decisions, administrative actions—all these do the job much better. To Luhmann it is a good thing that religion, values, and a moralistic posture have retreated to the sidelines of modern societies.

One of Luhmann's mentors was Talcott Parsons, who represented a sort of half-way house between Luhmann's position and the position of another of Parsons's students, Robert Bellah. Parsons celebrated differentiation and pluralism and those aspects of secularization that freed social life from direct regulation by a religious code. But he always insisted that societies—even highly modernized societies—need common values to legitimate the social order and to provide the motivational basis for social solidarity.[22] Bellah agrees with Parsons on this latter point, but some years ago he abandoned Parsons's relatively complacent image of American life and adopted a more disturbing one that emphasizes the decay of its core values and the growth of an ethos of amoral individualism that undercuts older notions of personal and civic virtue.[23] *Habits of the Heart*, which was widely read and is still being widely discussed, is an eloquent exposition of this perspective. To a certain extent Bellah and his collaborators echo the complaints that conservative pessimists have been making for years. But Bellah is much closer to critical Marxists like Christopher Lasch and Jurgen Habermas, who lay blame for the undermining of traditional values and morals on the capitalist system and its supporting structures of technology and government. They wish to rescue the orphaned elements of modernity not to restore a golden age but to renew these elements in an upgraded form so that a consensus can be generated that will command the systems of money and power to serve human needs. Neoconservatives also worry about the erosion of old value systems, but they believe that capitalism is the key to the economic abundance the modern age demands, and they fear it will not survive if its cultural supports are eroded. They blame much of the erosion on the anti-capitalist sentiments of the so-called "new class" of left-leaning intellectuals.[24]

These are difficult and vexing issues and it is not my purpose to resolve them here. Let me conclude by observing that if Luhmann is right, then only the thinnest consensus on values and moral codes is required under conditions of modernity. So long as larger systems are permitted to operate according to nonmoralized principles of their own there will be room for an ever greater diversity of world views, values, and lifestyles. Those who argue for a thicker consensus, as both Bellah and many of his neoconservative opponents do, are worried about the destructive side effects of an uncontrolled drift in the realm of values and morality. They, too, wish to preserve differentiation and pluralism, but their program involves a reshaping of public values and commitments on a broad front, and hence it also involves the implicit admission that even in modernity not all diversity is benign.

Part Two

Proselytism and Jewish Exclusivism

3

The Place of Other Religions in Ancient Jewish Thought, with Particular Reference to Early Rabbinic Judaism

ROBERT GOLDENBERG

From the earliest stages of its development, the religion of ancient Israel was marked by a burning hostility to the religious practices of other nations. The worship of foreign gods is denounced countless times in Pentateuchal law and prophetic exhortation alike as the ultimate evil—a danger to the well-being of the nation, an abomination to be destroyed with the utmost severity, and a monstrous folly besides.[1] Similarly, though such cases are fewer in number, Scripture offers stories of foreigners who came to recognize the power of the God of Israel and either explicitly or by implication renounced any further worship of that God's competitors.[2]

The Bible as a whole, however, is not without ambivalence on this very important question. Several other texts suggest that the worship of other gods was considered entirely appropriate for other nations, that such deities, while not Israel's "portion," were unobjectionable in their own right.[3] As Jewish religious thinking evolved out of its biblical foundations, it thus inherited two different tendencies: on the one hand a fundamental enmity toward the religious heritage of other peoples, but on the other simple avoidance of that heritage modified by an implied willingness to leave its adherents alone. As time went on, different heirs of the Bible could form attitudes toward their neighbors' religious practices under the influence of either of these models, and in the course of the generations each found its adherents. Jews in late antiquity produced both vitriolic denunciations of gentile religion and also remarkably balanced acknowledgments that pagans too could achieve righteousness. This ambiguity produced surprising consequences, which will become clearer as this inquiry proceeds.

Biblical writers did not often stop to distinguish between one forbidden cult and another. All worship other than worship of the One God of Israel was forbidden to members of the covenant community, and there was no occasion to examine whether certain other cults were more or less objectionable than the rest. From such well-known passages as the generic denunciations of idol-worship found in the latter half of the Book of Isaiah one receives no idea which actual religious traditions are being attacked. The impression one receives from surveying the Hebrew Bible as a whole is that all "other religions," as the title of this essay calls them, were more or less the same.[4]

This undiscriminating attitude was inherited by the postbiblical Jewish thinkers and writers who are the real subject of this study. The violent denunciations of the Wisdom of Solomon that will soon be quoted do not bother to identify the nations being ridiculed or the gods whom they worship. Even the more moderate Philo condemns Greek mystery religion and Egyptian animal cults alike,[5] while in the Talmud the very term used for non-Israelite cults is *avodah zarah*, or "alien worship"—that is, anyone else's religion. The very use of such a term suggests that the question of making distinctions between one gentile cult and the next need not arise at all.

It seems, to be sure, that with the rise of Christianity there was briefly a tendency on the part of some rabbis to distinguish between this movement—of Jewish origin, after all—and ordinary paganism. Such a tendency worked to the disadvantage of Christianity; R. Tarfon, an early second-century authority, is quoted as saying he would flee a murderer or a poisonous snake into a pagan temple but not into a house of sectarians *(minim)* because the former are merely ignorant of the truth while the latter know the truth well and deny it nevertheless.[6] Later authorities, however, lost track of this distinction, and once Christianity had become an overwhelmingly gentile religion it appeared no different in rabbinic eyes from all the other "alien worship" that surrounded them.

This failure (or refusal) to distinguish among gentiles meant, among other things, that for most Jews the distinction between Greeks and barbarians, a central feature of Hellenistic culture, was of no interest whatever. When Jews encountered the culture of the Greeks, they seem merely to have carried forward the biblical attitude of rejection. Early

Greek writers on Judaism were impressed by the apparently philosophical nature of the Jewish religion and by the high degree of educational attainment bred by its text-centered character,[7] but Jews in general did not return the compliment. By the second century B.C.E., an intellectual Jew like Aristobulus of Alexandria was well acquainted with the Greek philosophical tradition and quite willing to cite its conceptions or even its texts;[8] at the same time, however, Jews would always remind their readers that "Moses," that is, the Jewish version of international Hellenistic thought, is a better guide to ultimate truth than any of his rivals, imitators, or renegade disciples.[9] As Jews spread throughout the Hellenistic world, even as they began to absorb heavy doses of Greek language and culture, they seem to have carried everywhere a determination that their religion be kept separate from those of their many varied neighbors.

In keeping with biblical precedent, this determination could be accompanied by denunciation of foreign worship so fierce that any prophet would have been proud to be its author; a passage from the Wisdom of Solomon (first century B.C.E./C.E.) can illustrate this. Beginning with the idea that idolatry is grounded in a simple confusion of natural forces and divine power, then adding the standard biblical theme that artisans take mere physical objects and having shaped them into images proceed to worship them, the author of this passage concludes by attributing all known evils to the worship of heathen gods:

> For whether they kill children in their initiations, or celebrate secret mysteries, or hold frenzied revels with strange customs, they no longer keep either their lives or their marriages pure, but they either treacherously kill one another, or grieve one another by adultery, and all is a raging riot of blood and murder, theft and deceit, corruption, faithlessness, tumult, perjury, confusion over what is good, ingratitude, pollution of souls, sex perversion, disorder in marriage, adultery, and debauchery. For the worship of idols which should not even be named is the beginning and cause and end of every evil. (14:23–27; RSV, slightly modified)

Striking for its intemperate language and breadth of scope, this passage concentrates on the triad of cardinal sins—idolatry, bloodshed, and sexual corruption—so often linked in early Jewish thinking, and reflects the assumption that the first of these is the root of the other two. The vigor of the attack suggests that the rivalry between Judaism and paganism was still heated, that some Jews were still actively seeking gentile recruits and others were still genuinely tempted to join pagan religious activities themselves.

In any event, however, the other biblical tendency survived as well and ultimately became the normative rabbinic position on the subject. A famous passage from early rabbinic literature can illustrate:

> R. Eliezer says, "No gentiles have a place in the World to Come, as it is written, 'Let the wicked return to Sheol, all the nations who have forgotten God.'"[10] . . . R. Joshua said to him, "If the text said 'Let the wicked return to Sheol—all the gentiles' and then was silent, I would say as you do, but now that the text adds 'who have forgotten God,' this means there are righteous among the nations who possess a share in the World to Come." (*Tosefta Sanhedrin* 13:2)

This text reveals that at least one early rabbinic master considered the advantage of worshiping the true God, the God of Israel, to be a relative but not absolute advantage. There was an old tradition that promised future bliss to all Israel,[11] but in this view at least some gentiles would be there to share it with them.

As is commonly the case with disputes found in early rabbinic texts, the dispute just quoted is not resolved with an authoritative ruling. Only later discussion of this matter reveals that the lenient opinion in this dispute rather than the exclusive alternative came to prevail.[12] Despite ample biblical and postbiblical grounds for deciding otherwise, rabbinic Judaism came in the end to renounce the most powerful known instrument of religious propaganda—the threat of ultimate perdition. Instead, it accepted the milder of the biblical options; it insisted that Jews must keep away from the worship of foreign gods, but allowed at the same time that gentiles who find such worship attractive or satisfying can be judged on other criteria.

Ancient Jewish attitudes toward the gentile religions of late antiquity fell somewhere in the range of possibilities just reviewed. Some early Jewish writers equated polytheism or image-worship with utter depravity, while others considered such customs merely foolish; some Jewish reactions to Greek philosophy saw it as empty and pretentious, while others more kindly judged it similar to Judaism though inferior to be sure. On a closely related question, however, there was powerful unanimity: no Jewish writer in late antiquity would have doubted that Jews possess a religious heritage demonstrably superior to any of the known alternatives.

How were gentiles expected to become aware of this superiority? For one thing, Jews were constantly telling them. There is abundant evidence of an active Jewish drive for converts, a quest lasting for centuries that did not come to an end until Roman pressure, especially Christian Roman pressure, made it impossible to continue.[13] Jewish writers as varied in subtlety as the author of the Wisdom of Solomon already cited and his countryman Philo produced works intended to convince gentiles of the foolishness of their native traditions and of the desirability of adopting Judaism instead. It is not certain how much Jewish "missionizing" was an organized project and how much really consisted of little more than Jews privately haranguing anyone who seemed ready to listen,[14] but in either case Jews actively saw to it that gentiles heard about the benefits of adopting the God of Israel and His worship as their own.

In addition, gentiles quite on their own found Jews fascinating and spent a good deal of time watching them.[15] As already noted, the imageless monotheism of early postbiblical Judaism held much attraction for the Greeks who first discovered it, not merely because it was exotic but also because it seemed in consonance with very important trends in contemporary Greek thought.[16] Maimonides' notion that idol-worship was essentially the result of philosophical confusion is an idea much older than his own time;[17] it has important precedents in both Jewish and Greek thinking.

In addition to this more or less philosophical argument that Judaism had produced a better conception of deity than the other nations' religions, Jews offered a kind of moral argument as well: life according to the Torah, it was claimed, is purer and more honorable than the life recommended in pagan traditions. It has already been noted that the Wisdom of Solomon posits a link between idol-worship and sexual depravity; such a claim in fact was widespread in Jewish writing from the Hellenistic and early Roman periods. Borrowing themes at least as old as Plato's critique of the epic traditions, Josephus and others denounce Greek myths for the unedifying picture they offer of the gods' sexual adventures and frequent deceptions.[18] How, it was implied, can people be led to conduct upright lives if they worship divinities who behave in such a manner? The very fact of widespread gentile interest in Judaism, and widespread gentile observance of numerous Jewish precepts and customs,[19] was taken as evidence that the superiority of Judaism is evident to anyone who examines the question with an open mind. Just try living a Jewish life, went the message; you too will decide to adopt the Jewish God, and the Jewish law, as your own.

An appeal to gentiles along these lines speaks to a putative desire on their part to improve their own lives, from either the intellectual or moral standpoint. Writings addressed primarily to a Jewish audience— the Dead Sea Scrolls, for example[20]—might echo the ancient prophets' anticipation of the horrible downfall of the wicked, but gentiles were simply told that by remaining outside the Jewish fold they were living lives less wholesome or satisfying than they might, not that some awful punishment awaited them after those lives would be over.[21]

To be sure, Jews (or at least most Jews) were assured, as has been noted, that the bliss of the so-called World to Come was held in reserve for them, and the thought of losing their chance for such bliss may well have been an important factor in gentiles' being attracted to Jewish teaching. Nevertheless, while ancient Jewish literature contains horrific descriptions of the suffering, whether in this world or another, that waits in store for the wicked, such descriptions tend to concentrate on other Jews, Jews considered evil or wicked by the authors of various documents. Anticipatory gloating of this kind over the downfall of gentiles is very rare in ancient Jewish literature and usually reflects national or political rather than strictly religious concerns when it appears.[22]

It has already been noted that Jewish thinking was divided on the issue of how Jews should respond when gentiles simply remain loyal to their own ways of life. Some biblical passages, and some postbiblical Jews, violently denounced pagan beliefs and those who upheld them, while others were content to leave such people and their traditions alone—always assuming, of course, that they presented no threat and no temptation to Jews and their worship of the one true God. Under rabbinic tutelage, the latter, milder attitude became the normative Jewish stance toward the other religions of the world.[23]

Now any discussion of rabbinic Judaism proceeds against a double background, with both nonrabbinic forms of ancient Judaism (mostly earlier) and patristic Christianity (more or less contemporary) supplying materials for comparison and contrast. Rabbinic judgment of gentile religions was milder on balance than the judgment of both these others, and it will be useful now to consider why this was so.

From the earliest period, Greek reaction to Jewish religion had been quite favorable; Jews were no doubt encouraged by this to think large numbers of Greeks and perhaps other gentiles as well were ready to accept the argument against idolatry and come over to the God of Israel.[24] Thus it seemed appropriate on religious as well as political grounds for Jews to take the prophets' denunciations as their model and to fight against gentile religions in any way they could. As long as Jews saw themselves as acting a role in universal history, this role required of them that they attack gentile religion in the strongest possible manner at every chance they got.

In Jewish thinking, moreover, religious and political considerations have usually gone hand in hand.[25] The fate of the Jewish nation has been seen as linked to that of the Jewish religion, so that the growth of either normally requires (or leads to) the growth of the other while a threat to either is seen as threatening the other as well. As the Hellenistic age went on, numerous Jewish communities in many cities all over the Diaspora found themselves struggling for political equality with the dominant Greeks. In Alexandria, about which relatively much is known,[26] the Jews claimed such equality on the ground that their community had been among the significant elements of the city's make-up since its founding, that they were not mere "natives," but rather fully Hellenized immigrants not easily distinguishable from Greeks themselves. True, the Jews demanded the right to abstain from worshiping the gods of the city, but this was a national privilege that had been recognized by generations of rulers. Such abstention was also philosophically correct; the Jewish polemic against idolatry suggested that anyone who gave the matter thought would adopt the same attitude, and it was not proper that people should suffer a loss of civic equality merely for acting in accordance with reason.

Judaea was no different in this respect from the Diaspora. The Maccabees and their followers not only fought for the rededication of the Jerusalem Temple, but also destroyed all others that came into their power; the Hasmonean period was the only time in history that Jewish law (that is, Judaism) was forcibly extended to people who had not asked to come under its jurisdiction. A sudden flowering of Jewish national hopes entailed a new burst of Jewish religious enthusiasm. Some of the acts of the Maccabees and their followers can be seen as aiming to implement the particular biblical injunction to keep the Holy Land free of idolatry, but these actions also present the religious aspect of a broader national revival that the Maccabean victory called forth.

Seen in this light, the violent polemic of early Hellenistic Jewish literature can be seen as part of a larger cultural and political struggle to establish the full legitimacy of Judaism—with all its remarkable features—at the heart of Hellenistic civilization. Its aggressive tone can be seen as at least partly defensive in purpose. The Jews' struggle for equality reached its climax at Alexandria with the unrest in the time of Caligula and Claudius; this was their final effort to establish that their religious privileges should entail no loss of civic standing. The Emperor Claudius rejected this claim in a famous ruling confirming the Jews' privileges while sharply admonishing them to accept in consequence certain limits on their civic rights.

The decline in Jewish missionizing activity that gathered momentum throughout the subsequent history of the Roman Empire can plausibly be connected to this political defeat. Other factors too played a role, needless to say, but finally it had been resolved beyond challenge that adopting Judaism would always be an act entailing political cost; whatever advantages a convert might gain in some other world by entering the covenant of Israel, that convert would also have to pay a price in this one.

The circumstances of early Hellenistic-Jewish writers such as the author of the Wisdom of Solomon thus differed from those that had arisen by the time of Philo or Josephus, and differed dramatically from those in which the later rabbis had to work. All these lived when Jewish fortunes had reached or passed their highest point—Philo during the last futile struggle for equality already mentioned, the others after the disastrous wars against the Empire of the first and second centuries— and the attitude toward paganism expressed in these three great sources for the study of ancient Jewish thinking becomes progressively milder as one moves from the earlier to the later. Philo still argues quite forthrightly against Greek myths and religious practices, but Josephus constructs all of *Against Apion* as though it were a defense against attacks coming from outside. As for rabbinic literature, even the rabbis' name for idolatry—"alien worship"—implies, as already noted, that it belonged to other people, who were welcome to it. The rabbis' task, as they saw it, was merely to ensure that no influence from this "other-people's-worship" came to bear on the now beleaguered and increasingly downtrodden Chosen People.

In contrast to earlier Jewish and contemporary Christian thinkers, ancient rabbis were no longer engaged in a struggle to win over the world. As a result of important changes in the political circumstances of the Jews whom they led, and in the light of their own conception of Judaism and Torah, their sights were considerably lower. They were content to preserve a Jewish community relatively safe from the depredations and temptations of the outside world, and were willing to give up prospects for continued large-scale recruitment if such self-restraint was the only way to achieve that safety.

The rabbinic mildness toward other religions thus reflects a decline of Jewish aggressiveness in general;[27] it is part of a larger rabbinic effort to calm Jewish excitability that led as well to the disappearance of apocalyptic literature and messianic adventurism from Jewish life. Jews became less inclined to fight against other nations' religions—such hostility might turn gentiles against the Jews and add to the Jews' own sufferings, and would not likely produce any beneficial consequences— and thus became freer to acknowledge those virtues in gentiles that they might previously have intentionally or accidentally overlooked. For all these reasons rabbinic attitudes toward paganism could be more benign than earlier Jewish attitudes, and the righteous gentile began to play a role in the rabbinic scheme of things;[28] Saul Lieberman's rather circumspect observation that "the Rabbis understood the heathen society and credited it with the virtues it was not devoid of" understates a long and dramatic development.[29]

Under rabbinic guidance, the Jews would have no further claim on the nations of the world; they were finished trying to play a role in world history, and were now content to hope that world history would simply leave them alone. If the world would only agree to such a bargain, they were willing to leave the nations and their religions alone as well. Some day, of course, divine retribution would strike back at all these nations who for centuries had continued to worship false gods of stone, and to honor flesh and blood as though mere human kings could be divine, but this was a task Israel was glad to entrust to its God.[30] They would wait in patient silence.

Several additional factors as well contributed to this development but led nascent Christianity along a different course. Judaism is at heart a religion of sacred law. Stripping away the enormous deposit of valuation (both positive and negative) that the concepts of law and legalism have acquired over the centuries, it can fairly be said that the early rabbis saw Jewish life as ultimately a matter of adherence to a sacred law, possession of which was the surest mark of Israel's chosenness.[31] Individuals were free to explain the law or to propose reasons why it should be obeyed; one person's reasons did not have to be the same as another's, however, nor was it necessary to articulate any reasons at all—one could just take up the truly sacred task of studying and fulfilling the Torah. In rabbinic thinking questions of truth that had motivated Greek philosophy for centuries simply lacked the compelling force they were acquiring for Christianity. There was no need for rabbis to refute alternatives to their own point of view with the same systematic care that Christian thinking came to value so highly; they could merely say that gentiles had one way of life and Jews had another. To borrow a phrase from an unlikely source, the Jews' task as the rabbis saw it was to tend only their own garden.

This conception made it easier to conclude that gentiles might tend their own gardens as well; just as Jews could simply ignore the alternative presented by paganism and concentrate on a life of Torah, righteous gentiles could legitimately be allowed to feel there was no virtue in assuming obligations not incumbent on them to start with. It was a generally accepted principle of rabbinic ethics that there is more virtue in performing a commanded act than in performing the same act, however praiseworthy it may be, when one has not been commanded to do so.[32] This principle deeply offends modern ethical sensibilities influenced by Kant and his successors, but it accords perfectly with the rabbis' developing renunciation of the mission to convert the gentiles.[33]

Furthermore, turning on its head the older Jewish idea that human reason on its own should see the superiority of Judaism, rabbis now began to take for granted that the better gentiles could on their own discover and adopt principles of virtue to serve as a basis for their lives. This new conception implied that the Torah was no longer to be considered the indispensable foundation of righteous living, an implication against which Maimonides was still fighting almost a thousand years later.[34]

All the earlier Jewish motives for energetically combating paganism, however, had now been inherited by the Church. Under the pagan Empire, Christians had little hope even of the partial legitimacy that Jews had achieved. Christians were in constant danger of lapsing or being forced back into a paganism whose agents episodically threatened their very lives, and at the same time the only promising source from which new Christians might be recruited were these same pagans, who had to be convinced to renounce their previous loyalties and adopt this new one. In response to such factors, Christian attitudes continued the older Jewish model of constant denunciation and threat, even as the Jews themselves were renouncing it.[35]

Christian faith was from its beginnings a matter of affirmation or conviction, not behavior, and was from its earliest days emphatically not content to remain the possession of a small group of God's elect. The combination of these two factors—the refusal to accept ethnic limitation and the need to convince people's minds, not just govern their behavior—rendered the very existence of individuals who denied the superiority of Christian affirmations too painful to bear; all the considerations that enabled the rabbis to ease their polemic against paganism were thus negated, and Christian thinking was left under permanent obligation to attack alternatives to itself with every weapon at its disposal.

Before raising one final question, I should like to summarize the points made so far. I have tried to suggest that the biblical attitude toward the worship of other gods is always disapproving but not always aggressively hostile. One ancient opinion held the worship of foreign deities to be an abomination anywhere and any time it took place, but another considered that while surely the God of Israel should have the undivided loyalty of His own people there is little harm if other nations are left alone to worship their own gods as well. I have proposed that the rise to prominence of the rabbinate and the consolidation of rabbinic leadership over the Jews was attended by a shift in the Jewish stance toward other religions from the first of these alternatives to the second, that the more insistently hostile attitude toward paganism was bequeathed by early Israel to its Christian heirs even as the Jews were turning away from it.

I have tried to suggest some reasons for this development; these have included the general withdrawal of Jewish thinking from active engagement with an increasingly oppressive world, the different attitudes suggested by a view of religion as faith and a view of religion as law, and by the unbroken association between Jewish nationhood and Jewish religion, an association that the Christian religion was determined to sunder.

I have not said much about certain other developments that should at least be mentioned. Even before the Roman Empire became Christian, its laws began to restrict the possibility of conversion to Judaism, particularly for men.[36] Once the Empire had become Christian, the restriction of conversion to Judaism, at least from Christianity, became an outright ban as soon as the Church authorities could achieve this. If gentiles could not become Jews, however, there again was much less point in belittling their current religious loyalties, and in fact there was a certain unfairness in doing so. If gentiles were going to remain gentiles in any case, it made more sense in terms of both tactics and theological or moral principle to see the critical distinction as between those gentiles who had found a way of living that might be pleasing to God and those who had not. Such a shift in the dividing line also helped to rationalize abandonment of an ancestral struggle it must have been painful to lose.

I should like to devote my concluding remarks, however, to a comparison of rabbinic (at this point I can no longer simply say "Jewish")[37] and Christian conceptions of the place of their own respective religions in the world. I am especially interested here in the frequently linked terms "particularism" and "universalism"; there is an apologetic element in the following remarks, but I think as well that some real clarification of an often-abused issue is possible.

What do the rabbinic and Christian conceptions of this matter have in common? Each begins with the biblical conviction that those in covenant with the God of Israel are barred by that covenant from worshiping other deities alongside Him. Each draws from that conviction the theological conclusion that no other gods have any reality, a conclusion that is hard to avoid, since other gods, if real, can exact a fearsome revenge for being thus neglected.[38] At this point, however, the two conceptions begin to diverge. The classical Christian notion, in some ways the more direct continuation of the shared biblical heritage, was that gods which are not real should not be worshiped. On this basis the Church offered to all nations an invitation to live in communion with the one true God, but warned that those who declined this offer had devoted their lives to unreality and would pay a terrible price for this defiant error.

The rabbinic notion, ironically more continuous with the Greek idea that all human worship aims at a single but multiform divine object,[39] was that people who worhsip non-gods can nevertheless achieve some pale imitation of the righteous life that is possible through Torah; the rabbinic tendency—even while gentile religions were all lumped together as "alien worship"—was to judge individual gentiles by the degree of righteousness they were able to achieve. The rabbinic invitation was simply to live a righteous life. For Jews this meant a life according to the Torah, but for others it did not; for others the well-known concept of the seven commandments incumbent on all descendants of Noah provided a separate basis for judging the righteousness of an individual gentile or an entire gentile society.[40]

On the basis of these conceptions, outsiders who insisted on joining the covenant of Israel were dissuaded if possible and admitted only if they insisted on coming in.[41] One way of dissuading them was the rule codified in rabbinic law that those who do join the Jewish people must leave their previous lives behind in all respects. There could not be, as there was for contemporary Christian thought, the possibility that people might retain their previous identities save for the religious component. In rabbinic law a convert to Judaism has no parents and no heirs; in rabbinic law a convert to Judaism is as one newborn, without connection to the prenatal world (so to speak) that has been left behind.[42]

These rules expressed and preserved the link between Jewish religion and Jewish nationhood that had been posited for centuries. The separation between life before conversion and life thereafter was part of a more basic and much older separation between the Jewish and gentile worlds that rabbinic law sought to maintain. It has its counterpart in the dietary laws, in the ban on intermarriage, in the notion that the very soil of the Diaspora is impure.[43] An old rabbinic tradition offers a clear acknowledgment that all these prohibitions were part of a single whole:

> [The early sages] forbade their [i.e., the gentiles'] bread on account of their oil, and their oil on account of their wine. . . . Why should their oil be a greater matter than their bread? Rather they forbade their bread and their oil on account of their daughters, and their daughters on account of something else, and something else on account of something else still. (*B. Shabbat* 17b)

Thanks to the rabbis' penchant for euphemism, we do not know which "something else" is idol worship and which is sexual perversion. Rabbis do not seem to have worried that Jews of their time still were seriously tempted to worship foreign gods but evidently were quite afraid that gentile licentiousness would be irresistible to many.[44] By skillfully adapting these ancient religious motifs to the changed circumstances of Jewish life, however, rabbinic teachers managed to develop a new world view: now the legitimacy of gentile righteousness might be recognized without abandoning the Jews' ancestral determination to isolate themselves from their neighbors for the sake of their God. Gentiles could worship any gods they liked, so long as the covenant people itself remained unaffected.

But in this way it came about that despite Christian insistence that salvation is impossible outside the Church[45] it was rabbinic Judaism that came to be branded with the label "particularist." The rabbis were quite willing to let others cultivate any religion they liked, but the Jews' devotion to their sacred covenant imposed on them an obligation to remain forever a separate people, a nation distinct from all the other nations of the earth. The Hellenizers whom the Maccabees successfully opposed had tried to establish the different conception that Jews could legitimately dismantle all those separations and simply develop their own version of an international culture, but this effort failed. After the Maccabees' success, the notion of Jewish distinctiveness became one of the most tenaciously held dogmas of the Jewish faith; it remains so today.

Martin Hengel suggests that the great failing of Second Temple Judaism lay in its failure to overcome this separatism,[46] that its inability to become a universal religion stemmed from this insistence that converts renounce their previous national identity as the price of entering the covenant. He seems to think this demanded too great a psychological dissociation with one's past and also that it rendered Judaism too vulnerable to changes in the social and political status of the Jews in the various lands of their dispersion.[47] As long as Judaism retained such insistence, he suggests, it could harbor aspirations of becoming a universal religion but had no chance of achieving this goal.

The rabbis' great achievement—this has already been said, but it bears repeating because it so often goes unrecognized—was to combine the determined separatism of Jewish life with an acknowledgment that other nations too could develop acceptable traditions and live acceptable lives, not equivalent traditions or lives, but acceptable ones nonetheless. This took the sting out of Jewish particularism by freeing it of the implication that all other identity is utterly worthless in the absence of Jewish identity, and left other nations at liberty to cultivate their own ways to righteousness. It was a universalism of live-and-let-live that gave up none of the Jews' own claims to be the chosen ones of the Creator of the world.

Christianity, on the other hand, became universal by denying the value of anything outside its own framework. True, it strove to embrace the whole world while the Jews seemed content to remain complacently behind the protection of their laws. But Christianity developed its own particularism as well, which took the form of transforming the original Christian invitation to the gentiles into a threatening demand: people could become Christians without violence to the rest of their respective identities, but woe to those who declined this offer.

It is hard to know which form of particularism has more grievously distorted the universalism to which it is attached, and it is fortunate that the question need not be decided here. It is enough to take due note of the complex symmetry between these two responses to a shared dilemma, of their common roots in the Scriptures of ancient Israel, and of the long, too frequently painful encounter between them of which we are all the heirs.

4

Joining the Jewish People from Biblical to Modern Times

ROBERT M. SELTZER

The Jews have been, through most of their history, a relatively small and frequently vulnerable people. Perhaps under the influence of the modern threats of assimilation and extermination, popular Jewish history has tended to draw attention to the loss of Jews into other national groups or religions. The Assyrian conquest of 722 B.C.E. resulted in the Northern Kingdom's destruction and the deportation and eventual disappearance of much of its Israelite population. The Jewish revolts against Rome in the first and second centuries C.E. resulted in the decimation of the Jewish population of Judea, Egypt, Cyrene, and Cyprus. The mass conversion of Jews under pressure of popular violence, church persecution, and government restrictions in the Iberian peninsula during the late fourteenth and fifteenth centuries resulted in the drastic diminishment of the medieval Sephardim. The baptism of cultured and wealthy Jewesses of Berlin in the beginning of the nineteenth century, of German Jewish lawyers during the Restoration after Napoleon's defeat, and of Jewish bankers, writers, and artists in Europe toward the end of the nineteenth century are symbolic of more recent forces acting to subvert Jewish religious loyalty, as the Holocaust is emblematic of the threat of the physical destruction of the Jewish people by those who have feared and hated them. But apostasy in ancient or medieval times or drifting away to universalistic ideologies and assimilation in the modern period should not obscure a contrary movement that was always present to some degree: the absorption of non-Jews into the Jewish people. Although we can assume that the majority of Jews in each generation was inducted by birth and the males enrolled on the eighth day of their lives by the covenant of circumcision, there is evidence in almost every period of those who became Jews later in life. The boundaries separating the people of Israel from the "nations of the world" have always been open in both directions.

Conversion to Judaism has occurred for a wide variety of reasons, ranging from the desire to marry a Jew or Jewess to coercion by ancient Jewish rulers, from diplomatic considerations by Judaizing gentile rulers to individual decisions to take on the yoke of the God of Israel. At first, the incorporation of outsiders as full-fledged members in the Jewish group probably took place over two or three generations and in several distinct steps. The gradual metamorphosis of gentile to Jew was distilled by the sages of the Mishnah and the Talmud into a set of acts and rituals marking a total transformation of personal status according to Jewish law. More commonly at present, conversion entails a formal course of study in Jewish customs, values, beliefs, and history, leading to a declaration of the individual's acceptance of Judaism before the synagogue's open ark. Whatever the procedure or motivation, conversion to Judaism in the broad sense replenished the critical mass that sustained Jewish energies and added new perspectives and content to the personal meaning of Judaism to its adherents.

On the one hand, the history of conversion to Judaism refutes misconceptions about the immutable self-segregation of the Jewish people and the invariable relationship of ethnic to religious elements in Judaism. On the other hand, because conversion abuts on matters such as ritual purity and eschatology, it has more problematic sides, raising vexatious questions about continuity and innovation in Jewish law and the fine balance between Jewish piety and Jewish beliefs about the religious enlightenment of humanity. Quite evidently, it continues to expose considerable tensions and ambivalences in the Jewish community.

The starting point for historical analysis is the truism that the entrance of outsiders into the people of Israel was conditioned by the changing circumstances of the Jewish people and the Jewish religion. Much has yet to be learned about the ebb and flow of conversion to Judaism, but a considerable body of material has been published. In order to convey the variety, dynamics, and ubiquity of this phenomenon, we will survey four contrasting periods: ancient Israel from its origins to its absorption in the Persian Empire under the Achaemenid dynasty, Jewry in the pagan Hellenistic and Roman realms when conversion became a widespread phenomenon and formal procedure, the long span from the early Middle Ages up to the modern era when the Jews occupied a delimited and subservient status in Christian and Muslim states and conversion from Judaism occurred under threat of capital punishment, and finally recent times, when these sanctions have been lifted and there are signs of a resurgence of conversion to Judaism.

Conversion in Biblical Israel

The Hebrew Bible preserves indirect indication of the absorption of Canaanites, to use a broad term for the Hittites, Hivvites, Jebusites, Perizzites, Girgashites, Amorites, and other peoples that lived in the land of Canaan in pre-Israelite and early Israelite times. The tale of Ruth, set during the period of the eleventh-century B.C.E. tribal confederation, although probably written after the return from Babylonian exile, reports that the Moabite Ruth states to her Israelite mother-in-law, Naomi: "Where you go I will go, and where you lodge I will lodge; your people shall be my people, and your God my God; where you die I will die, and there will I be buried."[1] This averment (could it be an ancient formula rather than an invented speech?) indicates the complexity of responsibilities assumed: Israel as one's people, Israel's God as one's God, Israel's home as one's home, the mortal destiny of an Israelite as one's destiny—a social-religious unity that was to be characteristic of the elements involved in becoming Jewish throughout history.

There has been discussion in recent biblical studies concerning the extent to which premonarchical Israel might have been a coalescence of tribal, ethnic, or social groups into a confederation united by the worship of a singular God that was not the God of any other people. Perhaps only the ancestors of a part of the people Israel left Egypt (the "mixed multitude" of Exodus 12:38 and elsewhere) and lived as seminomads in the wilderness where they were imbued with the idea of an imageless, solitary deity who brought about redemption from slavery. When the wilderness group entered Canaan, disaffected Canaanites and *habiru*, alienated from the feudal society and cults of the second-millennium Canaanite city-states, may have accepted the Israelite God and come to view themselves as descendants of the suprafamily of *b'nai Yisrael* (Israelites). In favor of this argument, it is pointed out that regions of Canaan that played a conspicuous role in the history of biblical Israel, not mentioned in the books of Joshua and Judges as having been conquered in the initial decade of penetration, may have been included in the Israelite domain in a more voluntary manner. The classic picture of twelve tribes, each derived from the offspring of a son of the Patriarch Jacob, was probably a late schematization of a slow process of the accretion of subtribal and tribal groups involving the gradual absorption of new elements into Israel.[2]

The transformation in scope and make-up of the late thirteenth-century Israel into the Israel of the late eleventh and tenth centuries indicates that the pastoralists and warriors of the earlier period have become the agrarian, village, and urban people of the age of Samuel, Saul, David, and Solomon. Such a transformation could have involved intermittent assimilation during the two centuries of tribal confederation and one century of monarchical consolidation of considerable numbers of non-Israelite "neighbors."[3] A marginal stratum available for such assimilation in the early centuries was that of the *gerim* singled out for special consideration in biblical law.

In biblical law the *ger* is a legal category, like the widow and the orphan, that Israel is repeatedly commanded to protect; Israel was to remember their precarious circumstances because they had been *gerim* in the land of Egypt.[4] Distinguished from the foreigner or temporary visitor, the *ger* was a permanent resident of the land, yet not a bona-fide member of the people. (Ruth was a *ger* until her marriage to Boaz.) The analogous status in ancient Athens was the metic. To obtain permission to reside permanently in Athens, the *metoikoi* had to be sponsored by a citizen and officially registered. They were obligated to pay an annual head tax and entitled to contract legal marriages with citizens and to acquire houses or land only if granted this privilege by the polis assembly.[5]

While certainly not converts in any sense (religious conversion had not been invented), the *gerim* occupied an intermediate status that may have made possible the assimilation of their descendants into Israel. In the early biblical codes, provision is made for the *ger*, if circumcised, to share in the paschal lamb like "the native of the land" (Exod. 12:48). The text goes on to insist that "there shall be one law for the native and for the *ger* who sojourns among you" (v. 49). Presumably children of a *ger*, if married to Israelites, could be accepted as "natives of the land." Opportunity to be participants in the Israelite cult was not open to everyone. In a list of various people, such as eunuchs, who were not allowed to enter "the assembly of the Lord," Deuteronomy 23:2–8 specifies that Ammonites and Moabites were to be excluded; but the third generation of Edomites and Egyptians were to be allowed to enter the assembly. Restrictions concerning who could or could not enter testifies to the likelihood that there was such entering (again, witness the case of Ruth the Moabitess).

There is a clear distinction in biblical society between those who were recognized as part of *b'nai Yisrael* and non-Israelites who acknowledged the truth and might of Israel's God. The existence of the latter are duly recognized in the biblical narrative. Both Solomon's prayer and the story of Naaman, commander of the army of Aram, indicate that it was considered desirable and meritorious for non-Israelites to worship the God of Israel.[6] Why was the assimilation of Canaanites, if it took place, not recounted as evidence of the power and majesty of the God of Israel?[7] Most likely because of the Deuteronomic movement's role in shaping and editing the biblical history books.

The Deuteronomic reform movement expressed the revived morale of the Israelites during the reign of King Josiah of Judah in the 620s after a century of Assyrian domination and thereby obscured the historical record for theological reasons of its own. A persistent theme of the Deuteronomic writers and redactors was that the inhabitants of Judah were bound by the Torah of Moses as descendants of those present at Mt. Horeb (Sinai) in Mosaic times. The Deuteronomists insist on the voluntary acceptance of the covenant by all the people, beginning with the exodus ancestors at the formative moment at Horeb and extending down to the moving present.[8] The first generation of the covenanted people of Israel had been commanded to purge idolaters from the land:

> When the Lord your God brings you into the land which you are entering to take possession of it, and clears away many nations before you, the Hittites, the Girgashites, the Amorites, the Canaanites, the Perizzites, the Hivites, and the Jebusites . . . then you must utterly destroy them; you shall make no covenant with them and show no mercy to them. You shall not make marriages with them, giving your daughters to their sons or taking their daughters for your sons. For they would turn away your sons from following me.[9]

The Book of Judges indicates that no large-scale extermination took place.[10] Insistence that the bulk of the inhabitants of the kingdom of Judah in Joshua's time were descendants of the wilderness generation, therefore, may have obscured the absorption of individuals of Canaanite extraction over the course of the intervening six centuries up to the time when the core of Deuteronomy was composed.[11]

This doctrine of the Deuteronomic school had exclusive rather than inclusive consequences two centuries later when Nehemiah and Ezra came from Babylonia to Judah, with the permission of the Persian king, to reform the demoralized and disorganized city of Jerusalem. Nehemiah rejected the help of the inhabitants of Samaria, who were considered not to be the seed of Israel but descendants of settlers planted by the Assyrians 250 years previously. Ezra launched a campaign against any intermarriage whatsoever by Judahites with the peoples of the lands:

> Give not your daughters to their sons, neither take their daughters for your sons, and never seek their peace or prosperity, that you may be strong, and eat of the good of the land, and leave it for an inheritance to your children forever.[12]

All non-Israelite wives are to be put aside, regardless of religious behavior.

> The people of Israel and the priests and the Levites have not separated themselves from the peoples of the lands with their abominations, from the Canaanites, the Hittites, the Perizzites, the Jebusites, the Ammonites, the Moabites, the Egyptians, and the Amorites [most of these groups had disappeared from the land of Israel]. For they have taken some of their daughters to be wives for themselves and for their sons; so that the holy seed has mixed itself with the peoples of the land.[13]

To the generation of pious Jerusalemites in the mid-fifth century who accepted the guidance of Ezra and Nehemiah, the non-Judahite wives and the Samaritans were symptomatic of the faithlessness of the generation to its covenantal duties. These adherents were a contamination of the holy remnant because, at this juncture, there was no mechanism by which such admirers of the God of Israel could be brought formally into the people. If Israel was to be truly the Israel of God according to the Deuteronomic faith, Ezra was forced to exclude them.[14]

It has often been pointed out that Ezra's attitude differs rather strikingly from that of the classical prophets, where eschatological passages envision that at the end of days other nations will join in the worship of the God of Israel. One exilic prophecy even extends an explicit word of welcome to prospective joiners:

> And the foreigners who join themselves to the Lord, to minister to him, to love the name of the Lord, and to be his servants, every one who keeps the sabbath, and does not profane it, and holds fast my covenant—these I will bring to my holy mountain, and make them joyful in my house of

prayer; their burnt offerings and their sacrifices will be accepted on my altar; for my house shall be called a house of prayer for all peoples.[15]

Indeed, postexilic prophecy held that there would eventually be universal recognition of Israel's God: "For then I will make the peoples pure of speech, so that they all invoke the Lord by name and serve Him with one accord."[16] But the universal religious enlightenment anticipated by the prophets was at the end of history rather than in the immediate offing. And even after the whole world acknowledged the kingship of God, other peoples and nations would continue to exist alongside the people of Israel.[17] In short, the "conversion" of humankind predicted by the prophets was not contingent on everyone's becoming an Israelite.[18]

The prophetic notion of an eschatological awakening to the one God indicates that the *idea* of proselytizing entered the mind before the program to actualize it. Within about two centuries after Ezra and Nehemiah, the age of large-scale Jewish proselytism commenced.

Jewish Proselytism in the Hellenistic Era and in the Roman and Persian Empires

A signal of Jewish proselytism as a voluntary assumption by non-Jews anywhere of the Jewish way of life is the coinage of the verb *lehityahed* to describe how "many from the peoples of the country declared themselves Jews" during the clashes after Haman's fall from power.[19] With the Greco-Macedonian conquest of the Persian Empire in the late fourth century B.C.E. and the subsequent expansion of the Diaspora to include most of the cities of the Mediterranean basin as well as Babylonia, a significantly wider range of ways to bring people into Judaism takes shape that included: a vigorous Hellenistic-Jewish propaganda that attacked paganism as absurd and defective, a policy of forced conversion in newly conquered regions of the land of Israel by Judean rulers, and individual missionary activities by Jewish travelers and settlers. Enlargement of Judaism's orbit indicates the growing reputation of Jewish monotheism, of the Hebrew Scriptures, and of the Jewish people and its ethos as the most vibrant, assured, and distinctive pre-Hellenistic tradition of the ancient Middle East to gain new life in the cosmopolitan Hellenistic and Roman *ecumene*.[20]

Almost all of the Jewish sources and many Greek and Roman sources of the time refer to Jewish proselytism. Josephus relates that the Hasmonean rulers of the newly independent Judean commonwealth compelled the conversion of some of the neighboring population after

140 B.C.E. Campaigning south of Jerusalem, John Hyrcanus forced the Idumeans to convert;[21] John Hyrcanus' son Aristobulus I forcibly Judaized the Itureans in the Galilee a few decades later.[22] (The Hasmoneans were not able to integrate the Samaritans in a similar way, though they razed their temple, nor did they assimilate the gentile population of the Hellenized cities along the coast.) The political justification for forced conversion probably was to cement the loyalty of the population to the enlarged Judean state; the religious justification may have been an Elijah-like attack on paganism in the land of Israel, drawing on the eschatological fervor that surfaced during the Maccabean revolt.[23]

The source of our English term "proselyte" is the Greek *proselytos* ("one who has arrived"), used to translate the Hebrew term *ger* in the Septuagint, the Greek translation of the Torah produced in Alexandria during the third pre-Christian century. In the writings of Philo of Alexandria at the turn of the era, *proselytos* had come to designate someone who has left polytheism and arrived at a new and God-pleasing life. Philo's remarks on proselytes indicate that he was accustomed to their presence and held them in high regard:

> Having laid down laws for members of the same nation, [Moses] holds that the incomers [proselytes] too should be accorded every favor and consideration as their due, because abandoning their kinsfolk by blood, their country, their customs, and the temples and images of their gods, and the tributes and honors paid to them, they have taken the journey to a better home, from idle fables to the clearer vision of truth and the worship of the one and truly existing God.[24]

Elsewhere Philo insists that the proselyte is superior to those who are Jews by birth but not by virtue and observance:

> The proselyte exalted aloft by his happy lot will be gazed at from all sides, marvelled at and held blessed by all for two things of highest excellence, that he came over to the camp of God and that he was won a prize best suited to his merits, a place in heaven firmly fixed, greater than words dare describe, while the nobly born [i.e., native Jews] who had falsified the sterling of his high lineage will be dragged right down and carried into Tartarus itself and profound darkness.[25]

In like manner, traditions about the Pharisees of the first century allude to their enthusiasm about conversion. A pagan *nudnik*, notorious for wanting an instant education in Judaism such that he could learn the Torah while standing on one foot, provided the Babylonian Talmud with the opportunity to attribute to the first-century B.C.E. sage

Hillel a classic formulation of the golden rule.[26] Among Hillel's apothegms is the maxim, "Be of the disciples of Aaron; one that loves peace and pursues peace, that loves mankind and brings them nigh to the Torah."[27] Reflecting the religious conflicts between Jews and Christians at the end of the first century C.E., Matthew ascribes a veritable passion for proselytizing to the Pharisees: "Woe to you, scribes and Pharisees, hypocrites! For you traverse sea and land to make a single proselyte, and when he becomes a proselyte, you make him twice as much a child of hell as yourselves."[28] Later rabbinic traditions attribute proselyte ancestors to such sages as Shemaiah and Avtalyon of the first century B.C.E. and to Rabbi Meir and Rabbi Akiva of the second century C.E.

Judging from the frequent mention of conversion to Judaism in the whole range of extant sources, the first century B.C.E. and the first century C.E. were the high-water mark of Jewish proselytism among pagans in the Greco-Roman world. Josephus and various Roman writers allude to outright conversion as well as to the widespread adoption of some Jewish practices and beliefs among those who did not formally convert.[29] The Roman historian Tacitus speaks of Judaism's appeal as an unfortunate matter, but by doing so adds confirmation to its existence. Similar remarks can be found in the writings of Cicero, Horace, Juvenal, and Dio Cassius. Individual Diaspora converts of high status singled out for special mention are Queen Helena of Adiabene and her sons at the beginning of the first century C.E., and Flavius Clemens, a nephew of the Roman Emperor Domitian, and Fulvia, the wife of a Roman senator, later in the century. References to Jewish converts in Greek and Latin literature (Josephus wrote his books in the decades after the war and Tacitus at the beginning of the second century) indicate that the Roman victory in Judea in 70 C.E. did not inhibit the phenomenon.

We have no description of the rites of formal conversion to Judaism in the Diaspora at this time, but there is considerable material preserved in the Mishnah, Talmud, and Midrash about admission procedures, legal status, and attitudes to new Jews. In the land of Israel requirements by the second century C.E., if not earlier, were *milah* (circumcision for males), *tevilah* (immersion in pure water), and offering a Temple sacrifice.[30] Opinions and rulings in the Mishnah and Talmud indicate that with some reservations, the standing of proselytes in talmudic law was that of born Jews. Unlike the *mamzer* (a Jew born from a union within the biblically forbidden degrees of propinquity or of a married woman by a man other than her husband), a proselyte was allowed to marry anyone, even the daughter of a *kohen* (an Aaronide priest), with the restriction that a female proselyte converted after the age of three years and one day could not marry a *kohen*. (This technicality, part of the corpus of restrictions intended to protect the purity of the priesthood, probably had little effect on actual marriages since, if the female proselyte was already married to a *kohen*, she was not required to leave him.) There were limits on a proselyte's right to act as judge in criminal cases, but none on the children of proselytes to serve in that capacity.[31] In talmudic law, conversion to Judaism was a legal rebirth, the proselyte being considered to have terminated his ties with his former family. Thus if one died without heirs born after conversion, property not distributed by the proselyte before his death was not considered to belong to anyone and was literally up for grabs.

Talmudic terminology distinguished between the righteous proselyte (*ger tsedek*), who fully accepted the responsibilities of a Jew to observe all the commandments of the Torah as elucidated by the rabbis, and the resident of the land (*ger toshav*), who had rejected idolatry but not accepted the full burden of the *mitzvot*.[32] According to the Babylonian Talmud proselytes (*gerei tsedek*) are singled out for honor in the benediction for the righteous and the pious recited by Jews three times daily.[33] According to rabbinic literature, making proselytes was an especially honorable task, an imitation of Abraham. In one homily, the phrase in Genesis referring to "the persons which they had gotten [literally 'made'] in Haran" (12:5) was understood to mean that Abraham and Sarah made many proselytes there; the lesson was that "he who brings a Gentile near [to God] is as though he created him."[34] Elsewhere, Rabbi Jose ben Halafta answered the question, why did Solomon cleave to so many foreign women "in love" (1 Kings 11:2), by explaining that the expression "in love" meant "to make them beloved [to God], to bring them near [to God], to convert them and to bring them under the wings of the *Shekhinah*."[35] The Midrash Tanhuma called the proselyte dearer to God than all the Israelites who stood at the foot of Mt. Sinai: the Israelites would not have accepted the Torah had it not been for the thunder and lightening, the quaking of the mountain and the sound of the trumpets; the proselyte experienced none of these miracles, yet surrendered himself to the Holy One, blessed be He, and accepted the yoke of Heaven.[36] Another midrash interprets Psalm 128:1, "Happy is every one that fears the Lord, that walks in His ways," as referring to the true and sincere proselyte who is included, according to the homily's author, among the "happy." The proselyte may have no distinguished ancestry on which to rely to ensure reward in This World or the Next, but he will attain full reward through his or her own merit. Moreover, such proselytes will give birth to sons who will make themselves masters of Scripture, of Mishnah, and of good deeds, and to daughters who will be privileged to marry priests and give birth to children who will be priests that bless Israel with the priestly benediction.[37] The Babylonian Talmud discusses the question of sincere and insincere converts. Those who become proselytes from love of a Jew or Jewess are not deemed proper proselytes, nor are those who want to convert from fear, or because of dreams, or from motives of expediency or worldly advantage. It is noted that the law is according to those sages who maintained that, after the fact, the conversion of such people was unquestionably valid.[38]

These citations, which could be multiplied several times over, come from the first five centuries of the Common Era, during which there were, to be sure, ebbs and flows of conversion. The second century, which included the Jewish revolt in Egypt, Cyrene, and Cyprus against the Romans between 114–17, the Bar Kokhba revolt between 132–35, and the brutal Hadrianic persecutions, may have seen a marked decline in the previous scale of conversion. The talmudic interrogation of the sincerity of prospective proselytes may reflect the conditions prevailing after the promulgation of Hadrian's edicts:

> If at the present time a man desires to become a proselyte, he is to be addressed as follows. "What reason have you for desiring to become a proselyte; do you not know that Israel at the present time are persecuted and oppressed, despised, harassed, and overcome by afflictions?" If he replies, "I know and yet am unworthy," he is accepted forthwith, and is given instruction in some of the minor and some of the major commandments.[39]

Nevertheless, there was no letting up of interest in making converts, and the pace may have picked up again later. Perhaps the most frequently quoted defense of proselytizing is the statement attributed to the third-century amoras Johanan and Eleazar: "The Holy One, Blessed be He, scattered Israel among the nations for the sole end that proselytes should wax numerous among them."[40]

In contrast to the hospitable tone of such statements, other dicta express suspicion of the motives and behavior of proselytes. The remark that "they revert to their evil ways" may refer to the backsliding of some proselytes during the repressions after the Bar Kokhba revolt.[41] The most frequently quoted statement against proselytizing is Rabbi Helbo's observation that "Proselytes are injurious to Israel as a scab."[42] Among the interpretations of this put-down is that Rabbi Helbo was referring to idolatrous habits that converts brought into Judaism or that he was alluding to the danger facing a Jew who received proselytes when Christian Roman emperors imposed severe penalties on Jewish proselytizers in the fourth century.[43] We can conclude that the extent of the references to proselytes, both laudatory and cynical, in rabbinic literature testifies to the frequency of the phenomenon in the pagan Roman Empire and in Parthian and Sassanian Persia.[44]

In late antiquity, Judaism evidently continued to make many proselytes; Christianity made more. If the Jewish troubles with the Romans, especially in the second century C.E., affected the pace of conversion to Judaism, the Christians had their troubles with the Roman government too. The religious assets of Judaism and Christianity were similar: radical monotheism, denial of pagan deities' ontological reality, claiming the Hebrew Scriptures as the only revelation of the only true God, promises of resurrection and immortal life to qualified individuals, an extensive support system within the faith-community. The rabbinic "fences to the Torah," which limited ordinary intercourse with gentiles, constituted a deterrent to outreach in the towns and cities of the Roman Empire, but the Jewish requirement of circumcision may not have been as great an obstacle as some historians have assumed, since converts in this period were not looking for the most painless solution to their spiritual needs. Perhaps a nonrabbinic Hellenistic Judaism of the kind espoused by Philo would have continued to win large numbers of new Jews in the cities of Egypt, Syria, Asia Minor, Greece, and the western Mediterranean where Christianity was to do so well, but this Judaism was weakened by the revolt of the early second century and lost its assertive edge.

The adherents that the early Christians won among the Jewish people to the worship of Jesus as the Christ were dwarfed by their success in making converts among gentiles. For pagans the divinity of Jesus, the virgin birth, and the trifold nature of God were not problematic in the way they were to most Jews. When Christianity began its separate career, it had available to it the completed Septuagint, the Jewish Diaspora (especially Asia Minor and Greece where Paul's missionary efforts were channeled) and, presumably, an audience of God-fearers (*sebomenoi*) who had taken on some but not all Jewish observances and were receptive to the *kerygma*, the proclamation of the coming of the Messiah.[45] In the final analysis, Christianity's messianic-apocalyptic roots, its origins as a sect rather than the religion of a people, and its doctrine of salvation only through faith in Jesus as the Christ led Christians to proselytize with far greater intensity than Judaism ever contemplated.

After the Bar Kokhba revolt the rabbis had a strong predisposition against active messianism. While welcoming proselytes, they saw their primary task as raising the level of Torah-observance and Torah-knowledge among the masses of the Jewish people. Rabbinic Judaism was a quality-intensive enterprise, like a classical academy or a Christian holy order. The positive attitude toward proselytes in rabbinic Judaism was not conducive to a campaign of mass conversion: the assumption remained that the bulk of the people would be Jews by birth. The procedures of conversion as formalized by the rabbis showed a decided preference for sincere converts who came with no ulterior purpose except the desire to accept the Torah of the people of Israel. In line with the prophetic eschatology mentioned earlier, rabbinic Judaism did not expect humanity to accept the 613 commandments that were incumbent on all members of the Jewish people; it was enough that the gentiles carry out the seven Noahide laws. In effect, the rabbis accepted the status of a permanent minority for the house of Israel, whose mission was to sustain This World, the antechamber of the World to Come, in quite a different manner than through historic conversion of the nations. For the Christian, conversion was a necessary means of saving souls from hell; for the Jew, Israel's duty to witness for God lay in obedience to the covenant, not in proselytizing as such.[46]

Jewish Proselytism in the Middle Ages and Early Modern Period

When Christianity became the state religion of the Roman Empire in the fourth century, Judaism, unlike paganism, did not become illegal, but it did become unlawful for Jews to make converts. A law concerning Jews, heaven-worshipers, and Samaritans issued by the Emperor Constantine in 315 made attachment to Judaism by a non-Jew punishable "with the deserved penalties." An edict of Constantius in 339 that subjected intermarriage between Jews and Christians to the death penalty also prohibited the circumcision of Jewish slaves, and a novella by Theodosius II in 439 banning Jews and Samaritans from public office stated, almost parenthetically, that "he who misleads a slave or a freeman against his will or by punishable advice, from the service of the Christian religion to that of an abominable sect and ritual, is to be punished by loss of property and life."[47] In canon law, conversion to Judaism by a Christian, or abetting such conversion, was an act of heresy, punishable by death. Canons reaffirming and elaborating the proper degree of Jewish isolation were periodically reenacted by church councils, suggesting the limits of their practical effectiveness. But inclusion of these prohibitions in Christian law surely indicates the drastically changed context for the Jewish proselytism that continues to be noted in historical sources.[48]

The new situation was fully defined after the rise of Islam and its conquest of the Sassanian Empire, bringing Arabian, Mesopotamian, and Persian Jewry under the rule of yet another monotheistic religion that considered itself to have superseded Judaism. It was a common feature of many versions of the so-called Pact of Omar that *dhimmi* (non-Muslims) were warned not to prevent anyone from converting to Islam but that conversion of Muslims to Judaism and Christianity was a capital offense. Faced with the splendor of Christian monarchs, the success of Christian missionary activity, and the power and authority of the rulers of *dar al-Islam,* the attraction of Judaism to gentiles was considerably limited.[49]

There was, however, Jewish proselytizing on the frontiers of civilization, where certain kings opted for Judaism, perhaps to withstand Christian or Muslim pressure. In the early sixth century the conversion of Yusuf Dhu Nuwas, King of Himyar in modern-day Yemen, indicates a history of Jewish conversionary activity there.[50] (Soon after, Himyar was invaded by Christian Ethiopia, then by the Byzantines, the Persians, and finally the Muslim Arabs.) In the first half of the eighth century the Khazars, a pagan Turkic people in the Volga-Caucasus region, converted to Judaism, perhaps to avoid having to align themselves with the Eastern Roman Empire or the Muslim caliphate. Conversion of the royal family and perhaps other Khazars did not entail the forced conversion of all the people, as occurred when the pagan Germanic, Scandinavian, or Slav peoples were baptized into the Christian Church. The Khazar conversion is not mentioned in Middle Eastern Jewish sources of the eighth to the tenth centuries, such as the geonic responsa, but it did find a place in the literary imagination of medieval Hebrew writers in the West.[51]

A significant source of new Jews in the early Middle Ages, according to the geonic literature, was the conversion of Jewish slaves in the Middle East, where owning and trading of household slaves was still common.[52] In Christian lands, individual proselytes continued to be mentioned in Jewish sources and Christian chronicles, despite the danger of incurring the penalties for committing or abetting heresy. Many of these Christian converts to Judaism were clergy; others were nobles. Such converts often fled to Muslim lands, where Christian conversion to Judaism was not prohibited. Bodo, a court deacon of Louis the Pious in ninth-century France, resettled in Spain where he wrote several polemical letters against Christianity (extant are the letters by his Christian opponent, Paolo Alvaro of Cordoba). In the eleventh century, a priest in Mainz and a wealthy Christian woman in Narbonne were said to have attracted attention by converting to Judaism. Around 1100, a priest named Johannes, of a noble Norman family living in southern Italy, became a proselyte. Inspired by a dream and by the study of the Old Testament, he found his way to Judaism, renamed himself Obadiah, settled in Baghdad, and later lived in Aleppo, northern Palestine, and Egypt. Writings by him, found in the Cairo *genizah,* relate that he was emulating an Archbishop Andreas in the province of Bari who had converted to Judaism several decades earlier and fled to Egypt. Six liturgical poems by Josephiah, a proselyte of twelfth-century France, are extant. An Ashkenazic rabbi of note, Mordecai ben Hillel ha-Kohen, refers to the burning of a proselyte at Augsburg in 1264. In 1270, a proselyte from France was burned at Weissenburg. In 1275 Robert of Reading, an English monk, became a proselyte.[53]

No comparable list can be formulated for Muslim converts to Judaism in the Middle Ages. Was Christianity inherently more prone to Judaizing tendencies among those who studied Scripture and identified with the people of Israel?[54] Did the similarities between Islam and Judaism mute the conversion phenomenon, or is the absence of Muslim conversion to Judaism a misleading impression produced by the vagaries of history?

The most famous medieval responsum on the religious status of the convert to Judaism is Maimonides' Letter to Obadiah the Proselyte (not the same Obadiah mentioned earlier and apparently a convert from Islam). The Mishnah had given a rather complicated answer to the question: Can the proselyte employ such traditional formulas as "Our God and God of *our* fathers" in his recitation of blessings and prayers?[55] Maimonides cut through the complexities to the heart of the matter:

> Yes, you may say all this in the prescribed order and not change it in the least . . . Abraham our Father taught the people, opened their minds, and revealed to them the true faith and the unity of God; he rejected the idols and abolished their adoration; he brought many children under the wings of the Divine Presence. . . . Ever since then whoever adopts Judaism and confesses the unity of the Divine Name, as it is prescribed in the Torah, is counted among the disciples of Abraham our Father. . . . Abraham our Father, peace be with him, is the father of his pious posterity who keep his ways, and the father of his disciples and of all proselytes who adopt Judaism. . . . Do not consider your origin as inferior. While we are the descendants of Abraham, Isaac, and Jacob, you derive from Him through whose word the world was created.[56]

In contrast to Maimonides' deferring to the sensibilities of the rational human being who recognizes the full import of God's oneness, the poet and philosopher Judah Halevy postulates an inherent distinction between proselyte and born Jew. In a philosophical treatise set in the court of the pagan Khazar king about to choose between conversion to Islam, Christianity, or Judaism, Halevy explains the sheer facticity of Israel's revelation as the result of an inborn Jewish propensity to receive revelation under certain circumstances. To be sure, Judah Halevy speaks respectfully of proselytes (after all, the Khazar king did convert to Judaism), but he insists that converts to Judaism do not acquire the divine quality or genius (*inyan ha-elohi*), even after proselytizing: "Those who become Jews do not take equal rank with born Israelites, who are specially privileged to attain to prophecy, while the former can only achieve something by learning from them, and can only become pious and learned, but never prophets."[57] In this regard, Halevy was a harbinger of the Qabbalah as it developed in southern France and northern Spain in the thirteenth century. The classic Qabbalistic text, the Zohar, also ascribes an honorable task for proselytes as a means for transmitting the divine light to the lower worlds, but distinguishes between their connection to the divine structure of *sefirot* and that of born Jews.[58] This tendency to treat the Jews as a metaphysically distinct entity may reflect the increasing sense of spiritual and social isolation that Jewish intellectuals felt in the latter Middle Ages.

Acceptance of proselytes remained a formal duty in the later Jewish law codes, but by the fifteenth and sixteenth centuries some Jewish authorities warn against active efforts to subvert members of other faiths, citing dangers to the survival of the community. These centuries were perhaps a low point in the story of Jewish proselytism, expressing a defensive stance that assumed an unbridgeable barrier between the faiths and an expectation that Jews would not be understood or appreciated by gentiles.[59]

There may have been less conversion to Judaism during these centuries, but there was reconversion: the reconversion to Judaism of new Christians (Conversos or Marranos) whose ancestors had been pressured to accept Christianity in Spain and Portugal between 1391 and 1497. In the sixteenth and seventeenth centuries, new Christians fled from Spain and Portugal to Ottoman Turkey and Italy, later to Amsterdam, Bordeaux, and other West European ports, where they formally reentered the Jewish faith of at least some of their ancestors. As time went on, the Jewish knowledge of these Marranos became meager, and their return was a drastic reshaping of their lives, as the travails of Uriel da Costa in seventeenth-century Amsterdam attest. Most of the former new Christians, now born-again Jews, were exceptionally loyal to their old/new religion. Opinions as to whether the Conversos or Marranos were Jews returning in repentance (*baalei teshuvah*) or new converts varied, depending on their relationship to the Jews in the communities where they resettled. The phenomenon itself, however, did maintain the permeability of the membrane surrounding the Jewish people in an era of spiritual isolation when the Jews were more ethnically distinctive, perhaps, than ever before or after.[60]

If the fact of conversion to Judaism declined, what about Jewish hopes for the universal worship of the one God of Israel? There is no evidence that Jews significantly influenced the Judaizing trend in fifteenth- and sixteenth-century Muscovy or various sectors of the radical Reformation that placed a renewed emphasis on the Old Testament or rejected Trinitarianism.[61] But from the perspective of the long-range impact of Judaism, the Judaizing of Christianity (that is, the strengthening of the Jewish consituent of Christianity) needs to be noted, and did not go unnoticed in some formulations of the Jewish eschatological hopes.

In seventeenth- and eighteenth-century Jewish writing there was a tendency to develop the theme that Christianity was a Noahide religion, whose adherents had rejected idolatry and were to be regarded as monotheists. Jewish Enlightenment figures, such as Moses Mendelssohn, treated the Jewish reluctance to initiate conversionary activity as a logical consequence and factual demonstration of Jewish toleration of other religions. Thus in his well-known letter to Johann Caspar Lavater, Mendelssohn rejected the suggestion that he become a Christian:

> According to the principles of my faith, I must not seek to convert anyone not born a Jew. The zeal for making proselytes runs diametrically counter to the spirit of Judaism—assertions to the contrary by certain people notwithstanding. . . . Our rabbis are not only far from feeling any compulsion to proselytize but make a point of enjoining us to dissuade with the most serious arguments anyone asking to be converted. We are to tell any would-be convert how unnecessarily heavy a burden this decision would put on him . . . It should be evident, then, that my fathers' faith does not ask to be propagated.[62]

Still, the trickle of individual converts continued. Some of the most striking personalities were Johann Peter Spaeth, who took the name of Moses Germanus in 1626; Alexander Voznitzin, a retired Russian naval officer who was publicly burned at the stake in 1738 together with the Jew, Baruch Leibov, who helped him convert; the eighteenth-century Englishman Lord George Gordon, who spent the last years of his life as a fanatically pious Jew living in Newgate prison; and Warder Cresson, a

Quaker who was appointed United States consul in Jerusalem and became a member of the Sephardi community there after converting in 1848. They were among those that just could not be restrained from becoming Jews voluntarily, despite the evident dangers.[63]

Jewish Proselytism in Modern Times

A hallmark of Jewish modernity is Judaism's transformed situation in Western countries, as Jews gradually won civil equality and political rights and Judaism was freed from restrictions imposed by the legal supremacy of Christianity since the fourth century.[64] Although not all Western nations fully disestablished their state churches, each effected at least a pragmatic separation of Church and State, abolishing legal sanctions against a non-Jew who converted to Judaism. Yet conversion did not bring large numbers of new adherents into Jewry, and proselytism remained low on the agenda of modern Jewish issues—until a few decades ago. In the course of time the forces that inhibited Jewish proselytism weakened and gave way to the recent upsurge in the number of converts and renewed Jewish interest in furthering this trend.

As noted, there has always been some conversion to Judaism, more in certain places and times. The extensive proselytizing of the late ancient and early medieval periods was obscured by the self-contained, more withdrawn Jewish stance of the later Middle Ages and early modern era. Even in the era of Jewish emancipation, when legal barriers to non-Jews' conversion fell away, the disinclination lingered on. Therefore, we must distinguish between the historical conditions that permit voluntary conversion to Judaism and those that actually encourage it.

What attitudes might facilitate conversion among the general population? Judaism, certainly since the talmudic era, has not claimed to be the exclusive channel by which an individual can achieve immortality; indeed, from the perspective of traditional Jewish expectations, the non-Jew has a lighter burden in This World, inasmuch as he or she can attain a share in the World to Come by obeying the Noahide laws as a non-Jew rather than take on the full yoke of the commandments as a Jew. (In contrast, Judaism was the only organized monotheism before the middle of the first century c.e., when conversion may have had a stronger salvific force in the eyes of gentiles and Jewish missionizers alike, because the question of the non-Jewish share in the World to Come was yet undecided in Jewish theology.)

Undeniably, the image of the Jews and Judaism that predominated at the beginning of the modern era and for many decades thereafter hardly promoted conversion. Even people friendly to the Jews, who worked for their civil betterment, harbored negative stereotypes of the Jewish people and its faith. Modernity did not bring about the end to these prejudices, only their reformulation in more up-to-date terms. It was commonplace among enlightened nineteenth-century Christians, including some of the most eminent philosophers, that the Jewish religion was legalistic and tribal and that it had been superseded by Christianity, which universalized what was enduring in the Old Testament. Racial anti-Semites denied the very possibility of crossing the line dividing Jews from non-Jews, inasmuch as Jewishness was defined as a biological phenomenon and Jewish character a set of involuntary predispositions to arrogance, cowardice, and parasitism. The atmosphere generated by anti-Semitism sustained a long-standing negative valence of Jewishness in the eyes of many non-Jews (and of self-hating Jews as well) that acted as an overall deterrent to conversion.

The rate of proselytism is not only a function of the attitude of potential converts, but of the Jewish community as well. Nineteenth-century German Jewish religious thinkers responded to the Jews' emancipation by reversing the preceding centuries' posture of withdrawal and passivity vis-à-vis non-Jewish religions. The impetus for the development of a modern Jewish apologetics was internal and external: Judaism was thrust into the contemporary Western world of ideas and competing forces, impelled to offer a rationale for the continued loyalty of born Jews reared with a modern education and modern social aspirations.

Of considerable importance to nineteenth-century Jewish religious thinkers of all tendencies—Reform, Neo-Orthodox, and Positive-Historical—was the notion of the mission of Israel: that the survival and dispersion of the Jewish people entailed the positive task of inspiring humanity with pure ethical monotheism and the prophetic vision of universal peace and brotherhood. But this task was to be fulfilled by example (as in the Bible's prophetic writings), not by missionary zeal. Reform rabbis spoke of Judaism as the religion most suitable for the modern age and most at home with modern science and freedom, but no plans were formulated for an organized missionary endeavor; indeed, such proposals were greeted with embarrassment and no financial support. Reform rabbinical debates on conversion in the nineteenth century centered mainly on whether circumcision was still to be required of a male convert. The assumption remained that prospective converts would find a way to Judaism on their own.[65]

The orientation of modern East European Jewish intellectuals in the late nineteenth century was even less suitable to Jewish proselytizing. Many of these individuals, often men and women of great moral idealism and devotion to human betterment, had absorbed the view of the radical Russian intelligentsia that all positive religion was reactionary, an impediment to progress. When "freethinking" Jewish intellectuals returned to the Jewish people, they did so through participation in Jewish national and socialist movements, out of the conviction that it was politically necessary, ethnically natural, and psychologically healthy for Jews to accept themselves as Jews and express their modern cultural interests in a Jewish way. As militant secularists opposed to organized religion, they saw little sense in asking non-Jews to join them, except as allies in the struggle for Jewish and human liberation.

These circumstances have changed considerably in the last twenty years, and so has the pace of conversion. Blatant anti-Semitism in America has declined since World War II. In its stead there is a public fascination with things Jewish that is unprecedented perhaps since the Hellenistic era, as indicated by the recognition accorded Jewish writers in the literary mainstream (including some who draw on authentic Jewish symbols as well as modern Jewish experiences) and by the acceptance of Judaism in the American religious mainstream. In an increasingly secularized (one might say paganized) world, Judaism can offer without excuse its ideal of personal wholeness, spiritual values, cosmic vision, respect for learning, social ethics, and undogmatic approach to faith. Moreover, in contrast to the nineteenth-century rabbis' expectation that Jewish monotheism would be most attractive if stripped of its ethnic integument, Judaism's particularistic heritage has become one of its strongest appeals. In a homogenized culture, cultural identity is a precious matter indeed.

Paradoxically, while the ethnic has gained in general appeal, Jews are ethnically less distinctive—linguistically and culturally less peculiar—than they have been for centuries. They are more open to the general culture, play a more active role in the general society, and are more accessible to non-Jews. Perhaps it is this social factor mainly that stimulates conversion to Judaism on a large scale, rather than a growth in the limited number of individual thoughtful religious searchers. The most likely candidates at present for conversion are people caught up in the Jewish network: people who desire to marry a Jew or, having married a Jew, to establish a Jewish home.

The rate of interfaith marriage has increased so dramatically in recent decades that some sociologists suggest that the conversion to Judaism of the non-Jewish partner is a significant factor in maintaining the size of the American Jewish community against a shrinkage resulting from assimilation and a low birthrate. Recent figures suggest that 20 to 30 percent of intermarriages involve the conversion of the non-Jew to Judaism. By conservative estimate, more than ten thousand persons are embracing Judaism every year. When Jewish leaders, such as Alexander Schindler of the Union of American Hebrew Congregations, advocate a more active program of proselytizing among the "unchurched," a specific target group is the non-Jewish fiancées or spouses of born Jews.[66]

As we have seen, classical Jewish sources tend to place a premium on sincere conversions—conversions based solely on love for Israel's God without ulterior or practical motive. Moderns are more realistic and sophisticated about seemingly disinterested reasons, because they recognize that the distinction between sincerity and insincerity can be misleading and all too simplistic. Some of the purest of heart may in fact be desperately lost souls, acting out anger or resentment against parents or peers. More constructive and salutary may be the contribution of those whose conversion is rooted not only in respect for the Jewish heritage but also in a desire for family unity and for rearing children with an unambiguous religious identification. Pragmatically motivated conversions are not necessarily perfunctory ones: a person grows into mature Jewish religious faith over the course of years, and knowledge of the Jewish tradition may tap spiritual depths. One hears rabbis say that Jews by choice, who have married born Jews and undertaken the study of Judaism's beliefs and practices, are among their most active and committed congregants.[67]

The new prominence of Jewish proselytizing (still mild by Christian evangelical standards) has become a matter of some controversy in American Jewish religious circles and between American Jewry and Israel's Orthodox establishment. Must all conversions be conducted according to a strict adherence to traditional legal formalities (circumcision, immersion, appearance before a rabbinic court)? The question of the contemporary authority of the *halakhah* is a matter of heated opinion. There are rabbis who advocate more flexibility in the application of Jewish religious law than the rigorous Orthodox authorities. There are rabbis who treat Jewish law only loosely as a precedent. It is not infrequent in the history of religions that theoretical disagreements over authority have escalated into painful and prolonged confrontation over who decides what is allowed and what is prohibited. What legitimacy, if any, will be conceded by the Orthodox rabbinate to the Reform, Conservative, and Reconstructionist rabbinate in the Diaspora? In Israel, Orthodox authorities have been insistent on the invalidity of all conversions performed under Reform, Conservative, and Reconstructionist auspices, even when traditional legal formalities are respected—an issue with the potential to sunder Israel from American Jewry's non-Orthodox majority.

Especially since the Holocaust, Jews have been preoccupied with maintaining the unity of the Jewish people. While there have been some in modern Orthodoxy and Reform who have inclined virtually to separatism, most have been willing to place the good of the whole above theological purity or the strictest formulas of the *halakhah*. Some Orthodox rabbis in nineteenth-century America, inclined to leniency in order to save Jewish homes, deliberately overlooked the probability that certain converts would not observe the commandments in the traditional sense.[68] On the other hand, earlier in this century two rabbis of Argentina banned all conversions there "to the end of time" on the grounds that this was the only way to combat the "wanton" life in Buenos Aires.[69] Orthodoxy, like the other groupings in modern Judaism, has shown a wide range of views that can be applied to the contemporary scene. Some pessimistic observers predict that the current tension will split the Jews into separate communities by the end of the century. There are, however, tendencies working against schism. A recent effort in Denver indicates sufficient grey area in Jewish religious law that a conversion procedure could be evolved with which members of all the branches of American Judaism might live in good conscience.[70] Such a solution, or quasi-solution, would require the acceptance of ambiguity, the deliberate use of *halakhic* legal fiction, an overwhelming desire to sustain the continuity of the Jewish tradition, the acknowledgment of the priority of broadminded Jewish spiritual goals against limited denominational or ideological interests, a practical toleration of diversity and pluralism within Judaism—qualities not in abundant supply in certain periods of history, including the present.

What is the future of conversion to Judaism? There is yet one other consideration that places contemporary conversion to Judaism in a context almost entirely novel to Jewish history. The dichotomy between Jews-by-birth and Jews-by-choice has lost much of its force because so many Jews-by-birth are faced with deciding whether they chose to become Jews in a meaningful sense. Now that Jews no longer live in a ghetto or a *shtetl*, the inertia of traditionalist culture and the force of anti-Semitism do not suffice to maintain the Jewishness of numerous Diaspora Jews. Under present circumstances, living Jewishly means devoting time past childhood years to acquiring Jewish knowledge and deciding to involve oneself in Jewish actions at home, in a synagogue, or in various organizational contexts. This crucial step may occur any time from late adolescence to late in life. We live in a period when young *baalei teshuvah* (repentant Jews) go to learn Torah in traditional *yeshivot,* when adult Jews undertake to become *bar* and *bat mitzvah,* when Jewish students (and senior citizens) register for courses in Judaica in colleges and universities. If being Jewish is more voluntary and self-committing than ever before, then the situation of the Jew-by-choice is no longer exceptional. The blurring of the boundary between individuals born to and those maturing into Judaism may be disconcerting to those who adhere to the traditional model of how Jews should be recruited, just as the conversion of lapsed Christians to Judaism may be disconcerting to those who presume that the natural order is the reverse. But the new voluntary Jewishness and openness to newcomers can prove a vitalizing challenge, indicating that one of history's oldest continuous religious traditions can still adapt to the unprecedented, which, after all, is what history is about.

Part Three

---◆---

Proselytism and Christian Exclusivism

5

Proselytism and Exclusivity in Early Christianity

JOHN G. GAGER

Three Questions

I have taken as my subject the issues of exclusivism and proselytism in the early centuries of the Christian movement. I will limit myself primarily to the first two centuries with a brief look into an episode at the end of the fourth century. My questions are the following:

—What is it that gives rise to proselytism among early Christians?

—Where do we find evidence of exclusivism, in the sense of exclusive claims to truth, among these Christians?

—What relationship, if any, can be established between exclusivism on the one hand and the drive toward proselytism or missionary activity on the other?

Before trying to answer these, we should look at what modern scholarship has said about them. This will have the double advantage of helping to place my own observations in some sort of setting and even more important of creating targets for me to shoot at as I develop my own thoughts.

One of my arguments will be that in establishing their own identity and self-definition, the earliest Christians frequently set up exaggerated contrasts between themselves and significant outsiders in their cultural and religious environment. My favorite example of this behavior is a line by Tertullian, writing from North Africa toward the end of the second century. In making the point that Christians represent something entirely new in the world, with no links to pagan history or culture, he proclaims, "What has Athens to do with Jerusalem; what has philosophy to do with faith?"[1] But he is very careful to write this spiteful prose in the classically elegant phrases of Ciceronian Latin.

As we look at what early Christians said about outsiders, we need to resist the temptation to take their reports too literally, remembering that their view of outsiders is not like that of modern anthropologists. They are using the outsiders for their own purposes, and we should be prepared for a significant dose of overstatement and distortion. And so, too, what I have to say about previous work on these topics should not be taken too literally; I am using them in large part to clarify where I stand on these important issues. The fact of the matter is that until very recently there had been very little work on either exclusivism *or* proselytism in early Christianity and almost none at all on possible connections between them.

Proselytism

On the question of proselytism there has been very little written since Adolf Harnack's *Mission and Expansion of Christianity* first appeared in 1902.[2] Ironically, the most important contribution after Harnack came only in 1984 and was written not by a scholar of the New Testament or a church historian but by a thoroughly secular historian of the later Roman Empire.[3]

The time-gap between Harnack and Ramsay MacMullen's *Christianizing the Roman Empire* is surprising in its own right, but all the more so when one realizes that missionizing was a universal feature of the early Christian movement. What is even more surprising is that neither Harnack nor MacMullen nor those who wrote between them bothered to give much attention to the question *why* these Christians, or at least the very earliest among them, made proselytizing not just an important task, but in some ways the very center of their religion. The Gospels, the Book of Acts and the Letters of Paul project an image of the movement in which missionary activity is the central feature—to be a "real" Christian was in some sense to be a missionary, a proselytizer, an apostle—and this is true not just in the pictures that Christians drew of themselves, but in the pictures of them drawn by outsiders. At the very least, it seems reasonable to ask why this should have been the case. Was it a function of their monotheism? If so, why was Judaism not a missionary religion in the same way? Was it simply because the Gospels portray Jesus as urging his followers to preach the Gospel to others? In some sense, of course, this answer only pushes the question back one step, ignoring the further question of why Jesus' missionary commands in early Christian literature were singled out for special attention.

Exclusivism

If we turn for a moment to the issue of Christian exclusivism, the results are pretty much the same. As I searched my memory for titles that include the term "exclusivism," I found myself coming up short. Occasionally one finds stray sentences or even paragraphs concerning Christian attitudes toward beliefs and practices associated with pagan cults, but very little else.

There are two noteworthy exceptions to this observation. In his marvelous little book *Pagan and Christian in an Age of Anxiety* (i.e., the period between 150–300), E. R. Dodds speaks briefly about the psychological and social consequences of Christian exclusivism:

> . . . its very exclusiveness, its refusal to concede any value to alternative forms of worship, which nowadays is often felt to be a weakness, was in the circumstances of the time, a source of strength. The religious tolerance which was the normal Greek and Roman practice had resulted by accumulation in a bewildering mass of alternatives. There were too many cults, too many mysteries, too many philosophies of life; you could pile one religious insurance on another, yet not feel safe. Christianity made a clean sweep. It lifted the burden of freedom from the shoulders of the individual: one choice, one irrevocable choice and the road to salvation was clear. Pagan critics might mock at Christian intolerance, but in an age of anxiety any "totalist" creed exerts a powerful attraction . . .[4]

Or, as Ramsay MacMullen puts it somewhat more succinctly, "the Roman Empire seemed positively to invite a sharply focused and intransigent creed . . ."[5]

The second exception takes us in a different direction. Whereas Dodds and MacMullen offer a look at what might be considered positive aspects of Christian intolerance, Rosemary Ruether focuses on the negative aspects of what she calls Christian triumphalism as it grew out of Christian encounters with Judaism in the early centuries. Her general conclusion can be summarized in the statement that "for Christianity, anti-Judaism was not merely a defense against attack, but an intrinsic need of Christian self-affirmation."[6]

There will be more to say about both of these exceptions later on, but for the time being let me leave them with the comment that each takes Christian exclusivism as a given. For both Dodds and Ruether, exclusivism is the hallmark of Christianity from the beginning, a primary trait that requires no explanation. But I am skeptical. For me, nothing should escape examination, and it is precisely what seems self-evident that requires a second look.

Connections between Proselytism and Exclusivism

Finally, in this hasty review we need to ask what connections have been made between proselytism and exclusivism. Once again, the answer is: "Not many." But once again there are a few exceptions. Ruether notes that much of early Christian anti-Jewish literature—and this is where we find Christian exclusivism in its strongest terms—seems to arise from situations where Christian believers were engaged with local Jewish synagogues in various ways. In some cases this involvement was entirely positive, taking the form of what I call Christian Judaizing—attending synagogue worship services, observing the major Jewish holidays and that sort of thing; in other cases, the involvement took a more negative form, as when Christians found themselves the targets of religious and theological criticisms directed at them by local synagogues.

If this first exception points to an external stimulus, something happening outside the churches, for the generation of an exclusivist attitude, the second one points instead to an internal cause, though both are linked to situations of conflict. What I have in mind is a recent series on the subject of *Jewish and Christian Self-Definition*.[7] While neither proselytism nor exclusivism is treated as fully as they should be, two essays in particular deal with the rise of Christian orthodoxy in this period in terms that I find quite useful. William Schoedel's essay on Ignatius of Antioch—an important figure who wrote a series of letters around the year 110—and Robert Markus's essay on Christianity's transformation from a sect to a church both argue that orthodoxy represents a significant narrowing of options *within* the church.[8] Diversity and disagreement gradually gave way to a stiff distinction between orthodoxy and heresy. At the same time, this sense of internal exclusivism—roughly, the emergence of orthodoxy—goes hand in hand with the growth of institutional power in general and with the increasing tendency of ecclesiastical power to become concentrated in the hands of a new power-elite represented by the bishops. The theme that governs this period is nicely put by Schoedel, who asserts that "exclusion and unity are two sides of the same coin."[9] The one goes with the other. This line of development reached its culmination under Constantine, when the church suddenly found itself with access to more power than it had ever dreamed of. But as many Christians soon learned to their dismay, political power, like electricity, could be a very tricky thing; if you are not a skilled technician, it can do you great harm. And the greater the power, the more serious the potential for damage.

Issues and Texts

Proselytism

Few scholars have ever paused to ask what it was about proselytism that made it such an important feature of early Christian behavior. Such answers as have been put forward tend to confuse what I would call the settings of missionary activity, or even its content, with its causes or sources. Among the standard explanations are Jesus' command to preach the Gospel, the experience of Jesus' resurrection, and the expectation of the coming kingdom. Let me focus on the last of these, which argues that the basic drive behind early Christian proselytism was the belief that the end of history was approaching in the immediate future.

The early churches' missionary zeal was undeniably related to their eschatological consciousness. But this observation alone hardly settles the matter. The basic questions are still unanswered. Why, for instance, did the churches ignore those sayings in the Gospels that limited the mission to Israel or which swore the disciples to silence and secrecy? Why did missions persist long after most Christians had ceased regarding the kingdom as imminent? Why is it that some eschatological groups, both ancient and modern, retreat into isolationism and quietism toward the outside world and avoid any suggestion of a mission? In short, explanations that appeal to eschatology as the basic motivation for missions are not really explanations at all. They simply note that the early Christians were both eschatological and missionary and then proceed to assume that the one must have caused the other.

Rather than abandon any connection between eschatology and missions, I have argued that the precise nature of their connection can be understood by appealing to the social-psychological theory of cognitive dissonance as developed by Leon Festinger and others.[10] In its basic form, the theory holds, against common sense, that under certain conditions a religious community whose fundamental beliefs are disconfirmed by events in the real world will not necessarily collapse and disband. Instead, such a community frequently undertakes zealous missionary activities. The crucial element in the theory is that the presence of dissonance, a sense of discomfort arising from the disconfirmation or challenging of important beliefs, gives rise to pressures to reduce or eliminate the dissonance.[11] And among the various techniques used for reducing dissonance, Festinger argues, proselytism is one of the most common and most effective. The unconscious assumption, according to him, is that "if more and more people can be persuaded that the system of belief is correct, then clearly it must, after all, be correct."[12]

Now, I would argue, it is possible to return to the connection between proselytism and missions with a new set of questions. Specifically, is it possible to reverse the traditional explanation and to argue that early Christian missions began not in response to eschatological hopes but in an effort to keep them from collapsing? Can we imagine that missionary activity was born out of and sustained by disappointment and despair over the delay in the coming of the kingdom, a despair and disappointment that are amply illustrated in early Christian documents?

The theory of cognitive dissonance makes it possible to suppose that missionary activity in the early churches was undertaken in part as a means of reducing the sense of disappointment at unrealized hopes about God's kingdom. Of course, there were other sources of dissonance as well, such as the belief that Jesus was the expected Messiah of Israel despite the fact that Jewish opponents regularly pointed out that traditional messianic expectations left no room for a crucified Messiah. And there were also other responses to dissonance, including a tendency to rationalize or reformulate the basic beliefs so that they seemed less open to disconfirmation by external evidence. But the real point I want to make here is that missionary activity was neither inevitable nor universal in early Christianity. It was neither a direct inheritance from its Jewish heritage, though there were forms of proselytizing in ancient Judaism, nor the necessary consequence of biblical monotheism. Nor, as we have seen, is there any direct link between missions and an expectation that the world is about to end. So far, the only clear link is an unexpected one: missionary activity appears to be most likely when a religious community experiences the discomfort that accompanies the disconfirmation of important beliefs.

Exclusivism

With these thoughts about proselytism and its motivations in mind, I would like to turn to the question of religious exclusivism. And in doing so, I want to begin by citing three brief passages from various early Christian documents.

They answered him, "Abraham is our father." Jesus said to them, "If you were Abraham's children, you would do what Abraham did, but now you seek to kill me, a man who has told you the truth which I heard from God; this is not what Abraham did. You do what your (real) father did." They said to him, "We were not born of fornication; we have one father, even God." Jesus said to them, "If God were your father, you would love me, for I proceeded and came forth from God; I came not of my own accord, but he sent me. Why do you not understand what I say? It is because you cannot bear to hear my word. You are of your father, the devil, and your will is to do your father's desires. He was a murderer from the beginning and has nothing to do with the truth because there is no truth in him." (John 8:39–44)[13]

Do not be led astray by strange doctrines or by old fables which are now profitless. For if we still live according to Judaism, we as much as confess that we have not received grace . . . Put aside the evil leaven which has grown old and sour and turn to the new leaven which is Jesus Christ . . . It is monstrous to talk of Jesus Christ and to practice Judaism (*ioudaizein*). (Ignatius, *To the Magnesians* 10.3 [c.110])

If you admire the Jewish way of life, what do you have in common with us? If the Jewish rites are holy and venerable, our way of life must be false. But if our way is true, as indeed it is, theirs is fraudulent. (John Chrysostom, *Against the Judaizers* 1.6)[14]

In the early development of Christianity's self-understanding and self-definition, Judaism was a, possibly even *the*, primary factor. If this seems painfully obvious, let me reassure you that it has not seemed obvious to many others. When E. R. Dodds deals with Christianity's growth in the Roman world, he simply ignores Judaism. Ramsay Mac-Mullen's very stimulating book makes scarcely any mention of Judaism. And in the volume on early Christian self-definition, Judaism is prominent above all by virtue of its almost total absence.

Both in the early stages, when the followers of Jesus were still a reform or revitalization movement *within* Judaism, and later on when the two traditions had forged separate identities, Judaism remained the focal point of Christian efforts to discover and proclaim what it was. Wherever Christians moved in the Roman Empire, they found well-established and highly respected Jewish communities. When Christians sought to announce themselves as the true biblical people, they were met with disbelief from many pagans and active resistance from most Jews. And in the late fourth century, in the largely Christian city of Antioch, at a time when the Roman emperor himself was Christian, church leaders like John Chrysostom found members of their own congregations affiliating with local synagogues in a variety of ways, but not in such a way that they ceased regarding themselves as Christians.

When Christian leaders like Ignatius and John Chrysostom found themselves confronted with these circumstances, they frequently responded with various forms of anti-Jewish polemics, polemics that were all the more intense because these circumstances seemed to undermine what has been called the theology of Christian triumphalism. In other words, the earliest expressions of Christian exclusivism—which took the form of insisting that God had rejected the old people (the Jews) and replaced them with a new people (Christians/gentiles)—took shape in encounters with Judaism as they are reflected in the gospels. And the strongest expressions of Christian exclusivism some three hundred years later are still to be found in settings where the real facts of Judaism—its continued vigor and attractiveness for both gentiles and Christians—continued to belie the aspirations of Christian triumphalism. To paraphrase Peter Berger, the continued existence and vitality of Judaism as an alternative symbolic universe posed a threat to Christians like Ignatius and John because it demonstrated that their own symbolic universe was less than inevitable.[15]

Under these conditions, as Berger has put it rather ominously, the threatened party may seek to defend and reinforce its legitimacy through the process of what he calls conceptual nihilation[16] or, in slightly different language, through the religious and theological liquidation of whatever appears to threaten its own universe. This, I take it, is what Rosemary Ruether has in mind when she concludes that for "Christianity, anti-Judaism was not merely a defense against attack, but an intrinsic need of Christian self-affirmation."[17] In short, expressions of Christian exclusivism derive neither from Christianity's monotheism nor from its biblical heritage as such. Instead, they are born in and later sustained by Christianity's anxious struggle with Judaism over the question of who could claim exclusive rights to the status of True Israel and True People of God.

When we look elsewhere in the early centuries for expressions of exclusivism in Christian circles, the results are rather surprising. Among many Christian apologists and theologians, especially those immersed in the philosophical culture of Greek and Roman Platonism, there was a strong tendency to include wise philosophers who had lived before the time of Christ within the company of the elect. Of course, virtually all Christians agreed that the old-style pagan cults—what we usually have in mind when we speak of Greek and Roman paganism as opposed to Greek and Roman philosophy—were to be ruled out of court completely. But this view was hardly limited to Christians. In fact,

Christians borrowed most of their arguments against traditional paganism from Jewish and Greek philosophical sources. Even on the question of exclusivity vis-à-vis Judaism, a figure like the Apostle Paul, whose presence bulks so large in the New Testament, has been radically reinterpreted in recent years in a way that makes him not the author of anti-Judaism, as traditional Christianity has understood him, but the theologian of two covenants, one fulfilled for Jews in the covenant of Moses and the other fulfilled for gentiles in the covenant of Christ.

This suggests that in assessing the issue of Christian exclusivism, we need to take great care not to fall into what has been called the elitist fallacy. Both academic and religious assertions about Jewish-Christian relations in the early centuries have tended to assume that a final and painful parting of the ways took place sometime in the late first or early second centuries. These assertions are usually accompanied by explanations of what it was that led Christianity not just to part company with Judaism but to repudiate and denigrate it as well. In other words, from the Christian perspective the parting of the ways has always involved a theological exclusivism that left no room for Judaism. And the questions that are usually asked are: Why should this have been the case? Why was it necessary not just to leave Judaism but to dismiss it as well? Why was it not possible for Christianity simply to go one way while allowing Judaism to follow another?

Many historians, sociologists, and theologians have proposed answers to these. I confess to having made use of them myself. But I have much less confidence in them today than I did even a short time ago, and the reason is that I am no longer convinced that there was a final parting of the ways except among a theological and ecclesiastical elite. In other words, for many Christians of an ordinary variety and for others whose voices are difficult to hear because they wound up on the losing side of the debate, there never was a parting of the ways. For them, there really is nothing to explain. For if some Christians did insist on their exclusive right to represent the biblical truth, others not only refused to part company but actively resisted efforts from ecclesiastical leaders to force them to do so. Or, to put it somewhat differently, it can no longer be argued, as Ruether and others have done, that anti-Judaism is intrinsic and inevitable for Christian self-affirmation as such.

In short, the exclusivism and the triumphalism that characterize much of early Christian literature on Judaism does not tell the full story, though it does tell the official one. My general impression is that the dividing line between those who saw no need to repudiate Judaism in affirming their Christianity and those who did tends to follow the contours of power and authority. As we might expect, and here we can find plenty of parallels in our own world, those in positions of power tend to define and defend themselves by emphasizing the differences between *us* and *them*. This will be especially true when the competition involves closely related parties. As one sociologist has put it, "The closer the relationship, the more intense the conflict."[18] To which I would add the important proviso that this law appears not to be true for everyone. It is, I would argue, the additional factor of power and authority that turns competitors into enemies and insists on the conceptual nihilation of competing systems. When we add the factor of power to the earlier observation that exclusion and unity are two sides of the same coin, it should come as no great surprise that the most prominent opponents of both Christian heresy (the internal challengers) and Judaism (the external threat) are to be found among the new power elite of the recently Christianized Roman Empire, namely the bishops of great cities—John Chrysostom in Antioch, Ambrose in Milan, and Cyril in Alexandria.

Conclusions

Very briefly, and somewhat whimsically, I would like to return to the question of whether we can detect any important connections between exclusivism and proselytism in the world of early Christianity. There are such connections, I think, but not exactly where we would expect to find them.

The most thoroughly exclusivist document in the New Testament, and not coincidentally the most vocally anti-Jewish, is the Gospel of John. But there is no sense that the community of this Gospel was interested in spreading its message to Jews or gentiles. The figure of Jesus in John is an intensely private one; outsiders come to him—and misunderstand him; but neither he nor his disciples go out to the world.

At the other extreme, the most intense proselytizer in early Christianity, the Apostle Paul, is also the sole representative of the view that Jews and Christians stood side by side, as separate but equal beneficiaries of God's ancient promises to Abraham. Of course, Paul was thoroughly hostile and exclusivist about everything that stood outside the Bible, but for him the gentiles no longer fell into that category.

Finally, there is the peculiar case of John Chrysostom at Antioch in the 380s, although we are now beginning to realize that his situation is not quite as peculiar as it once seemed. What was the relationship between exclusivism and proselytism for him? It would seem that his radically exclusivist brand of Christianity, sometimes directed against other Christians and sometimes against the Jews, produced an *inner-Christian* mission. What John told his congregation was that they should go out and proselytize their fellow Christians, wean them away from their involvement with the local synagogues, and convert them to his exclusivist understanding of the relationship between Judaism and Christianity.

At the end, we are left with an intriguing possibility. Instead of supposing that missionary outreach arises from a stance of certainty and confidence, we must now consider whether it is not more likely to appear as an antidote to doubt and uncertainty. One noted historian has rejected the notion that the early Christians turned to missions because the kingdom failed to materialize as expected, that proselytism served as a substitute for eschatological hopes. We must now consider the possibility that the church carried on its mission precisely in an effort to maintain those hopes.

6

Christianity, Culture, and Complications: Protestant Attitudes toward Missions

WILLIAM R. HUTCHISON

One of the central queries for this volume is whether the proselytizing ideology and practices that have been so evident in certain eras of Christian history have owed more to historical circumstance or to originating and inherent ideas (such as monotheism or exclusivism or Christ's "great commission"). My response is that the drive to proselytize, while grounded in Christian Scriptures, has been given its opportunity by cultural forces largely extrinsic to the Christian movement of a given time. To say this is not to deny the place of religion or Christianity in the emergence of such "secular" phenomena as New World exploration or the rise of capitalism. Quite the contrary: the religious sources, components, and rationales of secular cultural developments are precisely what made it possible for contemporaries to find God's hand and will in virtually every historical event or movement—and particularly in those thought to demonstrate God's desire for a Christian conquest of the world.

What cultural development gives it can eventually take away. The opportunity to proselytize passes; and with its passing, much of the rationale for such activity disappears or becomes merely latent. In the intervening time—between the rise of the opportunity and its decline—the role of culture's secular components seems above all to be one of "complicating," of creating endless dilemmas within the seemingly straightforward programs for preaching a faith and converting people to it.

This dual functioning of culture, as facilitator for activities such as missions and then as complicator of the same ventures, has been especially evident in the case of Christianity's interdependent relation to modern Western culture. Without what William McNeill called the "rise of the West" after 1500,[1] without the economic-political expansion first of Catholic and then of Protestant Europe, it is doubtful whether "foreign missions" of any sort could have been launched on a substantial scale. More to our present point, it is even less likely that without the expansionist impetus the idea of actual proselytization in foreign settings could have taken hold. Proselytism was an idea that the Protestant reformers of the sixteenth century had not put forward.[2] When their successors did take up that idea, secular expansionism, construed as a latter-day revelation of God's will, did far more than Scriptures or texts could do to imbed proselytization in some forms of Christian orthodoxy.

You will note that, though we are presumably interested in such traits as exclusivism—the claim to final and preemptive truth—and in such convictions as monotheism, I am bearing down on the terms "proselytization" and "proselytism." These are emotionally laden terms that missionaries themselves were inclined to avoid. Yet when understood neutrally as denoting the desire to win conversions, proselytism does seem to be the key concept for comparative purposes. I wish to insist, moreover, that the distinction between this intention and characteristics such as exclusivism must be kept clear, especially within the kind of argument I am advancing.

Our various terms, in other words, are not interchangeable. The commitment to proselytize involves more than a conviction of superiority, more even than the presumption, to be found among many religions and peoples, that one possesses an exclusive and saving hold on truth. It is this "more," within the definition and career of proselytism, that I think depends so heavily upon historical circumstance and development.

The Question of Representativeness

The American Protestant effort in foreign missions is the only one I am at all equipped to analyze. Can we consider that effort and its guiding assumptions representative, at least for Protestantism? I believe we can to a very large extent. To be sure, the American movement presents clear variants from its British and especially its Continental counterparts—most of these relating to the American trait usually called activism. Americans in missions as in other pursuits were, as Philip Schaff put it, "uncommonly practical, energetic, and enterprising . . . more like the busy Martha than like the pensive Mary, sitting at the feet of Jesus."[3] American evolutionary optimism, American impatience and quantity-mindedness, and our special zeal to "civilize" as well as convert, were traits distinct enough to create serious tensions within the international Protestant venture. Disagreements and hard feelings, around 1900, between German pietists and Anglo-American activists have been virtually ignored in the history books, but they appear to have caused grave disruptions in ecumenical Christianity and to have exacerbated the mutual distrust that allowed the First World War to occur.

Even so, such internal differences were matters of degree. They were also matters of rhetoric: Americans and continental Europeans differed much more in what they proclaimed than in what they actually went out and did. The American branch of the enterprise, moreover, became so dominant, numerically and otherwise (this of course was one large reason for the hard feelings just mentioned), that its peculiarities became representative in another sense: Americans by 1900 were doing a great deal of the "representing."[4]

More broadly, the American instance may be archetypal, hence especially instructive, in what it tells us about the two functions of culture that I want to delineate and discuss, namely, its function as that which provided opportunity for missions, and then as the diverse reality that produced complications and terrible dilemmas for missionary thought and activity.

With respect to the first of these functions, I have suggested that zeal for proselytization was heavily dependent upon the opportunities presented by cultural development. I have moreover shown a readiness to change that "was" to "is"—in other words to argue that such is generally or generically the case and that the unfolding American experience is in that sense very broadly representative. With respect to culture as complication, I would say much the same thing, but would be cautious about claiming representativeness beyond the confines of Western civilization.

The most persistent American problem under this second rubric, the one usually identified as "evangelization versus civilization," is surely one that has dogged Christianity throughout its long and troubled love affair with the West. It is, moreover, a problem that has persisted and been especially troublesome *because of* the peculiar conditions of that partnership. The anxious and constant concern whether to "civilize" or just "evangelize" could have had meaning, probably, only in the thinking of Westerners—only, that is, where it was common to conceive and reify "religion" as something distinguishable from culture in the first place. (Most non-Western languages contain the adjective "religious," but not the noun "religion.")[5]

It would seem, then, that at some of its deeper levels the American story is that of all Christianity (culture as complication) or even of all expansionist religion (culture as opportunity).

Culture as Opportunity

Historians who feel a strong personal commitment to missions frequently have shied away from secular explanations for the rise and persistence of the modern missionary movement. For such historians or other advocates, the idea that missionaries set forth *because* treaty ports were opened or *because* Americans hoped to spread democratic ideology has been anathema. But in offering such defenses of the missionaries' purity of motive, the apologists have been somewhat out of touch with the people they write about. They have been speaking a language that nineteenth-century missionaries and mission theorists could scarcely have understood.

Modern defenders may think the movement must be protected against reduction to secular explanation; and indeed it must be, to some extent, given the crude reductionisms in much that has heretofore passed for analysis of missions. But to suppose that nineteenth-century missionaries or theorists themselves disdained cultural explanations is sadly to misconstrue their understanding of culture and of movements in human history. It is, putting it another way, to impose upon them a much narrower definition of the term "religious" and a far more limited conception of God's action in history than they in fact employed.[6]

Arthur T. Pierson, editor of *Missionary Review of the World,* outstanding evangelical leader, and a premillennialist to boot, in 1886 penned the following exultant appreciation of the opportunities presented in cultural development—past, present, and future:

We have seen God making a highway for his Chariot through the iron gates of heathen hostility and Christian apathy. . . . While God permitted Protestant England to plant an empire toward the sunrise, the Pilgrims were driven toward these shores to sow the seeds of a Christian republic beside the setting sun. . . . Then the providence of God, by the issue of conflicts in America and India, settled the question that in both hemispheres the cross, and not the crescent nor crucifix, was to be dominant.[7]

Mission publicists like Pierson, though they began turning down the volume on such rhetoric soon after 1900, saw the "opening" of territories, from Marco Polo to Matthew Perry and beyond, as God's strategy for preparing the world, in distinct stages, for reception of the Gospel. As the Pierson excerpt suggests, they understood democratic ideology as religious ideology. They also, to be sure, viewed human culture as steeped in sin and marked by recalcitrance; one did not have to be a premillennialist nor even a conservative evangelical to hold that view. Yet human cultural development was conceived, in whatever degree a particular theology and eschatology permitted, as representing some degree of realization, in history, of the greater glory of God. Whatever human progress one acknowledged, whether much or little, was understood as God's progress.

American theologies, taken across their entire spectrum, allowed for more extensive realizations of the kingdom within history than had any others, perhaps, in the history of Christian thought. Samuel Hopkins, stern purveyor of "consistent Calvinism" in the Revolutionary period and after, spent much of a long *Treatise on the Millennium* in depicting the technological and other everyday delights of a better day that would precede as well as follow Christ's return. Such catalogues of earthly, or at least earthly sounding, wonders had already appeared in the writings of Jonathan Edwards, and they became utterly familiar elements in the foreign-mission rhetoric of the nineteenth century. If we are to take American missionary thought (to which Hopkins himself contributed massively) at its word, I think we are bound to regard the impulse to proselytize—not just to hold strong and exclusive convictions, but to seek to win others to them in all parts of the world—as having been strongly conditioned by what were understood at the time as providential developments in contemporaneous human history.[8]

Warrants for aggressive foreign mission activity were of course prominently available in Scripture. Jesus's "great commission," the admonition to go into all the world and preach the Gospel, was merely the most explicit proof text and the most commonly utilized. But on the other side of the argument there were at least as many biblical warrants—exegeted at length by critics of conversionary missions from Roger Williams in the seventeenth century through Alexander Campbell, Horace Bushnell, and the Anti-mission Baptists in the nineteenth—for inquiring exactly who has been annointed to convert others; for viewing the Christian community in static terms as a city set upon a hill; even for insisting that God's people stay at home and strive toward the salvation and perfection of the little flock.[9] For every "go into all the world" verse there was at least one other that admonished Christ's followers to "go nowhere among the gentiles . . . but go rather to the lost sheep of the house of Israel" (Matt. 10:5–6). Scriptural marching orders could thus be countermanded from Scripture—or could be made to say, as the Bible had seemed to say to most sixteenth-century Reformers, that "this is not the time."

Given that not-unusual situation of disparity among prooftexts, a great deal depended upon what appeared to be (whether called exactly this or not) God's continuing revelation in history. For increasing portions of Protestantism, from the eighteenth century onward, God's message through history was clear: You are the people, and this is the time. That message, articulated in the rise and expansion of the West, helped one choose which traditions and biblical texts to emphasize. Culture, more than just the enabler for proselytization, could be regarded as presenting God's challenge, to which the seemingly obvious response in the case at hand was world conversion.

Culture as Complication

In any such discussion of the opportunities afforded by cultural development, we are relating culture to the ground plan, to the fundamental religious justification for the mission enterprise. The resulting commitment was in itself simple, straightforward, and nearly univocal, from the preparatory experience in colonial Indian missions; through the first actual "foreign" ventures beginning in 1810; right up until the years 1925–1935 when for the first time, in the controversies surrounding the so-called Laymen's Report, the commitment to conversion missions came to be questioned in a serious and public way within the American Protestant churches.[10] Before that shaking of the foundations in the 1920s and 1930s, liberals nearly as much as conservative evangelicals had been steadily insistent that God, through historical confirmations of His intent, had instructed His latter-day people not just to go, not just to serve, but to preach, to convert, and (as a church) to conquer. Yet throughout that classical period of missionary history, this rather remarkable consensus about the overall and central aim of missions appeared far less clear, at best, in everyday application. The problem, the complicating factor, was culture.

To use the alternative terminology common in the nineteenth century, the problem was not evangelization but civilization. The duty to evangelize the world, to make the Gospel known everywhere and convert as many as possible, was a matter of general and powerful agreement. The question was whether "civilizing" (educating, reforming, sharing one's technologies) was also part of the missionary assignment.

Often the missionaries were offered mixed signals. One typical set of instructions, given in 1819 to the first missionaries to Hawaii, directed them to "aim at nothing short of covering those islands with fruitful fields, and pleasant dwellings, and schools and churches," to raise an entire people "to an elevated state of Christian civilization." Yet a most influential line of missionary advocacy and policy, beginning at almost the same date and continuing prominently until late in the nineteenth century, adopted a nearly opposite approach, proclaiming with assurance and some acerbity that a noncivilizing approach was the only scriptural one. Francis Wayland, a prominent Baptist theologian and the president of Brown University, explained that

> the son of God has left us no directions for civilizing the heathen, and then Christianizing them. We are not commanded to teach schools in order to undermine paganism, and then, on its ruins, to build up Christianity. If this is our duty, the command must be found in another gospel; it is not found in the Gospel of Jesus Christ.[11]

The issue was not at all new to the nineteenth century. St. Paul, determined to "know nothing" in his approach to the gentiles "except Jesus Christ, and him crucified" (I Cor. 2:2), could easily be read as counseling against the imposition of one's culture on others. The Roman Catholic church in the seventeenth century had advised its missionaries not to try to change the "manners, customs, and uses" of the people they sought to convert. As the Roman authorities put it, rhetorically, "What could be more absurd than to transport France, Spain, Italy, or some European country to China? Do not introduce all of that to them, but only the faith."[12]

But the difficulties encountered when missionaries tried to heed such advice were also hardy perennials. One can put the case unequivocally: during the classic period of modern missions, as in earlier times, variations in missionary ideology stemmed almost entirely from the variety of attitudes toward what nowadays is called cultural imperialism.

In this area of discourse, the first or foundational question, "Is Western culture superior?" was answered almost as easily and unanimously as the one concerning the duty to evangelize: of course the West—Christendom—was superior! Though most missionaries, like their colleagues back home, were quick to deplore the moral condition, and sometimes the social structure, of their own societies, few doubted the West's essential and overall excellence. But as soon as one moved to the next question—whether or not, being superior, one had a "right" to impose Western values where one had the power to do so—disagreement became more evident. The question of a right to impose, or a right to exert strong persuasive influences, was in general answered negatively if it implied the power of the sword or even of economic prowess, but very affirmatively if one meant the power of superior schools or technology or literacy.

The most agonizing debates, however, and by far the gravest disagreements, lay beyond both of these issues. Given Western cultural superiority and then admitting a certain right to impose or at least proclaim Western values, one still had to ask an entire series of further questions. Even if it is theoretically right and proper to export Western culture, is it really possible to do so? If it is possible, is it politic? Is it, in particular, something that Christianity and its missionaries should be doing? Or do teaching and healing and social service, however valuable in themselves, interfere with the real work of missions?

For a multiplicity of reasons, each of which is a story in itself, the "civilizing" arguments generally prevailed. The most usual reason, among European missionaries to the Indians during the colonial era, had been that missionaries simply found the evangelizing task grievously impeded by cultural differences that their theologies and theory had not predicted or taken into account—whereupon they concluded that a preparatory work of civilizing was unavoidable. Father Louis Hennepin in 1697, announcing such a change in view on his own part, explained that his predecessors in French Canada had "always given it for their opinion, and now I own 'tis mine, that the way to succeed in converting the Barbarians, is to endeavor to make them men before we go about to make them Christians."[13] John Eliot in Massachusetts, a generation before that, announced that he had found it "absolutely necessary to carry on civility with religion."[14]

In the context of nineteenth-century foreign missions, the reasons for abandoning a "Christ only" approach tended to be more complex and multifarious. In some measure, to be sure, one would be justified in contending that the gigantic nineteenth-century movement merely rediscovered, over and over, what the tiny bands of workers among the Indians had learned to their dismay; namely, that for all its discouragements civilizing succeeded far better than evangelizing did. But for the later nineteenth century in particular, one is inclined to weigh just as heavily such factors as the increasing participation of women and of laymen (both of these cohorts being confined largely to civilizing functions) and the bounding confidence about the virtues and the seemingly manifest destiny of Western forms of civilization.

The fact that the civilizing arguments did, one way and another, exert such force makes it the more remarkable that the opposing or minority tradition, that of strenuous objection to cultural imposition, fared as well as it did. The sentiments I quoted earlier from Francis Wayland, the Baptist leader, were spelled out with far greater practical effect, through all the middle decades of the nineteenth century, in the writings and leadership of Rufus Anderson, who was the dominant figure in the dominant missionary organization—the American Board of Commissioners for Foreign Missions. In his most famous and most characteristic statement of the anticivilizing argument, a sermon of 1845 called "The Theory of Missions to the Heathen," Anderson argued that for missionary purposes the glorious civilization of the West, and the still more glorious civilization of New England, were as much a curse as a blessing. The very perfection of such societies was, he said, a "formidable hindrance" to the establishing of purely spiritual missions—which were the only kind commissioned in Scripture or in apostolic tradition. We are conditioned to identify Christianity with "the blessings of education, industry, family government, social order, the means of a respectable livelihood, and a well-ordered community. Hence *our* idea of piety, and *our* idea of the propagation of the Gospel," become clothed in forms that we mistakenly associate with the Gospel itself.[15]

Anderson thought that the earliest work of the ABCFM, like the efforts of most other mission agencies, had been seriously flawed. But the board had seen its mistake, had discerned that "a simpler, cheaper, more effectual means of civilizing the savage, was the Gospel alone." It was really Anderson himself who, as a young board executive, had seen and articulated the mistake and then had gained enough authority and persuasive power to effect basic and often wrenching changes in missionary operations. With the support of his own board in Boston, and of leading spokesmen among the Baptists and others, Anderson had virtually ended the practice of sending out "farmers and mechanics." He had also induced many mission schools to stop teaching in English, had proscribed or discouraged other pursuits that he considered remote from conversionary purposes, and had pressed the missionaries to ordain natives and put them in charge. In some instances he had seen fit to close schools, or even close down entire missions, by way of making his point.[16]

In the late nineteenth century, however, the Anderson-Wayland positions fared about as well as those of General Custer at Little Big Horn. Some elements of Andersonian policy, such as the insistence on indigenization, continued to receive lip service and minimal effectuation; other elements, such as the severe proscription of "civilizing" practices, went underground until about 1920. Even in Anderson's day—lest in this brief recital I have made it sound otherwise—his policy fell far short of gaining any full-scale victory.[17] The Anderson initiatives now sound startling and "modern" partly because we have known so little about missions and have had no idea that such advocacies existed; but they also occasion surprise because so few of Anderson's contemporaries, in the missionary movement or elsewhere, were even raising his sort of question, the question of cultural imposition.

If nineteenth-century missionary opponents of cultural (and other) imperialism sound especially prophetic or admirable today, however, it does not follow that they sound consistent. One reason, after all (though not the only reason), for their restraint about cultural intrusiveness was that it got in the way of religious intrusiveness. Anderson to some extent, and others to a greater extent, were saying what the Roman authorities had said in the seventeenth century; in effect, "We must undermine and if possible destroy China's religions, but we must and shall not threaten China's culture." If the cultural restraint was modern, this presumption of separability between religion and culture clearly was not modern.

Roads to Religious Collaboration

The only mission spokesmen, therefore, who in retrospect seem both prophetic and consistent are those who worried about religious as well as cultural imposition. Before about 1920 these were the very few theorists—backed, to be sure, by substantial numbers of working missionaries—who rejected "proselytization," or simply set it aside, in favor of the various nonproselytizing modes of missionary witness, healing, and service and who, by the same token, worked more in collaboration with other religious and spiritual forces than in competition with them.

Before the 1920s, reservations about proselytizing aims and programs were voiced almost exclusively by outsiders to the missionary movement. Spokespersons for the movement itself maintained a solid front: evangelization and the conversion of all whom God might have marked for conversion were agreed to be the ultimate grand aims of missions; worthy nonevangelistic activities were at best subordinate, contributory, penultimate. But between 1925 and 1975, a number of formerly heretical views made headway not only within "ecumenical" Christianity, where they achieved their greatest intensity in the later 1960s, but even among evangelicals who by then had withdrawn from the too-liberal ecumenical organizations. These reservations about conversionary or proselytizing missions, as they began to surface in about 1925, were both direct and indirect.

Ralph Cooper Hutchison, a young professor at the American College of Teheran, voiced both types of inquiry in *Atlantic Monthly* articles of 1926 and 1927. In the first article, on "Islam and Christianity," Hutchison expressed more brashly what many others had previously said or written—especially during the years since the sobering experience of the First World War: If Christian evangelists had made few converts over the preceding century, this was largely because neither the West nor the Christian church had embodied the sort of example that Moslems or others cared to follow. From the Crusades (of which Christendom had never really repented) to the recent war, Hutchison pointed out, Westerners had too often pursued their destiny by laying waste to the lands and persons of others. At the same time, the Christian church had presented a spectacle of division and confusion. Moslems, according to this observer, saw little reason "to give up their sectarianism for our sectarianism, their strife for our strife, their frenzied theological debates for ours."[18]

A year later, Hutchison published a second critique that came closer to being a direct assault on the idea of proselytism. The notion that all mission activities must conduce to the making of converts was, he wrote, a notion honored at home but largely ignored in day-to-day missionary practice. In their insistence that conversions are the only valid goal, church leaders "speak the thought of their great parishes" (although, he suggested, such talk may help to keep potential churchgoers from those parishes in the first place). They do not speak the thought of missionaries themselves. The latter, he said, believe in evangelism and practice it, but they are also perfectly willing to offer Christian witness and service with no thought of making conversions. And that stance is the correct one; Christianity, Hutchison insisted, proposes to make its contributions to human welfare even if "from this day to the end of time not a single person surrenders his indifference or deserts his own faith to become a Christian."[19]

The ardent young missionary-rebel was obviously making his points with the aid of hyperbole and also by indulging in a certain amount of contradiction. It was surely an exaggeration to suggest, as Hutchison did, that most Americans in (or near) the churches were ready to dispense with proselytization as the ultimate intention of the missionary enterprise; and contradiction appeared when he set that point against the earlier concession that the party line on evangelism "spoke the thought" of the great Protestant parishes. Other would-be revisionists, in any case, quite definitely assumed that the great parishes, and even more the smaller ones, needed a good deal of educating if they were ever to accept the essentials of a pluralistic world view.

The outstanding contributor to such educational work during the 1920s was Daniel Johnson Fleming, a professor of missions at Union Theological Seminary in New York. Fleming's numerous writings, most of which were distributed by small publishing houses such as the YMCA's Association Press, may have reached a more limited readership than that of the *Atlantic Monthly;* but Fleming, through the students in a powerful mainline theological seminary and later through the widely discussed "laymen's inquiry" in which he played a part, probably gained a broader and more continuous hearing than did any of the other radical spirits within the missionary movement.

Radical spirit he was, in the truest sense: Fleming's critique went to the roots. At times, like Hutchison, he seemed too sanguine about the openness and progressivism of ordinary churchgoing Americans. He proposed, for example, that "if Buddhists came to our town" and were running the best schools, American Christians would permit them to try to convert the children to Buddhism! But insofar as the folks in Wichita or White Plains might *not* be ready to offer equal time to alternative religions, Fleming was determined to put them through an exercise in role reversal that few others, up to that time, had even suggested. In the *Christian Century* article that was in fact called "If Buddhists Came to Our Town," Fleming offered the surprisingly novel suggestion that the Golden Rule be considered a guideline for missionary practice. American communities would undoubtedly resist, for example, "any dealing with our children in such a way that they would not later freely think for themselves," or that would permanently bind them to a point of view "alien to all their inheritance." Insofar as missionary educators in foreign lands might exercise a similar restraint, the people at home, and the mission boards they supported, ought to applaud, not complain.[20]

Fleming, who had served for a dozen years as a missionary in India, like other commentators (including alarmed conservatives) believed that most missionaries did avoid proselytization, almost as a matter of course. The greater problem, from his point of view, was that the people back home appeared to want their missionaries to repair to the streetcorners armed with harangues and tracts (even though, again, such behavior would have been considered unseemly back in Wichita).

Fleming nonetheless thought that everyone, working missionaries included, needed to adopt fundamentally different ways of picturing the world. Not only should Europeans and North Americans stop assuming that the civilization of those continents was automatically superior to the civilizations of Asia and Africa, they should also go farther and revise entirely their notions of "continents."

According to Fleming, traditional phrases like "Christian conquest of Asia" would have to go. Besides being offensive, such hallowed slogans were simply irrelevant. In a newly interdependent world, the "continents" requiring conquest were not landmasses at all but "the great transverse areas of human activity" such as industrialization, nationalism, materialism, racial injustice, ignorance, war, and poverty.[21]

Within a few years the Laymen's Report (financed by a liberal Baptist, John D. Rockefeller, Jr., and organized by a liberal Congregationalist, the philosopher William Ernest Hocking) had spelled out one of the most radical and unsettling implications in Fleming's new continentalism: If the real battles are to be fought within the "great transverse areas" where spiritual and altruistic forces contend against materialism and cupidity, then Christianity needs to meet the other religions of the world as collaborator and not as competitor.

Besides being Hocking's own stance, this collaborationist outlook was one that could be seen as pervading the entire commission-produced study. As such, it was almost immediately rejected by the mainline mission boards. Many of the Hocking Commission's recommendations, as set forth in seven volumes of field reports and detailed analyses, were welcomed and assimilated. But the churches, mission boards, and ecumenical organizations were not yet ready to substitute "collaboration" for "conquest" in the lexicon of Christian world relations.[22]

Thirty years later, the same mainline organizations had become far more ready, if not always to proclaim the virtues of collaboration, then certainly to curtail most of the proselytizing aims and practices that traditionally had stood in the way of collaboration. The tendency, very strong in national and international ecumenical bodies by the late 1960s, was to redefine mission as "Christian presence" and conversion as the conversion not so much of individuals as of social structures. Mission, said a document of the World Student Christian Federation in 1964, means "being there in the name of Christ, often anonymously, listening before we speak . . . involved in the fierce fight against all that dehumanizes, ready to act against demonic powers, to identify with the outcast, merciless in ridiculing modern idols and new myths." The kind of personal evangelism that had been the putative centerpiece of Christian mission seemed to have become marginal and conditional: "Once we are there, we may witness fearlessly to Christ if the occasion is given"; yet "we may have to be silent."[23]

Johannes Hoekendijk, a Dutch theologian and ecumenical activist who served after 1975 in the position Fleming had held at Union Seminary, went so far as to question the propriety of seeking any converts at all if that meant bringing them into "the present chaos of denominations."[24] When, by about 1968, that and other strongly anti-traditional attitudes seemed actually to have gained the upper hand within ecumenical Protestantism, one result was that entire bodies of "mainstream evangelicals" reacted by distancing themselves from their ecumenical co-workers.

Yet even mainstream evangelicals, as distinct from sects and mission agencies on the far right, by the 1970s had considerably altered their mission rhetoric and their modes of operation. Evangelicals' concern to avoid cultural imposition, to de-Westernize both service and evangelism, had come nearly to equal that of the ecumenical Protestants. Evangelicals, like their liberal counterparts, held their mission conferences in Third World settings; and the Westerners among them seemed as willing as were ecumenicals in the Western churches to accept equal or subordinate roles within the various structures and operations of "world mission."

Although the emphasis on personal evangelism remained significantly stronger among evangelicals than among ecumenicals, the former were now usually comfortable with the idea of a "dialogue" with non-Christian religions. And social definitions of missionary obligations, which once had been shunned as diverting and dangerous, had achieved a considerably enhanced status. John R. W. Stott, a British evangelical leader, represented a large segment of world evangelicalism when he announced in 1974 that he had come to believe that Christian mission involves "social as well as evangelistic responsibility." Stott's revised stance was virtually a paraphrase of R. C. Hutchison's argument, in 1927, for the independent validity of nonproselytizing mission activity. Social amelioration and evangelism, Stott proclaimed, "belong to each other and yet are independent of each other. Each stands on its own feet . . . Neither is a means to the other, or even a manifestation of the other. For each is an end in itself."[25]

From Proselytism to Pluralism

Since, despite the vast changes in both ecumenical and evangelical approaches to world mission, militant religious and cultural attitudes on the far right seem very much alive in the 1980s, one might insist that the old adage applies: The more things change, the more they remain the same. But for mainstream Protestantism the changes have been as distinct and irreversible as the historical forces, such as the end of colonialism, that have induced them. By the same token, from the new vantage point it appears that the widespread acceptance of proselytism in Protestant thinking depended heavily upon two sets of conditions that no longer obtain with anything like their nineteenth-century force: the historical condition of Western dominance and certain intellectual or presuppositional conditions that allowed free play to religious and cultural absolutism.

Galloping modernity and the usual slow canter of cultural maturation. Mounting contact with non-Western peoples yoked to a persisting unreadiness to deal with these peoples in their own terms. However one states the combination of elements that produced the older commitment to proselytization, it was a potent combination and, we may well say, a destructive one. I am not suggesting that these conditions have entirely passed in the 1980s or that the mission ideology they induced no longer operates anywhere within the ecumenical and mainstream-evangelical worlds. Yet the revised stance that became so prominent in those precincts during the 1960s testified to a new birth of pluralism in Protestant consciousness. Christians, Western or otherwise, were being warned against arrogance, not merely in thinking they could proclaim God's answers to all human problems, but even in presuming to phrase God's questions. In entering into the concerns of others, said an ecumenical manifesto of the 1960s, one is bound to accept "their issues and their structures."[26]

From such a perspective, the story of Protestantism's extended and serious flirtation with proselytism clearly cannot be called premodern. It was part and parcel of modernity and of modernization. But it can appropriately (if not very elegantly) be called prepluralist. It is the story, played out on the stage of world Christianity, that the late Sydney E. Ahlstrom believed was also the central theme of American religious history—the drama of "pluralism struggling to be born."[27]

7

Changes in Roman Catholic Attitudes toward Proselytism and Mission

ROBERT J. SCHREITER

When examining claims to exclusivity and patterns of proselytism, the Roman Catholic Church provides material for a particularly useful case study. For, until quite recently, it not only held strongly to the Christian exclusivist claim on truth, but also went even further in maintaining that it alone represented the true form of Christianity. Roman Catholicism has maintained a long history of proselytizing efforts as well. With the beginning of the so-called voyages of discovery at the end of the fifteenth century, it mounted an extraordinarily large mission effort, something sustained more or less down to the present time.

Yet significant changes have come about in both the claims to exclusivity and in the understanding of proselytism and mission within the Roman Catholic Church in the past twenty-five years. These changes in both official position and in attitudes appeared in the course of the Second Vatican Council, held in Rome from 1962 to 1965. Some dramatic shifts took place. While Roman Catholics still saw their form of communion as the best manifestation of the church of Jesus Christ, it was no longer to be considered the sole or the complete manifestation of that church. The other Christian churches were accorded a new respect, a respect extended to other forms of religious faith as well, especially to Judaism. And that respect went further than general esteem; these religions were seen as possible ways to the salvation preached heretofore as the exclusive property of Catholicism.

The missionary movement went into a ten-year decline immediately following the Council. Many factors contributed to this downswing. Part of it was due to the exodus from religious orders. But more importantly, there was the most profound questioning of the missionary movement, both in its principles and its practice, that the Catholic Church had ever undergone. While the number of missionaries coming from First World countries has declined, there is a growing population of missionaries coming from Third World countries.

Why have all of these shifts taken place? What has been their effect on Roman Catholic self-understanding? And what might they teach us about the themes under examination here? This presentation will try to trace these shifts in understanding of mission and proselytism through the twentieth century. The question of exclusivity will not be addressed directly, but will be viewed from the perspective of mission and proselytism. The question of Christianity's relation to other religions is probably the most thorny and important theological question before the church today, but a full examination of that would take us too far afield. Rather, how understandings of exclusive claims to truth affected the sense of mission will be the window upon this vexing problem.

The presentation here will divide the history of these changes in attitude into four periods: (1) the period prior to the Second Vatican Council (1919–62); (2) the period of the Council itself (1962–65); (3) the period of the missionary crisis (1965–75); and the period of the rebirth of the missionary movement (1975 to the present). In examining this history, we will want to attend not only to official pronouncements and statements by theologians, but also some of the social factors that were at play. Having done this, I will then try to distill out of this history any salient points that might prove useful for our discussion here. Given the compass of this presentation, the overview of that history must be rather summary, touching only the high points of these periods. But I hope that even with this the contours of a remarkable history will be evident.

The Period of Certainty (1919–62)

Roman Catholics experienced the same surge in missionary activity during the nineteenth and early twentieth century as did Protestants. Although the Catholic Church had kept a high level of missionary commitment since the mid-sixteenth century, the nineteenth century nonetheless represented a significant increase. New religious orders were founded exclusively for mission work. National missionary societies were founded in Europe and North America (the United States missionary society, Maryknoll, being founded in 1911), and missionary patronage societies were developed on the national and international levels.

The popes, too, were encouraging of missionary activity in the lands outside Europe throughout this period. But the history we wish to trace here can be dated from 1919, when Pope Benedict XV issued the encyclical letter *Maximum Illud,* subtitled "On Spreading the Catholic Faith throughout the World."[1] This was to be the first of five encyclicals issued on missionary work between 1919 and 1962. Pius XI issued *Rerum Ecclesiae* in 1926; Pius XII issued *Evangelii Praecones* in 1951 and *Fidei Donum* in 1957; and John XXIII issued *Princeps Pastorum* in 1959.[2]

Remarkable about all of these letters is that virtually no attention is given to the theological foundations of missionary work. Generally, Christ's commission to the apostles to go out, preach, and make disciples of all nations (Matt. 28:20) sufficed. This commission to the apostles was now passed on to the successors of the apostles, the bishops. These were to go out and rescue those lost in darkness and the shadow of death (*Maximum Illud,* 6; *Evangelii Praecones,* 16). Standing behind the commission to go out and preach was God's will that all be saved. When addressing the more specific purpose of mission, the encyclicals revert to the two classic formulations of purpose: the winning of converts *(conversio animarum)* and the establishing of the local church *(plantatio ecclesiae).* Benedict XV and Pius XI emphasize the former; Pius XII and John XXIII, the latter. The bulk of these encyclical letters, however, are taken up with methods in mission: problems of education, financing, roles of bishops, and the like.

One theological question starts to figure more prominently, though still indirectly, in the letters of Pius XII, namely, the value and status of local customs. In his letters, Pius reiterates the principle, going back to Pope Gregory the Great, that whatever is good should be preserved, purified, and elevated by its contact with the Christian religion. He sums up the principle thus: "Although owing to Adam's fall, human nature is tainted with original sin, yet it has in itself something in itself naturally Christian; and this, if illumined by God's grace, can eventually be changed into true and supernatural virtue."[3]

Direct reflection on the nature, purpose, and methods of mission also begins more or less with this period. The first chair of Roman Catholic missiology was established at the University of Muenster in Germany in 1911, and the first handbook of missiology appeared in 1919.[4] The author of that handbook, Joseph Schmidlin, devoted approximately 60 of its 460 pages to the question of why engage in mission. Typical of the period, it is cast in apologetic form.

Throughout this period, the theological grounding for mission was devoted to expanding the two basic principles of the *conversio animarum* and the *plantatio ecclesiae*. The former focused especially on God's universal salvific will; the latter on the church as the concrete manifestation of that will. German missiologists emphasized the former; Francophone missiologists in Belgium and France, the latter. And these two principles provided the foci around which a closed ellipse could be created. The more fundamental question of why mission at all was not being asked; or, when asked, was responded to with the universal salvific will of God. If one looks to the last great handbook to appear before the Council, Thomas Ohm's *Machet zu Jüngern alle Völker,* which appeared in 1962,[5] a great deal more space was devoted to mission theory. But that additional space represented the elaboration of the familiar principles, rather than any advancement on them. The questions that were to become so important in the next period—the meaning of the church, the meaning of salvation in other religions—still found no place here.

This period prior to the Council, then, was a period of certainty, at least in the public positions of church magisterium and of the theologians. In the mission fields, however, things were beginning to change. The nascent struggles for independence from colonial rule were to reverberate in the mission stations in Africa and Asia. When this combined with the impact of the Second Vatican Council, the effect would be seismic. We need to turn now to the work of that Council.

The Period of Ferment (1962–65)

In 1962, the first session of the Second Vatican Council convened. Already in 1960, a Preparatory Commission had been established under the chairmanship of Cardinal Agagianian, the Prefect of the Propaganda Fide, for the purpose of preparing a schema for consideration by the Council, with the working title *De activitate missionali Ecclesiae.* The commission included a considerable number of people with missionary experience. The initial draft presented to the commission followed the traditional lines of the papal encyclicals, dealing primarily with the governance of missions and missionaries with little about the theology of mission. This first draft was composed mainly by people resident in Rome rather than those engaged in the ferment of the current missionary scene. It met with little approval by the Council Fathers and a fundamental revision was undertaken.[6] This and a subsequent revision were considered unacceptable to the great majority of the Council Fathers. The reasons, it seems, were that it did not reflect the contemporary mission experience and did not take adequately into account other theological developments that were happening in the Council.

It became apparent that the Council Fathers wished a more substantial and theologically weighty document. The commission preparing the document reorganized itself, with Cardinal Agagianian gracefully moving into the background. The figure who emerged as the effective leader in preparing a new draft was Father Johannes Schuette, the Superior General of the Divine Word Missionaries. In fact, it is to him that we owe the draft which was approved by the final session of the Council in 1965.

What elements emerged in the final draft that made it acceptable and which reflect the changes in an understanding of mission? It would go beyond the scope of this presentation to discuss those doctrinal elements in detail. It might be more helpful to focus upon three major developments that, in their own way, define the tensions that were to surround Catholic understandings of mission in the following two decades. The three elements are: (1) a trinitarian locus for the origin of mission; (2) an expanded understanding of the church; and (3) a new understanding of the nature of other religions.

The first part of the "Decree on Missionary Activity in the Church," known by its opening words in Latin, *Ad Gentes,* locates the origins of missionary activity in the Trinity itself, in God's eternal plan of salvation for all seen in the sending of the Son and the Holy Spirit into the world. Now the idea of grounding missionary activity in the Trinity itself had been gaining considerable current among theologians prior to the Council. In itself, this is not an entirely new idea. But the implication of making the Trinity the locus of the origin of mission, rather than the great commission of the Gospel ("Go out and preach to all nations"), is that mission is no longer simply a duty incumbent upon Christians, but becomes part of the very nature of being a Christian at all. The decree is quick to pick up on this implication and to show where this leads. While one can continue to define certain activities of the church as specifically missionary, on a more fundamental level the church has to come to see itself as missionary by its very nature. Thus, the church goes from "having missions" to "being missionary." This was to be the most fundamental shift that theology of mission and proselytism was to experience. Mission became, therefore, more than an extending of the perimeters of the church; it was to be something motivating the very heart of the church: not because some command had been laid upon the faithful, but because by being missionary the church was drawn into the life of the Trinity itself. For this reason, Roman Catholic theologies of mission since that time tend to speak of missionary activity as "mission" (in the singular), rather than "missions" (in the plural), to emphasize the unity of mission in the Trinity—albeit the plural usage does survive in some official usages.

What have been the implications of this shift in theological basis from the great commission to a trinitarian basis? Perhaps the most significant has been a change in the metaphors used to describe missionary activity. Prior to this shift, Roman Catholic missiological language shared with the Protestant missiology of the time (still to be found in some conservative evangelical circles) a predilection for military metaphors. Referring to Matthew 28 as "the great commission" is already indicative of that. Since the trinitarian foundation in *Ad Gentes* uses primarily the language of love, the whole tone of what constitutes missionary activity changes. To be sure, some of the more military language remains, but the tone of confrontation with the nonbeliever moves away from conquest to invitation, dialogue, and sharing. Effective proselytism, then, is not so much marked by conquest and submission, but is a more complex process that acknowledges the work of the Holy Spirit already active in the life of the potential convert long before actually hearing the Gospel. And the act of conversion itself is seen to be only the beginning of a long, complex process of growth away from sinfulness into the full life of grace. While proclamation is not played down in this approach, it clearly has to make room for a more dialogical approach, mirroring the intimate communication between those who love. For again, the purpose of missionary activity is not just to convert, but to bear witness to the trinitarian life, to bear witness to the very life of God. When one begins to think in these terms, one begins to feel a new set of tensions in missionary activity. Whereas previously missionary activity was the specialized and clearly defined task of winning converts and establishing the church, it now became the general task of all believers, involving a more complex combination of proclamation, witness, dialogue, and service. It had become at once more fundamental and less well-defined.

To understand the full implications of what this was to mean in the succeeding periods, we need to turn to the second element that emerged in the Council, namely, a shift in the understanding of the nature of the church itself. This shift is best seen in another document of the Council, the "Constitution on the Church," known as *Lumen Gentium.* In that document, two differing (although not necessarily contradictory) understandings of the nature of the church are juxtaposed. The first is a more refined form of the sense of church that had been formulated at the First Vatican Council in 1869, refined by subsequent popes, especially Pius XII in his 1944 encyclical *Mystici Corporis*. This ecclesiology had its roots in the Catholic Reformation, notably in the work of such theologians as the sixteenth-century Jesuit Robert Bellarmine. The dominant image of this understanding of church was that it was a *societas perfecta* or "perfect society," mirroring the celestial society surrounding the throne of God. It was hierarchical in nature and represented on earth the most complete possible presence of God. This self-understanding of the church was the basis for the policy it was to follow subsequent to the First Vatican Council in trying to create an alternate, self-sufficient culture against the onslaught of modernity. Pius XII was to begin the softening of the harder edges of this image with his theology of the church as the mystical body of Christ, taking up the Pauline imagery. However, while this enriched an understanding of the church as a *mysterion* or manifestation of the divine reality, it kept with it a firm sense of hierarchy, considerable self-assuredness, and confidence in its mirroring of heaven.

Juxtaposed to this understanding of church, we find in the second chapter of *Lumen Gentium* the presentation of the church as the pilgrim people of God. It was to be this image that captured the imagination of so many of the bishops at the Council and of others who saw the need to create a new relationship with the world. Instead of being an already perfected society, the church as the pilgrim people of God saw itself perhaps as the vanguard of that perfect society, but in highly modest and provisional terms. The image of the pilgrim people was dominated by the story of the Exodus, of a people indeed liberated from their captivity, yet far from the Promised Land. The image came to evoke for many the idea of the church as a collection of people engaged in a common quest for the fulfillment of the kingdom of God. No longer could the church be identified as the kingdom of God; it would be seen rather as pointing to that kingdom. To be sure, the constitution would continue to see the current presence of God's kingdom as "subsisting" in the church; but the compromise of using the word "subsisting" rather than the simple copulative verb "is" already opened up considerable latitude where virtually none had existed before. The real charter for mapping out the implications of this shift was to be the "Constitution on the Church in the Modern World," *Gaudium et Spes*. This document, like no other in the history of the Catholic Church, called for a positive and constructive dialogue with the world (or more specifically, with the industrialized and secularized West).

What were the more specific implications of the introduction of this considerably different understanding of the church for the sense of mission and proselytism? Most notably, it had a profound effect on one of the two great motives for mission, the *plantatio ecclesiae*. The establishment of the church, although still important, no longer in and of itself was the be-all and end-all of mission. And the reason was that the church itself was but a herald, an envoy of the kingdom of God, not the kingdom itself. That would be only realized in heaven, when the church as such would pass away. To be sure, the Council documents continue to speak of the necessity of the church and membership in the church as the visible sign of the fullness of salvation to which we might attain here on earth. But in almost the same breath, speaking of the church as pilgrim and provisional necessarily opened up the question of just how necessary was the church—really—to salvation. Might not conversion to a better life along the lines one's life had already taken be a better task for the missionary rather than insisting upon formal membership in the church? And what was to come into greater evidence in the succeeding period was that the boundaries of church itself, once so clear and secure, were now beginning to appear considerably more vague.

When this shift of awareness of what constitutes the church is paired with the aforementioned shift in the understanding of the nature of mission, a new kind of paradox is set up. On the one hand, the missionary task of going out and imparting the message of the Good News of salvation becomes something of the very nature of the church and of the individual Christian. But on the other hand, what one is witnessing to (at least as regards the visible community of Christ) has become considerably more vague. The conjunction of this paradox set the stage for the missionary crisis in the next period. Before turning to that period, however, we need to take into account the third element that was to emerge from the Council, namely, a new understanding of other religions.

In many ways, the Council's understanding of other religious traditions was not new. As the text goes to great pains to show, its understanding was rooted in patristic thinking and a theology of creation. Since the patristic period, there had been a strain of thought which held that there were indeed noble elements in non-Christian religions that served as a *praeparatio evangelica*, a preparation for reception of the Gospel. These elements were not to be abolished or set aside in the evangelizing process, rather they were to be purified, transformed as needed, and elevated to the realm of divine grace. While there had always been a great deal of controversy in Western Catholic Christianity as to what those elements might be and how they were to be engaged (for example, the seventeenth-century Rites Controversy in China), this was a principle that had remained part of the tradition. The encyclicals of the twentieth-century popes had reaffirmed these principles, especially those of Pius XII and John XXIII. What we find in *Ad Gentes* essentially reaffirmed the principles of those encyclicals without going beyond them in any special way.

The catalyst here was yet another Council document, the "Declaration on the Relation of the Church to Non-Christian Religions," *Nostra Aetate.* Originally intended to address Catholic relations with the Jews (which was to remain its principal purpose), it was extended to include all the great religious traditions. *Nostra Aetate* builds upon that tradition and in so doing takes it a step further. The document goes to great pains to reaffirm the positive values of Judaism, Buddhism, Hinduism, and Islam, noting the parallels in these traditions to Christian faith. The call found in *Nostra Aetate* was not so much to conversion as to dialogue. And the point of dialogue with other religious traditions was not only to come to understand those traditions better; its purpose was also to come to learn religiously from them about pathways to God. The stance of the Christian believer in approaching people of other faiths was to be one of humility and hospitality rather than superiority.

Nostra Aetate was one of the most hotly contested documents of the Council. It opened up new pathways by posing the question most seriously about the role of salvation in other religions. It continued to affirm that all people were redeemed in Christ, but the way the question of other religions was raised carried with it the possible implication that the church was not the sole agency through which that salvation might be realized. This, therefore, takes the redefinition of the nature of the church discussed above one step further. Not only is the church seen as a provisional sign of the coming kingdom of God, the very nature or purpose of the church is also challenged by this new relationship to other religions.

With twenty years of hindsight, it is now clear that the Council rarely spoke univocally on any subject and that it raised more questions than it provided answers. In the matter of mission and proselytism, selective readings of the Council documents can provide support for a considerable variety of interpretations. Yet if one looks at the changes that the missionary movement underwent in the years following the Council, it seems clear that the frontiers pointed to by questioning the nature of mission, the church, and the relation to other religious traditions marked out the territory that would need to be explored. And with that we turn to the third period of this history.

The Period of the
Missionary Crisis (1965–75)

Missionaries in the field and leaders of missionary orders were quick to catch the implications present in the conciliar documents. The fact that many of their concerns had finally been heard in the drafting process of *Ad Gentes,* albeit interpreted still in a somewhat conservative manner, gave many the impetus to explore more deeply the implications of what the Council had said. And indeed, in the initial period following the Council the number of missionaries entering the field continued to rise until 1968. Thereafter, the numbers moved into a steady and often precipitous decline. Much of this can be attributed to the large-scale exodus of priests, sisters, and brothers world-wide in those years. But the growing insecurity about what was the exact nature of mission in a post-Vatican II church surely fueled this development as well.

By the late 1960s the implications that could be drawn from the Council documents and the exodus of many missionaries from the field had set the stage for reflection on the profound challenge that traditional mission was facing. While mission was to be at the very heart of the Christian vocation, what was to be its acceptable form, given the new understanding of the church and of non-Christian religions? The old motives of the *conversio animarum* and the *plantatio ecclesiae* no longer exercised the same attraction, yet could not be relegated to the dustbin of history. Where was the acknowledgment of the good conscience of the non-Christian to be located in missionary strategies aimed at conversion? (This had been something affirmed in the "Declaration on Religious Liberty," *Dignitatis Humanae.*) And how was the new stress on dialogue to be related to evangelization?

A landmark attempt to deal with these dilemmas occurred early in 1969, in the form of a theological conference sponsored by SEDOS (Servizio di documentazione e studi), an association of the mission-sending orders of men and women.[7] This conference gathered together some of the most able minds reflecting on mission at that time. The conference took the most radically neuralgic point in the missionary crisis as their theme: why mission at all? The collected papers from that conference represent perhaps the single best attempt to grapple with the theological foundations of mission in that period.

The most cohesive and persuasive paper is that of Johannes Schuette, the man responsible for the final draft of *Ad Gentes.* The very title of his paper sets forth the question: "Why Engage in Mission Work?"[8] Schuette frames the dilemma by using theologian Karl Rahner's phrase "anonymous Christian." Put simply, the idea is that if

God wishes the salvation of all and Christ is the source of that salvation and if those who live uprightly according to the best dictates of their conscience do therefore experience that salvation, they are Christians, although "anonymously." Schuette sets forth the question directly: If God through unfathomable mystery is leading these upright non-Christians to salvation along other ways, what right do we as Christians have to disturb them? Having said this, he proceeds to develop a theological answer that is to serve as a foundation for motivation to mission.

What Schuette does is develop the eschatological aspect of mission; that is, following the early Christian vision that all things are ultimately to be brought together in Christ (Eph. 1:10), the task of mission is to help build up that *pleroma* or plenitude in Christ. This is to be achieved by continuing to proclaim that Christ stands at the center of human history. Secondly, the task of mission is to carry further the incarnation of Christ into every culture. And thirdly, the task of mission is to work toward peace and reconciliation, since such peace and reconciliation are to be signs of the imminent return of Christ and the establishment of his sovereignty.

To my knowledge, Schuette's paper remains the best articulation of a theological response to the missionary dilemma of that period. Its influence is evident in the concluding statement of the conference, where the motivation to mission is seen as helping people discover the mystery of God at work in their own lives and in their own situations. The statement also emphasizes the place of development within the missionary enterprise. But no real headway was made on the question of relation to other religious traditions. One finds in the concluding statement the same juxtaposition of the exclusivity of salvation to be found in Jesus Christ with an affirmation of the authentic values of other traditions.

The eschatological argument for establishing the motivation of mission remains probably the most effective one available to Catholics to this day. Seeing God at work in mysterious and hidden ways and helping to make that more explicit through the proclamation of Christ have become a standard part of contemporary Catholic missiology. It would generally be seen as a more convincing motivation than the trinitarian argument used in *Ad Gentes*. Such an approach, as we shall see, leaves room for dialogue within mission, but it does not address sufficiently the role of other religious traditions within the scheme.

What this period presents in terms of our understanding of mission and proselytism is a consolidation of some of the implications suggested by the positions taken during the Council. For proselytism to fit within a different understanding of the church, a church more provisional and exploratory in its nature and more vague in its boundaries, the motivation has to be shifted from a clear point of departure to a more anticipatory vision of a future. That allows for considerably more change and development than does the more deductive style of the trinitarian argument. This extra leeway has the advantage of at least buying time to construct a more ordered approach. The anticipatory approach also has the advantage of tying in dialogue and development more closely to the motivating factors for mission. Dialogue and development need not be grounded only in the general love of neighbor; they are part of bringing about the incarnation of Christ in every culture and in heralding the fulfillment of all things in Christ.

This approach, then, goes some way to meet the challenge of plurality without exactly addressing pluralism itself. To carry it a step further, we need to turn to the fourth and final period of this history.

The Rebirth of the Missionary Movement (1975—)

The fourth period of this history is marked at the beginning by the publication by Pope Paul VI of his apostolic exhortation *Evangelii Nuntiandi* in 1975. This document grew out of the synod of bishops held in Rome in 1974, which took up the question of mission and evangelization in the modern world. The synod itself was not able to agree on a concluding statement and turned its material over to the pope, who then issued it as an apostolic exhortation. It has often been remarked that *Evangelii Nuntiandi* is the document that *Ad Gentes* was intended to have been. It remains to this day the subject of close study in Catholic missionary groups around the world.

For our purposes here, the most important section of this document is the second chapter, which deals with the nature of evangelization. Paul VI begins by noting the complexity of the evangelizing process. Although the direct proclamation of Christ is central to evangelization, there is much more involved, and to deny this runs the risk of distorting the meaning of evangelization. Evangelization, Paul continues, involves the renewal of humanity in all its aspects, both individual and collective. It involves, too, the evangelization of cultures, by which he means a creative encounter between the Gospel and cultures. He assigns a certain priority to the witness of life as a form of evangelization alongside direct proclamation. He sums up evangelization as "a complex process made up of varied elements: the renewal of humanity, witness, explicit proclamation, inner adherence, entry into the community, acceptance of signs, apostolic initiative."[9] In the related matter of relationships to non-Christian religions, Paul reaffirms the teaching of the Council, attesting to the dignity of these traditions while reasserting the right to missionary activity of Christians among them. Thought on the issue is not advanced further, although Paul recognizes that the issue "raises complex and delicate questions that must be studied in the light of Christian tradition and the Church's Magisterium, in order to offer to the missionaries of today and tomorrow new horizons in their contacts with non-Christian religions."[10]

In 1981 SEDOS again convened a seminar to assess developments in mission.[11] The editors noted that there had been considerable development in thinking about mission since the 1969 conference. If the question then was the *why* of mission, six years after *Evangelii Nuntiandi* it was the *how* of mission. In its concluding statement, the seminar saw four principal directions in the *how* of mission: proclamation, dialogue, inculturation, and liberation of the poor. In the matter of proclamation, two differing but complementary models were presented: one of extending the visible communion of the church, and the other of recognizing and furthering the values of the kingdom. Participants in the seminar saw the second model as gaining prominence in mission over the first.

In many ways the concluding statement of the 1981 SEDOS seminar remains the charter of the contemporary missionary movement in the Catholic Church. In its fourfold emphasis on proclamation, dialogue, inculturation, and liberation, it continues themes that were first consolidated in the documents of the Second Vatican Council. The question of relation to non-Christian religions arose in the seminar but did not achieve much prominence in the discussions.

It is with a brief examination of this last point that we conclude this survey. Two church documents deserve mention here. The first is the so-called Venice Statement of 1977, actually a paper presented by Professor Tommasso Federici to a meeting of a liaison committee between Roman Catholics and Jews.[12] While the document does not have official status, it has been widely recognized as reflecting official Vatican thinking. This document rejects "any action aimed at changing the religious faith of Jews." In subsequent official documents this position has been reiterated. This was certainly the first time that the Catholic Church abdicated any right to evangelization among a given group.

The second document was issued in 1984 by the Vatican Secretariat for Non-Christians, entitled "The Attitude of the Church toward the Followers of Other Religions: Reflections and Orientations on Dialogue and Mission."[13] In the section on mission and conversion (arts. 37–40), the document reaffirms the Christian's right to proclaim the Gospel and to seek the conversion of others, as long as this is not forced upon the unbeliever. In the same breath, it reaffirms also the primacy of conscience, especially in religious matters.

The document does not break new ground but consolidates once again the thinking of the period since the Vatican Council on the nature of mission and the complexity of the dialogue process. Following out the title, the document can be said to be rather long on reflections and short on orientations.

A number of theologians have pointed out the ambivalences of the Catholic Church in facing the implications of the two differing sets of principles it holds: the necessity of mission and the integrity of other religious traditions. Methodist missiologist Gerald Anderson raised the question forcefully a number of years ago in responding to a paper by then-Secretary Pietro Rossano of the Secretariat for Non-Christians.[14] More recently, Catholic theologians Paul Knitter and especially William Burrows have raised this question especially.[15] The problem comes down essentially to this: How can the church retain its absolute claim to exclusive possession of the truth and of salvation and at the same time affirm the goodness and even validity of other religious traditions? What both Knitter and Burrows have said in effect is that the Catholic Church has yet to grapple seriously with this. It wants to have it both ways and ends up in a great deal of confusion or vagueness. I would have to concur with their challenge. The question of the relation of the church to other religious traditions is, to me, the single most important question facing us today. This is the case not only because of missionary activity; it has to do with the very identity of the church itself.

Conclusion

What conclusions might be drawn from this history of the Roman Catholic church's attitude toward proselytism and mission? The history relates a considerable change of opinion in the course of this century. Let me suggest a few things that strike me as useful.

First of all, proselytism works best when there are only two parties within the purview of the proselytizer: the proselytizer and the one to be proselytized. When the one to be proselytized fragments into a plurality, there are more possibilities of challenge to the proselytizer. In other words, the world of that other comes at the proselytizer in many different ways, and so raises more questions than would otherwise have been the case.

Secondly, proselytism requires that the proselytizer has a firm sense of his or her own identity. That identity must have clearly established boundaries so that one can tell quickly and simply when one is or is not a member of the group. When that sense of identity or the boundaries of the identity become porous or vague, proselytism becomes more difficult. As we saw in this history, when the meaning of the church shifted during the Second Vatican Council, the conversion aspect of mission came into difficulty.

Third, when competing groups give priority to acknowledging their similarities over their differences (usually this is done to assure some peaceful coexistence), proselytism loses much of its energy. Thus, when the Catholic Church affirmed the positive values in other great religious traditions in *Nostra Aetate* and emphasized the value of dialogue, this necessarily undercut more straightforward proselytizing efforts. Put another way, when the post-Vatican II church opted for a more inclusive approach to other traditions, it became more difficult to see why one would want to switch from one to the other.

Fourth, when boundaries surrounding identity became unclear, the complexity of the conversion process comes more into evidence. As Paul VI noted in *Evangelii Nuntiandi,* not to acknowledge this distorts the very process itself. And missionaries have become more aware of how long conversion takes, even after the primary symbols of Christianity have been embraced. This seems to take the urgency out of proselytism in one kind of way, since conversion is always a more gradual process than it might seem on the surface.

Fifth, if the proselytizer wishes to acknowledge pluralism and not simply plurality (i.e., the existence of many different forms as legitimate), then the proselytizer will have to shift the values involved in mission and proselytism to a broader context. In terms of our discussion here, the shift was made from rescue from damnation to "renewal of humanity" (Paul VI) or "furthering the values of the kingdom" (SEDOS, 1981). The values attained are no longer the exclusive property of the proselytizer; they are open, at least in principle, to others. The proselytizer participates in the realization of these values rather than claims to have exclusive right to them. This allows some form of mission to continue, but under considerably different auspices.

And finally, the identity of the proselytizer will tend to be more anticipatory than participatory in the ideal. This allows for sufficient ambiguity to permit the considerable and largely unforeseen kinds of change that is likely to come upon the proselytizer in the course of interaction within the pluralist framework. We saw a general shift in the motivation for Catholic mission away from a deductive trinitarian argument toward the anticipatory eschatological argument. This provides a reasonable amount of firmness in the identity of the proselytizer without foreclosing the possibility of changes. There is a good deal more flexibility in a church as "pilgrim people" than there is in a church as "perfect society."

Much more no doubt could be said about the changes that the Roman Catholic Church has undergone. They are indeed remarkable. What is noticeable today in the Catholic Church is the large proportion of missionaries now coming from Third World churches. This seems to grow out of a deep sense of the missionary nature of the church itself.[16] Whether they will teach us something new about mission and pluralism—as they already have in so many other places—remains to be seen. Suffice it to say for now that great challenges still lie ahead, especially in the more direct confrontation of how the salvific role of other religions is really to be assessed.

8

Fundamentalists Proselytizing Jews: Incivility in Preparation for the Rapture

NANCY T. AMMERMAN

Fundamentalism, by definition, stands in opposition to the modern world. From the beginning, fundamentalists have identified themselves as those who opposed accommodation to pluralism, secularization, subjectivism, and—yes—even civility. While the "modernists" of the late nineteenth and early twentieth centuries were discussing how to adapt theology to the realities of the modern situation, a group of conservative leaders began to formulate what they saw as the irreducible truths of Christianity. Their intellectual leaders were at Princeton Theological Seminary, while their organizational leaders were found in Bible and Prophecy conferences and in prominent pulpits throughout the urban Northeast. Followers began to rally around these leaders and around publications such as *The Bible Champion,* the Scofield Reference Bible, and finally a series of pamphlets that gave them their name: *The Fundamentals.*[1] They insisted that certain doctrines, like the virgin birth and the resurrection, could not be compromised. But most importantly, they insisted that the Bible was divinely inspired and not subject to human error. Any attempt to "explain away" what the Bible said came to be seen as the Protestant equivalent of mortal sin. One either believed the Bible and was saved or doubted the Bible and was lost.[2]

By the 1920s, fundamentalists were convinced that the denominations had fallen to the error of modernism, and they took it upon themselves to restore the churches to proper orthodoxy.[3] They failed, of course, but they did not disappear. Rather, they withdrew from the denominations to form a patchwork of independent churches and agencies, small new denominations, Bible colleges, and thriving broadcast ministries.[4] Throughout the 1930s their evangelistic and missionary efforts grew, but by the early 1940s the movement was facing division. One side thought it essential to maintain an aggressive antimodern stance, advocating what they called "second-degree separation." They not only wanted to avoid sin, but also to avoid being seen with sinners. The other side began to disdain this aggressive stance, claiming that it was enough simply to avoid sin. (Not surprisingly the two groups also began to differ on just what constituted sins to be avoided and just how literally the Bible should be taken.) The separationists, epitomized by Carl McIntyre, formed the American Council of Christian Churches, while the accommodationists, later epitomized by Billy Graham, formed the National Association of Evangelicals.[5]

Both were still very conservative in theology, but they differed in their stance toward the civility required in a modern, pluralistic world. Evangelicals (as the more accommodating wing has come to be called) might still tell a good practicing Catholic that she needs to be saved, but at least they know she is likely to be offended. Fundamentalists will tell her where she is eternally headed and firmly believe they have done her a favor for which she should thank them. Though Hunter may correctly note a decline in the amount of hellfire and damnation issuing from the pulpits of evangelicals,[6] such subjects are not shunned by fundamentalists. Fundamentalists are simply evangelicals who believe that nothing, not even civility, should get in the way of proclaiming the truth about the need for salvation.

One of the reasons fundamentalists are so adamant about their evangelistic mission is that they firmly believe the end of this present age is at hand. Most are dispensational premillennialists. And as such, they expect—at any moment—the return of Christ for his church, an event they call the Rapture. After the Rapture, there will essentially be no opportunity to redeem one's soul; so it is essential that salvation be guaranteed *now* and not later. Those who will be taken in the Rapture are only those who have truly accepted Christ as their personal savior. For fundamentalists, the most important decision anyone can make, then, is the decision to accept Christ, and it is important that the decision be made with all possible haste.

Boundaries of the Brotherhood

The necessity of personal salvation is the fact around which fundamentalist theology is organized, but it is also the status around which the fundamentalist community is organized.[7] Being saved is not only one's "ticket" to eternal life; it is also one's ticket into the community of the faithful, one's badge of brotherhood or sisterhood, the sign that one belongs. Such an invisible spiritual state, of course, is hard to discern. Believers are forced to make inferences about another's eternal destiny based on more visible outward signs. They are helped in this task by hundreds of cues, some conscious and some not so conscious.

First of all, certain groups of people are automatically assumed *not* to be true believers. Unless proven otherwise, Catholics, liberal Protestants, and of course, Jews (and the rest of the world's religious and irreligious people) are taken to be among the unsaved. In the fundamentalist mind, one simply cannot go to heaven if one does not believe the right things, so groups that preach "wrong doctrine" are assumed to be populated with unsaved people. In addition, because fundamentalists see evangelism as the most central task of God's people, they also assume that groups that do not openly practice evangelism must not really be God's people.

In addition to checking for group membership, believers also look for individual attitudes and actions as clues to eternal destiny. Certain behaviors can quickly place a person on the doubtful list. People who enjoy drinking and dancing, who listen to rock music, who use profanity, or who are unfaithful to their marriages are very unlikely, in the minds of fundamentalists, to be headed for heaven. In fact, most believers expect all the strangers they meet to be unsaved. They expect to be a minority voice in most social situations outside their own churches. When they do meet a fellow believer they are pleasantly surprised. They listen for whether the other person can talk about the Lord in the same language and with the same enthusiasm as they do. Only then are they convinced that they have found a fellow believer, one who can be a friend, one to whom they do not need to witness.

The multitudes who are not believers are, for the fundamentalist, held at some distance. Any bond that may develop between the unsaved and the saved is unlikely to be described by the believer as "friendship." Even family members suffer from the distance created between saved and unsaved. Believers do not expect to enjoy the company of unbelievers, nor do they expect unbelievers to understand or enjoy them. When they venture into the world outside their fold, it is primarily to witness, to attempt the rescue of as many souls as possible.

Such a clear separation of oneself from the outside world can, of course, result in prejudice. Some of the signs of salvation can easily coincide with other social categories that also divide insider from outsider. There is in this tendency to see the world in black and white a strong leaning toward exclusion and even persecution of those who are on the outside. Among the fundamentalists I have studied, for instance, there were subtle tendencies to equate the ills of the public schools not just with "secular humanism," but with behavior associated more with blacks than with whites. Historically, some other fundamentalists have seen the pope as anti-Christ and Catholics as, at best, hopelessly duped. The social position of many (but not all) fundamentalists has made them likely consumers of ideologies that scapegoat racial and ethnic groups.[8] As a result, a variety of "hate" groups have littered American history from time to time, claiming some version of conservative Christianity as their legitimation. What distinguishes them from most fundamentalists, however, is their almost complete lack of attention to evangelism. For groups ranging from the Ku Klux Klan to the American Nazi party, outsiders are past redemption—to be hated, not evangelized.

That tendency toward exclusion is, in fact, counterbalanced in much of fundamentalism by a tendency toward inclusion. Born-again Christians do not simply baptize existing social boundaries; they often assault them with every evangelistic tool available to them. Though the temptation to exclude never quite goes away, most fundamentalists care too much about evangelism to let most social barriers get in their way. When we look closely at many groups of fundamentalists, we are likely to discover inside that fold a remarkable variety of ethnic and social-class representatives we might not have expected. To the evangelical, it does not matter whether a person is Jew or gentile, Hispanic or Anglo, black or white, rich or poor—just so long as she is saved, she is a sister in the Lord.

Fundamentalists have the audacity to believe that *everyone* needs to be saved, and because of the sense of urgency about the evangelistic task there is no time for deference. Even if the other is from a different social class, speaks a different language, or thinks he has a perfectly good God already, believers are willing to strike up a conversation with the intent of witnessing. For people who believe that the Rapture will soon whisk all believers off to heaven, leaving the unbelieving world in Tribulation, the business of becoming a believer is of crucial importance. And again, it does not matter whether a person is Jew or gentile, Hispanic or Anglo, black or white—fundamentalists will witness to anybody. Just as salvation draws the boundaries between insider and outsider, so it also can destroy all other social barriers.

Having noted the urge toward inclusion that is inherent in evangelism, I should add that evangelism is not an easy task. It is approached by most believers with fear and trembling. Fundamentalists are no different from the rest of us in our reluctance to be rebuffed by a stranger. They are also no different from the rest of us in sizing up those strangers most likely to respond positively based on the stranger's similarity to themselves. The urge toward inclusion has to overcome the very ordinary human urge toward homogeneity. Not surprisingly, most fundamentalist churches are unremarkably reflective of whatever social groups are dominant in their particular community. Nevertheless, the very recognition that the Gospel is to be preached to everyone often overcomes those social forces to create congregations of sometimes surprising composition.

Fundamentalists Proselytizing Jews: The Jews for Jesus

One of the most interesting and controversial of these "incivil" efforts at rescuing people from damnation has been the "Jews for Jesus." This group represents a forthright statement of the extent to which ethnicity is irrelevant to salvation. Jews are urged to acknowledge Jesus as their Messiah *and* to nurture their Jewish traditions and distinctiveness. As if "Hebrew-Christians," as they call themselves, were not anomaly enough, Jewish Christians also include in their ranks a certain number of gentiles who speak of "converting" to Hebrew Christianity from their ordinary Protestant variety. Though many Jewish parents of converts are quite convinced that no real Jew could be for Jesus, this group challenges many easy assumptions on both sides. Fundamentalists are forced to recognize Jews as brothers and sisters, while Jews are confronted with Christians who retain their "Jewishness."

Currently Jews for Jesus claims three hundred thousand members and defines itself as "Jewish people who believe that 'Y'shua' (Jesus) is the Messiah and whose lives have been changed as a result of that belief."[9] They describe themselves as devoted to understanding and reconciliation, though it is clear that most of those efforts are directed at Christians who need to "appreciate the Jewish heritage." To this end, they keep a variety of music and education teams busy visiting conservative Christian churches. Their touring groups include "Israelight," "Kosher Salt," "Messiah's Shofar," and "Lion's Lambs." But most of their energy is directed toward evangelism and witness training. They seek "creative" ways to communicate the Gospel to their Jewish, but unsaved, brothers and sisters.

Jews for Jesus was an outgrowth of two separate streams of Protestant proselytizing. From the beginning of the modern Anglo-American missions movement, there were groups aimed at converting the Jews.

In London, a Society for the Evangelization of the Jews was begun in 1819. Until that time, Christian relations with Jews often involved either hit-and-miss preaching or generalized condemnation. This and several subsequent groups throughout the nineteenth century sought (with small success) to evangelize individual Jews through the establishment of ongoing mission stations, often staffed in part by Jewish converts. In addition to missionary activity, these groups served as support groups for recent converts. In America, it was not until 1915 that a stable Hebrew Christian organization was formed. This, of course, coincides with the reawakening of Jewish national consciousness. Over the years since, organizations such as the Hebrew Christian Alliance and the Jewish Missions of America have taken on quasi-denominational form.[10] And it is within the Jewish Missions of America that Jews for Jesus first existed.

The other stream from which Jews for Jesus came was that turbulent little tributary known as the "Jesus Movement." During the 1960s and early 1970s, youth who had burned out on the free life of the streets and communes began to discover a new "high." They discovered religious experiences that replaced drug experiences and religious answers that replaced the chaos of individualistic hedonism.[11] They discovered—or created—a religion quite unlike any they had observed before. Many came from homes characterized by the kind of Protestant-Catholic-Jewish American respectability that Herberg and others had written about in the 1950s.[12] These youth had long since given up respectability, and getting saved did little to change that fact. They still shunned the middle-class churches and synagogues where they saw religion as too easy. They chose instead a more rigorous discipleship, embraced more enthusiastically.

These two streams first came together in the person of Mordecai Steinberg, an adult convert to Christianity who had become a missionary with Jewish Missions of America, spreading the Gospel among his Jewish brothers and sisters.[13] During the 1960s, he became concerned about the large number of Jewish youth who were to be found in the counter-culture, and he also came in contact with the Jesus Movement. He was impressed with the enthusiasm and aggressiveness of the Jesus People and began to model his ministry after theirs as a way to reach Jewish youth. He began by distributing literature at peace demonstrations in New York and continued with a ministry to San Francisco's young street people. A small group eventually gathered around the charismatic Steinberg; and in 1971 they took the name "Jews for Jesus"—an epithet used against them by a local college Hillel rabbi in a campus newspaper.

Steinberg's ministry departed from accepted practices in Hebrew-Christian missions in several ways, not the least being his insistence that Jews need not give up their Jewishness upon accepting Christianity. In those early days, he began to develop a renewed emphasis on Jewish traditions, creating a new Passover Seder and a special marriage ceremony. He and his young converts often rediscovered (or discovered for the first time) holidays and traditions given little attention in secularized, assimilated homes. Just as many Protestant parents were chided for their neglect of prayer and Bible-reading, so many Jewish Jesus People became, ironically, more "Jewish" than their parents.

From the beginning this group has existed in tension with both the Jews and the conservative Christians to which they are most closely related. Their very claim that "Y'shua is the Messiah" flies in the face of the way both Jews and Christians have identified themselves since the Diaspora. Christians worship "Jesus," not "Y'shua." Not all fundamentalists are willing to admit the possibility that retaining some of the customs of "the law" can coexist with the dispensation of grace in which believers see themselves living until the Rapture. And, of course, Jews have identified themselves as people who do *not* believe "Y'shua" was the Messiah. Many have not taken the conversion of several thousand of the "best and brightest" of their youth lightly. Some estimate that converts to Christianity now account for nearly one percent of the U.S. Jewish population.

There is more to the hostility, however, than even this. American Jews have taken much of their identity in the American polity from their defense of human rights, their insistence that every person's life, liberty, and beliefs must be protected from the encroachment of government or any other group. In short, American Jews have often thought of themselves as very civil people and as having the function in the larger society of protecting that civility.

Jews for Jesus, on the other hand, are anything but civil. Their roots in the Jesus Movement predisposed them to the sort of street evangelism that violates the sensibilities of most urban Americans. We have learned to define public areas as collections of individual private spaces, places in which each person's private agenda should be respected. Likewise, we have thoroughly defined religion as a private affair, not something to be displayed where others who disagree might be offended by it. To invade the public world at all is bad enough. To invade it with religion is more than many believers in civility (Protestant, Catholic, and Jewish) can tolerate.

Taking a page from Saul Alinsky, Jews for Jesus seek to attract attention, present the message creatively, use the opposition effectively, and learn from experience. They often deliberately enter confrontational situations, having practiced at telling a good story and handling hecklers. They distribute massive amounts of literature, actively seeking Jewish prospects in likely "Jewish" locations. They also use the media to make their cause look bigger than their actual numbers might warrant. When they demonstrate against some immoral cause, the name of Jews for Jesus is prominently displayed. They even show up at synagogues, openly displaying their identity. They invite every rabbi in town to a "dialogue." In short, they go directly into the Jewish community, seeking converts, and then chide Jews for refusing them the rights of free speech so often defended by American Jews. It can be a no-win situation for their targets.

The ultimate insult of the Jews for Jesus, however, is not even their incivil tactics, but their claim to be "fulfilled" Jews. These believers not only claim the Christian identity and all its cultural implications (from Christmas to Easter); they have the audacity to argue that those Christian distinctives are really "Jewish." They do not simply argue for equal time or equal respect. Theirs is not one option among many religious alternatives. What they propose is that to be a Jew and a believer is somehow a higher state than to be either a Jew or a believer alone. And as evangelicals, they are not content to bask in their own eternal status. They feel compelled to share their good news, and they are aggressive enough to find for themselves a wide public audience.

Fundamentalists, Jews, and the Age to Come

Another of the interesting twists on the relationship between Jews and fundamentalists is the special place accorded Jews in dispensational eschatology. Jews are not just any other ethnic group in need of salvation. They are and will always be God's chosen people. Those who read the Bible with an eye toward its prophetic message see there a continuing role for the Jews after the Rapture, during the Tribulation, and in the millennial kingdom.

John Walvoord, president of Dallas Theological Seminary, describes the system in his book *Israel in Prophecy*.[14] He begins with the covenant set forth in Genesis 12 between God and Abraham. God promises to bless Abraham and to make of him a great nation, adding "I will bless them that bless thee, and curse him that curseth thee" (v. 3). This covenant, say the dispensationalists, is permanent. They point to Genesis 17:7 as proof that God intended to be related to Abraham's seed forever (and that the land of Canaan would be theirs forever). They go on to note that God's promise to David is also permanent. God promised, say dispensationalists, that there would always be a kingdom and that a descendent of David would always be on the throne. Though they are willing to concede this promise as "interrupted," they still look for some future time when David's throne will be restored. They recognize that God's *blessing* has always been contingent on obedience to the law, but the establishment of the nation (and later the kingdom) of Israel, they say, is not contingent on anything. It is a promise an omnipotent God can be trusted to keep.

They recognize, of course, that Israel apparently disappeared as a nation for many centuries but, as with other historical facts, fundamentalists are usually able to find references in Scripture to explain what has happened in the world. They look at Scriptures referring to Israel's return to the land and see in them a prediction of twentieth-century Zionism. When Ezekiel quotes Yahweh as promising to "take you from among the heathen, and gather you out of all countries, and bring you into your own land" (37:24), fundamentalists marvel at the way ancient prophecy is being fulfilled today in the 1948 establishment of the state of Israel.

Dispensationalists are also not deterred by the assertions of other Christians that Israel is superseded in the covenant with God by the church. Walvoord claims that the New Testament still recognizes differences between Jews and gentiles among both believers and nonbelievers. He claims that the plan for God's relationship with the Jews is distinct throughout time. Though in this dispensation of grace Jews may receive salvation by believing in Jesus, they have a history in past dispensations and a future in times to come that is distinct from the role of gentiles.

The coming of a new age is hinted at, in fact, by the establishment of the modern state of Israel. Dispensationalists see this as "a token that God is about to fulfill His Word concerning the glorious future of His chosen people."[15] What they expect is that one day soon the trumpet of God will sound (heard only by believers) and Christ will appear on the clouds. All those who truly believe will be whisked into heaven, leaving the world in chaos behind them. Almost immediately, Israel will sign a covenant with her gentile neighbors and for three and one-half years will live in peace and prosperity. There is some speculation that the Temple will be restored then and that ancient sacrifices will be resumed during this time. In addition, a "remnant" of Jews (the 144,000) will believe in Jesus and will serve as evangelists in the world during this Tribulation period.[16]

After the first three and one-half years, however, the peace will be broken by a time of terrible upheaval. Israel and all the rest of the world will suffer in wars, earthquakes, famines, even stars falling from heaven. In part this is seen as God's judgment on the unbelieving world; in part it is interpreted as Satan's attack on the only remaining believers—the Jewish remnant. Finally, a climactic world war will close the period. Then Christ will return with the saints to set up his millennial kingdom. Apparently a few of those remaining in Israel (and in the rest of the world), having survived the Tribulation, will pass Christ's judgment and will be allowed to participate in the kingdom. Christ will rule from Jerusalem along with a resurrected King David and the twelve apostles. Israel will again occupy her ancient territories and will prosper, as will the rest of the world. Finally, at the end of the thousand years, all will be translated to heaven for eternity.

Such beliefs about the future of Jews in the Tribulation and eventual millennial kingdom would seem to be rather irrelevant to the current state of relations between Jews and fundamentalists. After all, this is the dispensation of grace, and everyone—regardless of ethnicity—must go by the rules of grace. Salvation is to be obtained through right belief, through the acceptance of Jesus as savior. However, the belief that God has always, and will always, treat the Jews as separate and special, as chosen, means that fundamentalists are prepared to do so as well. They are prepared to expend special efforts to induct Jews into Christian belief now, and they are prepared to expect Jewish distinctiveness, even among believers in "Y'shua."

Fundamentalists and
the State of Israel

Even more important than support for individual Jewish distinctiveness, of course, is the nearly unqualified fundamentalist support for the nation they believe God established in the promises to Abraham and David, the nation of Israel. This has become most evident in Jerry Falwell's very visible support for the state of Israel. As a dispensational premillennialist, Falwell believes that the Jews remain God's chosen people and are important as players in the great dramas that lie ahead. He says, "Israel is moving to front and center of God's prophetic stage."[17] But Falwell the literalist also sees the Jews as important simply because they are God's chosen people. When God promised to make of Abraham a great nation that would endure forever, Falwell believes it.

Many fundamentalists, especially since the beginning of modern Zionism, have looked at events in Israel as signs of Christ's imminent return. They had read the prophecies about the Jews being regathered into their homeland in the "last days," and it was hard to avoid equating this new nation with those prophecies. Its apparent prosperity and success in making the desert bloom were seen by many as a sign of God's blessing and favor. Anything that made Israel look like its ancient counterpart (such as using its ancient language or currency) played into this scheme by making the apparent parallels to Hebrew Scripture more striking. In the everyday thinking of ordinary fundamentalists, Israel is seen as a "sign of the times."

Falwell (like most fundamentalist preachers) is a bit more sophisticated (and cautious) in his assessment. In his view, the true restored Israel of Scripture will be a believing Israel—believing in Jesus, that is. Though it may be an advantage to have Jews regathered in one place before the Tribulation, it is only after the Rapture and Tribulation that the biblical restoration will take place. "When Christ returns in glory [the Second Coming, not the Rapture], He will deliver Jews from their gentile enemies. As a result, the Jews individually and as a nation will acknowledge Christ as their Messiah."[18] Falwell is careful to say that Christ's return is not dependent on any human activity, whether Jews living in Palestine or Christians evangelizing the whole earth. The most he is willing to concede is that the restored nation of Israel is "suggestive" of an immanent Rapture.

Falwell's support for Israel comes as much from his political ideology as from his theology. He asserts that he supports Israel for three reasons, each of which can be seen as both political and theological. First, he claims that all peoples have a divine right to a homeland and a national purpose; and for Falwell, the claims of the Jews to Palestine simply take precedence over the claims of any other peoples. Here his appeal is as much to ideas about human rights (and legal maneuverings in defense of those rights) as to any biblical principle. He and other conservative preachers often tell the story of Israel's birth as a twentieth-century parallel to the American struggle for freedom, independence, and dominance over the land. Americans, in this view, should support Israel's efforts to do what we did two centuries ago.

Second, Falwell points out that Israel is the only democracy, and therefore the only bastion of anti-communism, in the Middle East. America should simply recognize her own best interests and support this ideological ally. Here he builds out of the evangelical Christian conviction that communism is inimical to the spread of the Gospel and should be opposed on those grounds as well as on grounds of democratic rights. Falwell takes a very dim view of the governments of neighboring Arab states, seeing most as dictatorships friendly to terrorists. It makes no sense to Falwell to support governments like that in opposition to a staunch Free World ally.

Finally, Falwell caps his argument about support for Israel by noting simply that it *is* the Promised Land. It is the land promised to the Jews from the beginning. As he reads Scripture, the land from the Jordan River to the Mediterranean is the least Israel has a right to claim. Judea and Samaria were "eternally" promised to Abraham and should be Jewish.

Falwell has made the issue of support for Israel one of the cornerstones of his Moral Majority. And he does not seem to be seriously out of step with rank-and-file fundamentalists in doing so. Most have not thought about all the reasons, but supporting Israel simply seems right to them. Supporting Israel seems to be a way of being on God's side. If the Jews continue to be God's chosen people, the state of Israel should be supported.

It also means that anti-Semitism is not looked on with favor in the fundamentalist community. If the Jews are God's people, Christians have no business persecuting them. Falwell (at least in his mature, public, years) believes all racial and ethnic prejudices to be creations of Satan that should be condemned by Christians. But anti-Semitism is particularly heinous because of God's promised protection of the Jews. Falwell's peculiar reasoning can let him proclaim that no *true* Christian ever persecuted a Jew.

This clear opposition to anti-Semitism has existed in tension with a more passive position born of waiting for the end. Just as some believers saw Israel's success as a "sign of the times," so others saw rising anti-Semitism as a similar sign. Some past fundamentalists have seen anti-Semitism as inevitable and part of God's cosmic calendar of events. They have even sometimes been afraid to interfere so as not to interrupt the world's movement toward the Rapture.

Falwell, however, is not so fatalistic. On this, as on other issues, he is not willing to sit back while the world becomes worse in preparation for the Rapture. And, in fact, there have always been voices like his raised among fundamentalists, voices reminding believers that the one who blesses the Jew is blessed by God, and the one who curses the Jew is likewise cursed by God.

These tensions between passive and active support for Jews were never more apparent than during the 1930s.[19] While some fundamentalists could find biblical explanations (and thus excuses) for the events unfolding in Europe, others spoke out forcefully against Hitler's program. Owen documents the presence of extensive missionary efforts among the Jews in Eastern Europe in the early 1930s, and many of those missionaries were actively engaged in protecting Jews from the growing Nazi threat.[20] Their letters home were printed in fundamentalist publications and warned the people in America that they should act to stop Hitler and his threats against the Jews. Many fundamentalist leaders saw this persecution of Jews as completely alien to anything taught by Jesus (who was, after all, himself a Jew). They responded by organizing relief efforts, refugee funds, and world-wide days of prayer. Though we would not want to claim for fundamentalists in the 1930s or otherwise a clean record on anti-Semitism, it is true that their dispensational eschatology has lent itself to a consistent chorus of pro-Jewish sentiment among Bible believers.

Fundamentalists, Jews, and Civility

The relationship between Jews and fundamentalists, then, is no simple matter to analyze. On the one hand, believers must be taken at their word (and by their actions) as firm supporters of the nation of Israel and of Jewish people in general. In addition, both their words and their actions speak to their tolerance—even encouragement—of Jewish ethnicity. They are content to have Hebrew-speaking, yarmulke-wearing keepers of the law in their midst. I think we must take fundamentalists at their word that they are not anti-Semites, at least in any usual sense of that term.

We must also realize, however, that believers are not content for Jews simply to be Jews. Though fundamentalists may be quite tolerant and civil in matters of ethnicity, they cannot be tolerant in matters of religion. To say that believers should respect the right of Jews to practice their religion as they choose is, for a fundamentalist, like saying that people have a right to sit in a burning house, if they choose, and we should not bother them. Whatever the past or future role of Jews in God's kingdom, *this* is the dispensation of grace, and those who wish to be saved must accept Jesus, Y'shua, as their messiah and savior. Those who do not accept Jesus are doomed to eternal hellfire and by virtue of that will never be seen as true brother or sister by the believer. Though fundamentalists may be very civil in matters of ethnicity, their intense evangelicalism prevents any such civility in religious matters.

Even here, however, the question of civility is not so clear as it first appears. We may vehemently disagree with our fundamentalist neighbor's diagnosis of our eternal danger and wish she would leave us in peace to practice our own religious traditions, but perhaps we should thank her for being willing to talk to us. One of the ironies of pluralism and civility is that we pluralists spend most of our time talking to those who already understand us and agree with us. We rarely make occasions to say anything of consequence to those who might differ with our views. The joke goes that we are so tolerant that the only thing we cannot stand is intolerance.

In a curious way, the fundamentalist's willingness to confront strangers demonstrates a kind of bridging of barriers not often tackled by those of us who are so concerned to be civil. They are so convinced that their beliefs are of critical value that they are willing to talk with anyone—rich or poor, black or white or Hispanic, Jew or gentile. Because they think their message might make the difference between eternal life and eternal death, they are willing to set aside social niceties that sometimes keep the rest of us from saying what we really mean, and therefore from saying anything at all. The fundamentalist's problem, of course, is an inability to live with a pluralism that does not yield to their evangelistic efforts. But they have the audacity to think they can talk to *anyone* and talk about things that are important, and in that way they may be more "civil" than we think.

Part Four

Social Science
Perspectives

9

The Psychology of Proselytism

H. NEWTON MALONY

Proselytism is the practice of making proselytes—those who have changed from one faith to another. It is a special type of persuasion in which an individual decides to forego one set of convictions in favor of another. In fact, proselytism may not simply be a unique type of persuasion; it may be the only type of persuasion. If Fowler is correct, persons are never without "faith."[1] While the qualities of faith may differ from time to time, persons always have a faith. Thus, when persons become convinced to change their faith, it may always be a matter of "proselytism." It may never be a process of changing from no-faith to faith. Instead, it is likely to be a process of changing from one faith to another.

Be this as it may, the set of events whereby late adolescents are persuaded to leave the faith of their upbringing and embrace another religion seems different from changes that might occur in children or among those who are less mature. Even though "faith" may always be present, the faith of those who have "come of age," who have self-consciously embraced a given faith, seems to be qualitatively different from the implicit faith of childhood. Proselytism usually refers to intentional efforts to change this more overt, self-conscious kind of faith.

While my attempt will be to discuss these persuasive efforts dispassionately, there is no question but that many persons have thought of them in a distasteful, negative manner. As a young pastor I well remember the disdain with which we looked upon those who proselytized. These were the evangelists who tried to convince Methodists to become Baptists, Baptists to become Church of Christs, Church of Christs to become Jehovah Witnesses, and Jehovah Witnesses to become Catholics. We were possessive of each and every one of our church members, and it pained us deeply to lose one of them to another group. We were more willing for them to become inactive and drop out of church entirely than for them to become members of a neighboring church. I can remember saying, "Since there are so many unchurched persons around, why do these people spend their time trying to steal our members?" I disliked proselytizers immensely and worked strenuously to make my church so attractive that members would not want to leave under any circumstances. I must admit I was never fully successful.

In an article on "Jewish Attitudes Toward Mission and Conversion," Daniel Polish reflects on an even more negative judgment about proselytism. He states:

> From my earliest childhood, I remember being importuned, evangelized, or witnessed to in one fashion or another by all kinds of people who professed to have my best interests at heart. I often felt as if the very fact of my Jewishness constituted me as a special challenge . . . I have been a rabbi for a little over a decade . . . Scarcely a month has gone by since my ordination when I have not received one form or another of these conversionary solicitations. They have become, in my mind, one of the intrinsic features of the American rabbinate, though certainly not one of its more edifying aspects . . . Within the Jewish community, missionary activities contribute to a sense of being beleaguered and set upon by a "hostile world." They are perceived as yet another "assault" upon us by the various forces that would put an end to our existence. In terms of Christian faith in particular, they are understood to be yet another act of ill-will in a history of malice.[2]

Even in the advertising community, proselytizing was, until recently, considered anathema. The professional code of advertising prohibited comparing one product to another. For example, all of us can remember when margarine was compared to "the high-priced spread." Even this was a bit suspect because everyone knew the high-priced spread was "butter," and at that time in our history we did not think it appropriate to win customers on the basis of comparing one product to another. Advertising could laud the good qualities of a given product, but it was not allowed to claim superiority by downgrading the competition.

Times have drastically changed. Proselytizing has become permissible. The majority of ads nowadays compare antacids, automobiles, peanut butters, diet meals, and a myriad of other products with one another. I am sure many would agree with me in feeling that these are in poor taste. I prefer the old standards in which proselytizing was prohibited.

Although I acknowledge this negative evaluation of proselytism in myself, Daniel Polish, and many others, it is my intent in this essay to be descriptive rather than prescriptive in my evaluation. By this I mean that I intend to describe the motives, processes, and results of proselytizing in a neutral fashion. In spite of the fact that I recognize that authors from Aristotle to the present have emphasized the crucial importance of ethics in the persuasive process, I leave to others the task of moral evaluation. My job is to detail the psychological and behavioral dynamics of proselytizing rather than to evaluate their efficacy.

I acknowledge that for elders whose children depart from their traditions and embrace other religions, proselytism may be anything other than a dispassionate issue. These parents might prefer that I take a strong negative stand toward proselytizing. This is understandable. As one father said to me, "I would not mind if my daughter married a Christian, but I would strongly disapprove of her becoming a Christian." Such changes as this are a threat to parenthood. They imply that one has not done a good job of rearing one's children. They violate the biblical promise "Train up a child in the way that he should go and when he is old he will not depart from it" (Prov. 22:6).

While I might have some of these same feelings, as a behavioral scientist I choose to resist the temptation into which others of my ilk have fallen, namely, to see in generational independence-strivings and in the application of persuasive technology devious and diabolical maneuvers that differ in *kind,* rather than degree, from other normal psychological processes. As Erikson and others have noted, adolescence is greatly prolonged in Western society, and the pressure to challenge, test, and reform the culture of the parents is persistent and strong.[3]

There is no question but that parents experience much anxiety during this period, nor is it surprising that religion becomes that focus of youth's individuation-striving. The parameters of this maturation process, however, have not differed from the time of the ancients to the present day. In this regard, Charles Stewart noted that there are three basic responses of youth to the religion of their parents: affirmation, rejection, and deviation.[4] I have witnessed each of these options in my three sons. One affirmed my faith; one rejected it; and another kept it but in a different form. They have also exemplified these alternatives in their choices of ways to make a living—the other major issue about which parents become most disturbed.

Better, as a behavioral scientist, I should recognize the naturalness of many aspects of these experiences and I should resist the tendencies of such behavioral scientists as Martin Ofshe and Margaret Singer who insist on projecting all of the responsibility for adolescent faith-changes onto groups which, they claim, deceive or coerce.[5] In my opinion, the type of reasoning exemplified by these scholars is inflammatory, and it ignores not only the normality of developmental questioning, but also the radical differences between mind control and brainwashing during the Korean war and proselytizing by religious groups in Western society. Studies have shown that, by far, the great majority of these changes in religious affiliation involve willful association with a new religious group and are devoid of the overt physical control of bodily movement such as characterized the pressures in prisoner-of-war camps.[6]

In this regard, the testimony that Larry Wallersheim was the innocent dupe of forceful compliance in both his decision to enter Scientology and to stay with it for eleven years is contrary to the facts, in my opinion—quite apart from the jury decision in the recent trial involving the church. In a recent article, I have analyzed this case and suggested that Wallersheim's experience illustrated the typical collaborative processes that occur between converts and groups wherever such events occur—at least in our society.[7] In my judgment, to call his experience "mind control" or "brainwashing" is incorrect. His participation was of his own volition.

There is no question but that many religions capitalize on these generational differences between parents and children, but this should not provoke us to take a prejudicial stance toward them simply because they make us anxious and uncomfortable. Nor should proselytism be judged as negative simply because it does not fit one's understandings of what a religion should be. As Bryan Wilson points out, Christianity stands in stark contrast to both Eastern religions and to Judaism. In regard to the former, Eastern religions were introduced into well-developed and sophisticated civilizations, while Christianity was the prime agent in the development of most of the Western culture. Christianity has played a much more assertive historical role than Buddhism or Hinduism. In regard to the latter, while Judaism shares with Christianity the belief in one, universal, and omnipotent God, it has differed dramatically in the way it has applied this belief. Wilson states:

> . . . whereas the Jews came, in time, to use religious exclusivism to reinforce ethnic exclusivity, Christians were from the outset a proselytizing people. Their God was exclusive, but they, unlike the Jews, were not

an exclusive people. Indeed, the fact that they were competitive, and sought to convert others, made their claims all the more audacious.[8]

Christians have always tried to convert persons to their beliefs. Jews have not. Evangelism, the Christian word for proselytism, has been thought to be a mandate stemming from the admonition of Jesus to

> . . . go and make disciples of all nations, baptizing them in the name of the Father and of the Son and of the Holy Spirit, and teaching them whatsoever I have commanded you. . . . (Matt. 28:19–20a)

It is not legitimate, therefore, to discount a given religion solely because it is what it has always been—as offensive as its practices may be in terms of social customs and the ideals of tolerance or mutual respect.

Thus, I intend to take a descriptive rather than prescriptive stance in my discussion. I assume this point of view at the same time that I question the oft-made distinction between "communication" and "persuasion." For example, Bettinghaus suggests that while all persuasion is communication, all communication is not persuasion.[9] He suggests that when a professor walks into a room and says "Hello," communication without persuasion occurs in the sense that nothing is demanded of the student. But when the professor walks into a room and says "Will you go to the library for me?" communication *with* persuasion occurs.

Polish, among others, would have us believe that communication without persuasion can occur between persons of differing faiths.[10] He assumes that persons can share their faiths without attempting to influence one another. I do not agree. I think the Marxist analysis of communication is more correct. Herein, it is asserted that all communication involves persuasion, defined as attempts to influence others' thoughts or actions—even if influencers are only minimally aware of their intent and even if the desired result be only recognition and approval.[11] I make the assumption, therefore, that it is better to look on proselytism as an extreme example of the very essence of communication, namely persuasion and influence. Thus, the distinction between communication and persuasion is moot, in my opinion.

Proselytism:
A Definition and Model for Analysis

As noted earlier, proselytism can be understood under the generic term "persuasion." Several authors have proposed definitions. All of them agree that persuasion involves an attempt by one person to influence another through speech and behavior. Scheidel states that persuasion is ". . . that activity in which speaker and listener are conjoined and in which the speaker consciously attempts to influence the behavior of the listener by transmitting audible and visible symbolic cues."[12] Bettinghaus simplifies this by contending that persuasion is "a communication situation which involves a conscious attempt by one individual to change the attitudes, beliefs, or the behavior of another individual or group of individuals through the transmission of some message."[13]

Without making proselytism synonymous with persuasion, let us define proselytism as the kind of persuasion in which the attempt to change other persons' beliefs is grounded in the conviction that these persons' present beliefs are essentially wrong. Now, it could be said that such an assumption is inherent in *all* persuasive attempts, and I would agree—in an absolute sense. But it occurs to me that, while we might affirm that these are only differences in degree rather than kind, the focus of proselytism is much more on the wrongness of a present stance than is typically true in such persuasive efforts as automobile sales, toothpaste ads, and dietary programs. I would hasten to agree, however, that this distinction breaks down when it comes to antacids, cereals, and political parties. Here the differences between the selling of products and evangelistic efforts to change Jews into Christians seems to me to break down. All are proselytism in the sense in which I have defined it.

I would now like to propose a model for analyzing proselytizing from a psychological point of view. It attempts to describe the motives, actions, and perceptions of these kinds of social interactions. I have labeled the model "the proselyte tree" after the distinctions proposed by William James in his analysis of religious experience. Using the analogy of a tree, he suggested that both the "roots" and the "fruits" of behavior should be noted.[14] These terms refer to motivations and results respectively. My model simply inserts the term "trunk" in between these two to refer to the proselytizing actions themselves. As can be seen in diagram 1, this allows for a threefold model encompassing most of the dynamics of proselytism from a psychological point of view.

There are two other dimensions that need to be added to this proselyte-tree model: First, there is the need to provide a way of distinguishing between the behavior of those who proselytize and those who are proselytized. The dynamics are different. Second, there is the need to distinguish between those dynamics that enhance and those that impede the process. It is obvious that not everyone who engages in proselytism nor do all persons exposed to such influences succumb to

DIAGRAM 1

The Proselyte Tree Model

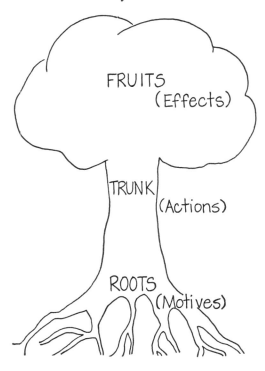

them. Thus, an expanded depiction of the proselyte-tree model resembles a $3 \times 2 \times 2$ block figure as can be seen in diagram 2.

As diagram 2 shows, it should be possible to analyze proselytism in twelve distinct manners:

1—The motives (roots) of those who proselytize;
2—The actions (trunk) of those who proselytize;
3—The results (fruits) of those who proselytize;
4—The motives (roots) of those who are proselytized;
5—The actions (trunk) of those who are proselytized;
6—The results (fruits) of those who are proselytized;
7—The motives (roots) of those who do *not* proselytize;
8—The actions (trunk) of those who do *not* proselytize;
9—The results (fruits) of those who do *not* proselytize;
10—The motives (roots) of those who are *not* proselytized;
11—The actions (trunk) of those who are *not* proselytized; and
12—The results (fruits) of those who are not proselytized.

DIAGRAM 2

The Expanded Proselyte Tree Model

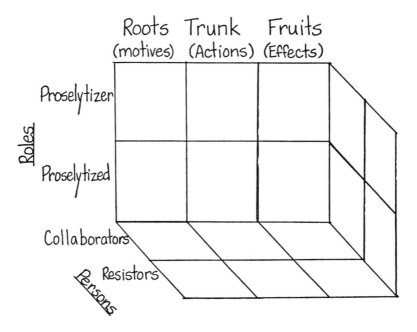

These dimensions could be subsumed under the rubrics of "the evangelizer" (numbers 1, 2, 3), "the converters" (numbers 4, 5, 6), "the decliners" (numbers 7, 8, 9), and "the resisters" (numbers 11, 12, 13). Although there are important psychological processes involved in each of the dimensions, for the purpose of this essay I will only discuss numbers 1 and 2 under the evangelizers and number 4 under the converters. Thus, the remainder of the discussion will be concerned with the roots or motives of evangelizers as well as their methods or behaviors. Further, the roots or motives of the converters will also be considered.

The Evangelizers

As noted earlier, Christian evangelizers, i.e., those who proselytize, often refer to the command of their leader, Jesus, as the rationale for their behavior. This command to "go into all the world . . ." (Matt. 28:19–20) is referred to as "the great commission." On the basis of these words, many Christians look on attempts to convert others to their faith as a duty or an obligation. An example of this is the dictum "show me a person who is not leading people to Christ and I will show you a defeated Christian."[15] The reasons for proselytizing, however, are probably more complex than this. At least two other motives should be considered. They are the need to persuade others to accept totalistic answers to life's problems and the accompanying need for the reassurance that converts bring.

Galper suggests that "totalism" is a phenomenon that characterizes new religious movements that arise during times of radical historical change.[16] It is interesting that he, along with other authors to which he refers, freely apply this designation of "totalism" in a derogatory manner to such groups as the Unification Church, the Krishna Consciousness Movement, and the Children of God, but ignore the fact that all religions are essentially totalistic. If, as Yinger concludes, religion is the way in which persons handle the enigmas, the tragedies, and the mysteries of life,[17] then it should come as no surprise that any and all religion provides for a person's total answers to the meaning of existence.

A recent printed statement by the president of a college related to a church that neither Galper nor the scholars he quotes would call "new" attests to this "totalistic" point of view. The president stated:

> Many people, including some Christians, have compartmentalized their lives. They have social lives, spiritual lives, family lives, sexual lives, and recreational lives, to name a few . . . Integrating faith, learning, and living suggests that we tear down the walls of these little partitions to let our faith invade every area of our lives. In reality, every facet of our lives, then, becomes informed and influenced by our spiritual lives. Christ is Lord of all, not just of our spiritual pursuits.[18]

Certainly this is how many Christians look on their religion. It is "the Good News," meaning it is the solution to the problem of life. They repeat the words of Jesus: "I am the way, the truth, and the life." (John 14:6). It is not just the new religions that are totalistic. All the great religions of the world are totalistic in essence. They are utopian in their basic beliefs. It is probably an accident of history that much modern religion has become compartmentalized and respectable. "Sects" may be more true to the essence of religion than "churches," to use Troeltsch's dichotomy.[19] "Churches" may be sects that have accommodated themselves to modern society. Just as it is probably not unreasonable to assume that "Jihad," or Holy War, underlies the assumptions of all Muslims—fundamentalists or moderates[20]—so it is not incorrect to assume that "totalism" underlies most religions—respectable, mainline or not.

Thus, it is a questionable procedure to differentiate among religions that are and are not totalistic or to conclude that affiliation with a totalistic group is an index of inferior mental health or social marginality. In my opinion, such interpretations likely reflect an unexamined American penchant for individualism, agnosticism, and that type of personal freedom which never exists in concrete form. The presumption that anyone has found a complete answer to the meaning of existence seems to be an offense to the American character. The issue may be more one of culture than of logic. Suffice it to say that there exists a strong impulse among many who take their religion seriously to share their totalistic answer to life's problems enthusiastically, and to persuade others to join them in affirming these things.

Another dimension of this impulse to convince others is that unless they accept a given point of view their lives are in danger. Although this motive is less influential now, it was a dominant theme in eighteenth-century America as could be seen in Jonathan Edwards's classic sermon "Sinners in the Hands of an Angry God." This approach is not entirely missing today, however. A famous Baptist pastor in Dallas, Texas, still preaches annually a sermon entitled "Pay Day, Some Day." While many would consider this motive presumptuous and messianic, it has been an impelling influence among many sincere religionists who have felt a genuine concern for others. They have been convinced that "there is no other name under heaven whereby a man may be saved" (Acts 4:12) and that they would be judged by God as unfaithful if they did not engage in trying to convince others of that fact. Preaching "hellfire and damnation" is, therefore, something they *have* to do.

This leads to the second motive, namely, an ever-so-subtle need to have others agree with one. It should not be forgotten that religion is a matter of faith, not proof and, thus, in these matters the comfort of group agreement becomes its own motivation. There is reassurance in numbers, and the more who agree, the more comfortable the individual believer becomes. This is the opposite of the need to *conform;* it is the need to *confirm.* Alcoholics Anonymous knows well the reassuring power of one alcoholic converting another alcoholic to the AA way. The same is true for proselytizers. They proselytize, in part, for their own good. Many of the classic experiments in social psychology attest to this fact. The pressure to conform is great and people feel better when others agree with them. Every salesperson knows this dynamic. The conviction as to the goodness of the product grows as a function of the number of sales.

The psychological theory underlying this phenomenon is that of "balance theory," described by Fritz Heider in the 1940s.[21] Herein it is presumed that there is an innate need to have persons agree with oneself on matters of great conviction and importance. This is termed "balance." This urge lessens on matters of less importance and conviction. The theory predicts that where there is imbalance people will attempt to change the attitude of the other person, change their perception of the other person's attitude, or change their own attitude. Only after one of these has occurred will the person feel satisfied, i.e., in balance. The presumption is that such a need is in all humans.

Turning next to *behavior*, it should be noted that the model being used here makes no presumptions about the specific *types* of persuasion used in proselytism. Some writers, such as Cronkite, are inclined to exclude the use of force.[22] I would, however, include all types of influence among the options available to proselytizers. I am inclined to agree with Minnich that a revolver held to the head is as viable a method as are argument and debate.[23] Many will remember the statement made by the commandant to Paul Newman in *Cool Hand Luke* just prior to committing him to solitary confinement for failure to obey prison rules: "What we have here is a failure to communicate." A better use of force in proselytizing persuasion has yet to be made!

The point is that my definition of proselytism makes no distinction among the variety of strategies for gaining compliance. All have been used. The Crusades and the Inquisition are but two questionable examples of this fact. Brainwashing during the Korean war was another. However, it is probably helpful to distinguish those methods that severely curtail physical movement and decision-making from those that involve the noncoercive, but intentional, application of techniques gleaned from the social/behavioral sciences. In the modern world, the ideal of making decisions freely without physical coercion is a worthy one. Most proselytizers would agree. As noted earlier, coercion has not been found by most researchers on new religious groups, popular impressions notwithstanding.[24]

However, it is one thing to affirm the ideal of individual freedom and another thing to ignore the extent to which we accept without question in everyday life the same pressures to conform that we decry when they are observed in religious proselytizing. I agree with Engel who concluded that religious persuaders are ". . . justified to make use of any insight from the behavioral sciences, persuasion, advertising, and so on; but every action will be judged by . . . rigorous biblical standards."[25] These "rigorous biblical standards" must eschew manipulation, according to Engel. Manipulation includes any method that restricts another person's freedom to choose. As an illustration of the Bible's disapproval of manipulation, Engel quotes Phillips's translation of 2 Corinthians 4:2–7:

> . . . we use no clever tricks, no dishonest manipulation of the Word of God. We speak the plain truth . . . For it is Christ Jesus as Lord whom we preach, not ourselves, we are your servants for Jesus's sake . . . This priceless treasure we hold, so to speak, in common earthenware—to show that the splendid power of it belongs to God and not to us.

As noted in the above quote, however, adherence to this ideal would not mean that Engel did not recommend the use of numerous available and commonly accepted methods in evangelizing.

Marwell and Schmitt list sixteen such persuasive methods.[26] They range from coercion, threat, and promise to altruism, logic, and moral appeal. Raven and Kruglianski provide a somewhat more manageable taxonomy that should be held in mind as we consider further the methods of proselytism, i.e., the "trunk" of the proselyte tree.[27] Among their list of seven types of power are the following:

Coercive power— based on the use of fear. Those who proselytize on this basis do so by threatening harm to others who do not conform.

Connection power— based on influence with others. Those who proselytize on this basis do so by reference to connections they have with important people.

Expert power— based on expertise and skill. Those who proselytize on this basis do so by demonstrating their agility at solving problems or performing tasks.

Information power— based on access to valuable facts. Those who proselytize on this basis do so by sharing information and engaging in logical arguments.

Legitimate power— based on the holding of a position. Those who proselytize on this basis do so by calling attention to the status that is theirs by virtue of the office they hold.

Referent power— based on likeableness and on personality. Those who proselytize on this basis do so by the force of their personal attractiveness and social skills.

Reward power— based on the possession of reinforcement. Those who proselytize on this basis do so by giving gifts and positive incentives.

As Engel notes, one of the most agreed-upon rules of communication is that "the probability of change in beliefs is directly proportional to the credibility of the sender."[28] In other words, the proselytizer must be believed or there will be no response. All of the above strategies are ways of legitimatizing the proselytizer.

The content of the message is parallel to the credibility of the messenger in importance. Whereas earlier theory contended that persuasion involved separate appeals to reason (the logic of the message) and to intuition (the feeling of the persons), current thinking does not divide humans into separate mental states. A valid distinction, however, could still be made between "direct" and "indirect" approaches. These relate to the difference between a "search-" and a "problem-" focus among converts to which I shall return in a later part of this essay.

The direct approach most resembles the recommendation of the Protestant theologian Karl Barth, while the indirect approach has most affinity with the thinking of Emil Brunner. In a spirited dialogue these scholars debated whether it was necessary for persons to have a need for God before they could become religious.[29] Brunner said yes. According to him, there needed to be a "point of contact" between human need and the answers of faith. Barth said no. According to him, God broke into life and established His own "point of contact." God revealed Himself through His word (i.e., the Bible and the life of Jesus), and this was a powerful enough stimulus to evoke the response of persons. Thus, for Barth, God spoke to the world without any mediation. Therefore, communication about Him should follow that approach. It should be direct and should emphasize the content of the proclamation, i.e., the truths of faith. For Brunner, God spoke indirectly. His message to the world came as answers to the problems of life, and communication about Him should be related to the difficulties being faced at a given time.

Both strategies have been utilized. James Sellers's book, *The Outsider and the Word of God*[30] is a clear example of the indirect approach. Using the Kantian categories of time, space, causality, and substance, Sellers concludes that twentieth-century persons can best be evangelized by demonstrating that faith in God is the best solution to peoples' anxieties over these existential realities. He follows the theologian Paul Tillich in this approach.

Of related concern is the issue of "contextualization" in proselytism. At the simplest level there is the question of language. While persons who speak all languages may have anxieties of time, space, causality, or substance, they will not understand the answers of faith unless they are communicated within the language that they speak. The persuader must put the message within the context of the thought forms and linguistic sounds of the receiver or the message will fall on deaf ears.

Missionary anthropologist Ralph Winter has proposed a model that illustrates this necessity.[31] He terms it the E–0, E–1, E–2, and E–3 model. "E" stands for evangelism and the numbers (1–3) stand for degrees of contextualization. E–0 evangelism is for someone who speaks the same language and with whom there is no need to adapt the message; an example of this would be a Christian talking with an inactive member of the church. E–1 evangelism is for someone who speaks the same language but who does not share the same faith; an example of this would be a Christian talking with a non-Christian in the same culture. E–2 evangelism is for someone whose language is similar but not identical; an example of this would be a Christian talking with a Jew. E–3 evangelism is for someone whose language is entirely different; an example of this would be a Christian talking with a Buddhist. There would be some contextualizing in each case; however, it would be less in those settings where the language was most similar.

In the case of Christians and Jews, their common grounding in the Old Testament and in their hope for a messiah makes proselytism resemble a family affair. Although it is widely recognized that the difference between the Jewish and Christian messiahs is great, there is still the keen urge on the part of Christians to convince Jews that their hope has been realized in Jesus. The dynamics of family relationships are unique and probably very applicable here. There is certainly the need to prove one part of the family wrong, but my suspicion is that it would be an error to assume that it was entirely a condescending impulse to degrade one member of the family. I suspect that many Christians would speak with love and concern instead. They would see themselves as engaging in a sensitive effort to contextualize.

The Converters

The converters are those who are proselytized. They reject one faith in favor of another. Much of the discussion in recent literature has focused on the situational determinants influencing decisions to change from one faith to another.[32] I choose to emphasize the internal dynamics of those who convert, however, feeling that these predispositions are of equal, if not more, importance than environmental pressures. I will discuss these motivations to become proselytized under four rubrics: (1) problem-solving; (2) friendship-finding; (3) meaning-seeking; (4) role-discovering; and (5) preparation-lacking.

For over two decades the Lofland and Stark model has been identified with the problem-solving understanding of predispositions toward conversion.[33] The model suggests that, initially, those who convert experience enduring, acutely felt life tensions within a religious, problem-solving perspective. These tensions lead persons to define themselves as searching for answers. Near to the time they are experiencing these problems in their lives, they encounter a religious group where they find answers and establish friendships that become the major focus of their social life. This approach would appear to be supportive of the assumptions underlying the indirect approach to persuasion mentioned earlier. It would imply that without such a predisposition there would be no conversion because the new faith would not be answering any questions the persons were asking.

It should be said that the awareness of the tensions can be overt or covert. On the one hand, overt awareness might lead to an explicit search for groups with answers. On the other hand, covert awareness might reverse the order of events. Inquisitiveness might lead to an initial encounter during which the person becomes aware of how the new faith addresses the problem. Although advocates of the religion from which the person converts might insist that the individual already possessed solutions to such problems, in many cases the persons does not see the connection or feels that the new faith offers a novel, if not superior, answer.

In a study utilizing the Lofland and Stark model, however, Austin found that only a small percentage of his college sample reported major problems prior to converting.[34] The one fact that was characteristic of all of these converts was intense interaction with others in the group. Friendships are, therefore, the second motive that determines susceptibility to proselytism. It is no accident that many groups begin with social contacts from which strong friendships result. In studies of who attends which church, people report friendships to be the dominant cause. Of course, the friends of those who convert are inclined to see the solution to life crisis within a religious perspective. Thus, friendship reinforces the importance of the credibility of the persuader referred to earlier.

The third motive that seems to characterize converts is that of "meaning-seeking" as opposed to problem-solving. As a counter to the accusation that proselytizers seek out youth with problems, Richardson contends that many youth are "seekers" for meaning in life.[35] Although their parents might assume that they have settled these major issues earlier, they may not have done so.

Such a presumption that the meaning of life, as adults understand that term, may not be clear to late adolescents when they encounter a new religion is consonant with what is known in developmental psychology. Erik Erikson suggests that this period of life is characterized by a search for "integrity versus despair."[36] If his analysis is correct, the religious training that is received in childhood and early adolescence should not necessarily be considered sufficient in the search for meaning that is encountered in later years. Persons become awakened in late adolescence to a life-long search that may lead them from one group to another. Richardson calls these "conversion careers." This point of view would lend support to the direct method referred to earlier. The totalistic answer that a given religion might provide to this search for meaning is experienced as satisfying and understandable.

"Role-discovering" was suggested as the fourth motive behind the converting of persons to other religions. In many situations the person has only a participant role in the old and is provided with an official position in the new religion. The opportunity to have an official title and to achieve a leadership role is presented very early in the encounter with proselytizers. Very often, youth who remain in the religion of their parents are followers. Their parents are the leaders. The appeal of having a position in another group is strong. Certainly, this coincides with the analysis of development maturation during which youth yearn to find a place with which they can identify. Many youth do not experience this in the religion of their childhood. Being offered a position in a group that is run by their peers is very attractive.

The final motive behind converting is a sequel to the motives to find meaning, to solve problems, and play significant roles in one's religious faith. This motive has been termed "preparation-insufficiency." A number of leaders in groups from which youth have departed have suggested that leaders should spend less time in complaining about the persuasive techniques of proselytizers and more time in preparing youth for meeting these pressures. Although there is a sense in which this makes the victims the perpetrators, there is a need for groups to take some responsibility if a large percentage of their youth defect. Many converts report that their former faith simply did not deal with the same issues addressed by the new faith or, if it did, that their knowledge of their faith's answers paled in the face of the superior knowledge of the adherents to the new religion. To assume that catechetical or synagogue training in late childhood is sufficient for meeting the psychological needs of late adolescence may be delusional. Many converts report themselves unable to deal with their faith in a sophisticated manner when they encounter those whose faith is alive and up to date. Preparation for these experiences has been insufficient.

If Stewart is correct, however, in saying that there will always be those who react to the religion of their parents by defecting, parents should not tyrannize themselves unduly.[37] Yet, there is no denying that most of the mainline religions have done inadequate thinking about how to upgrade the religion of their children in order to meet their developmental needs for the solution of life's problems, for discovering the meaning of existence, and for finding realistic roles to play.

In conclusion, some comments should be made about predisposing conditions that have been presumed to be present in converts but which have not been found to be true. Sargant, among others, proposed that conversions tended to occur in those who were hypersuggestible owing to cerebral weakness.[38] According to Sargant, this hysteric tendency to embrace religious ideology as if it solved all of life's problems was due to "reciprocal inhibition" in which certain parts of the brain became overstimulated while other parts became inert. This resulted in the ability to cut off from awareness complexities, to deny difficulties, and to think in absolute terms. Sargant felt this tendency varied from person to person and that those who experienced religious conversions were inclined to possess more of this physiological state.

Sargant's theory has been subjected to much study but has not been widely confirmed.[39] There is little evidence to support the contention that those who convert to new religions are physiologically weaker than those who do not. The judgment that the proselytized are hypersuggestible hysterics who are preyed upon by unscrupulous mind-benders has not been found to be valid. A case in point was the recent claim made by Larry Wallersheim in his suit against the Church of Scientology. While I lack sufficient information to evaluate his experience fully, it is difficult to imagine that an individual could be said to have been imprisoned and coerced against his will to participate in a group for eleven years during which he rose to a position of leadership at the same time that he lived and worked at jobs and apartments of his own choosing. What I do feel able to judge, however, is the question of his predisposition toward proselytism within the Sargant model. Wallersheim's social history reveals he was anything but a naïve, passive college student who was seduced by a temptress into Scientology on a spring-break trip to San Francisco. As I have stated in an earlier essay, ". . . he was a lad who had dyed his hair purple while in high school, had left his Roman Catholic background and joined an Eastern religion, had walked naked around the office of his draft board to convince them of his instability, and had made failing grades in two colleges."[40] Clearly, here was a young man whose demeanor was characterized less by a weak, physiological state than by inner turmoil and a desire to find meaning in life. He was more a seeker than an innocent bystander.

Summary

This essay has considered the psychology of proselytizing. Proselytism was presented as essence of persuasion, and communication was presented as essentially persuasive. However, proselytism was specifically defined as attempts during the post-childhood stage of life to change the faith of those who were identified with another religion. A model for examining the psychodynamics of proselytism was proposed. Called the "proselytism tree," this model suggested that proselytizing could be studied in terms of motives, methods, and results for both those who engaged in the process and for those who were persuaded by it.

The motives and behaviors of proselytizers (evangelizers) and the motives of proselytized (converters) were considered. In regard to the former, obligation and reassurance were stated as the prime motives while friendship and information were stated as the prime methods. The need to find answers to problems, to find the meaning of life, to have friends and a role to play, and to have a faith that is adequate were mentioned as the motives for converting.

The sociodynamics of group influence were not discussed, although it was noted that research suggested little evidence of undue or coercive pressure being exerted by contemporary proselytizers.

10

Proselytizing Processes of the New Religions

JAMES T. RICHARDSON

America is a proselytizing nation and has been since its inception as a country with formalized separation of church and state. No religious tradition has a monopoly in America, and none is formally sanctioned by the state. This forces religious groups that desire permanence to compete in an open religious market.[1] This competition for members, resources, and legitimacy has resulted in many religious traditions being somewhat evangelical. They have had to proselytize or die (or at least not grow very much or very rapidly). Even religions from the Hindu tradition have become more oriented toward proselytization within the context of American society.[2]

This structural fact of free-market competition among religions within the American context does not, of course, explain why certain religions grow more rapidly than others or why certain religious ideas and practices seem to "catch on" in certain time periods and locations. Also, the simple fact of competition does not itself explain why some people respond to proselytizing appeals while others ignore them. Much more psychological, sociological, and historical information is needed before one can even begin to understand the varying effectiveness of various religious groups' proselytization processes in America.

America has a history of amazing vitality, even volatility, when it comes to religious movements. As Smelser has noted, American society is accustomed to interpreting its problems and their solutions in religious terms.[3] Such actions occur, he says, at the level of norm-oriented movements rather than value-oriented ones. This basically means that we spend much energy on the issue of what specific religious beliefs or practices are best but seldom focus on the fundamental values upon which American society is built. Smelser's work suggests that religious norm-oriented movements serve, therefore, something of an "escape-valve" function for our society.

America's religious orientation is probably directly related to the fact that there is no state religion. Ironically, this lack of a state-sanctioned religious monopoly has apparently led to more of a propensity to see the world through religious-colored glasses than would have been the case had some group obtained a religious monopoly.

The tendency toward proselytizing has led to American culture's being infused with religious ideas. The marketing and promotion that has taken place (and still does) has the effect of doing what all advertising is supposed to do—it develops a demand for products that probably would not have existed (at least at the same levels) had there not been the advertising and public-relations efforts. All the activities designed to promote specific brands of religion have, in concert, caused us to think more about religion and to incorporate religion more into discussions of problems and solutions. When social turmoil develops, many in America are prone, almost expected, to view its solution religiously.[4]

Thus, America has always had its share of "new religions." Some die out while others develop a "market niche" for themselves. Some of yesterday's new religions are today's accepted denominations, while others arise to take the place of those that have failed. The religious fervor of American society continues, even in (or perhaps because of) this most secular of times. The question to be addressed here is why certain groups are able to last and become a part of the religious landscape in America.

New religions' proselytizing processes have been examined in considerable depth in what is called the "conversion literature";[5] however, that literature, immense though it is, has a different focus from this effort. It typically examines the individual convert, often with a decidedly psychological bent. We will attend mainly to the *structural arrangements* set up by groups and organizations to recruit new members and to resocialize them to new norms and values. Some of this material can be gleaned from a close examination of the conversion literature, because often some discussion of the organizational efforts to recruit is included in such research reports. Also, some limited subset of the literature on new religions contains rather thorough discussions of the recruitment/resocialization mechanisms developed by the groups.

We will discuss several such efforts taken from the literature. Before this is done, however, one point needs to be made. There is little evidence that these groups have some mysterious or magical techniques to attract and hold new members. There are no "Manchurian Candidate" types of processes being used. What takes place is remarkably normal and ordinary.[6] The greatest evidence for this statement is these groups' extremely high attrition rates.[7] They are usually experimenting to develop techniques that work, and more often than not have difficulty recruiting and retaining participants. With that caveat, we will now examine several ways in which new religions have tried to recruit and resocialize their members.

The Moonies

The Unification Church, better known as the "Moonies," is perhaps the best known of any of the newer religions. This is in part the result of deliberate tactics on their part to use the media to communicate their message to as many as possible. They have also achieved notoriety through some of their activities, such as group marriage ceremonies involving hundreds of young Moonies, and through the Rev. Moon's much-discussed trial on tax-evasion charges. A major share of the notoriety, however, derives directly from the allegations of brainwashing that have been made against the Moonies by ex-members and other detractors.

The term "brainwashing" is, of course, not a scientific term with a readily understandable meaning in the scientific community. The term is used in popular parlance, however, and often therapists and other professionals use it to refer to techniques used by groups such as the Moonies to recruit new members.[8] As we will see, however, the Moonies' techniques may be intense in some instances, but they are neither new nor especially potent.

The recruitment methods have been well described.[9] Lofland, in fact, offered a systematic discussion of proselytizing methods, using the early efforts of the Moonies as examples for this theorizing. At the same time, he presented a great deal of specific information about the Moonies' proselytizing methods and some important theorizing about proselytizing.

His analysis begins with a contrast between *embodied* and *disembodied* access, and *covert* and *overt* methods.[10] Embodied access refers to face-to-face methods, whereas disembodied access does not (e.g., use of media, printed brochures, newspaper ads, handbills, posters). Overt and covert carry these terms' usual meaning. Lofland also distinguished between proselytizing in secular as opposed to religious locations, focusing on different target populations (leaders vs. ordinary people, young vs. old, etc.). Thus he offered an analytical structure for describing the proselytizing done by the Moonies and other groups.

Lofland's book on the Unification Church (he called them the "Divine Precepts") described the haphazard way in which various methods of recruitment were tried, usually with little success. The Moonies initially shifted back and forth between overt and covert methods and used both embodied and disembodied access to attract converts. We are told about paltry efforts to get people to listen to Moon's message and of gatherings where the main center of attraction was a tape recorder playing tapes of the Rev. Moon describing his views in broken English. These efforts were directed at anyone who would listen, and those attracted by these unsystematic attempts were usually people on the fringes of society—social misfits of sorts.

In the later edition of his book Lofland included a lengthy epilogue, updating developments in the Moonie organization. He claimed that the Moonies had become more duplicitous, and he reported the development of much more systematic proselytizing tactics, with a focus on the affective or emotional level. He also described large media events planned during the early 1970s and other ways in which the Moonies sought attention.[11] We will use his analysis of the social-psychological processes of conversion/recruitment to illustrate the development of perhaps the most sophisticated set of recruitment procedures of any newer religion.[12]

Lofland states that the Moonies' recruitment methods changed dramatically around 1972, becoming much less haphazard and more focused on the emotional.[13] He presented five "quasi-temporal phases" to this process: picking-up, hooking, encapsulating, loving, and committing.

Picking-up refers to the way in which casual, face-to-face contact between Moonie recruiters and members of the public was used to interest potential recruits. Moonies systematically approached young men and women in areas frequented by such people. They would sometimes do this covertly, using a "front organization" and general talk about changing society or improving the world. Out of this initial contact would come an invitation to a lecture or a dinner to meet and discuss important issues with people similar to the recruit. Note the emphasis on public, secular places of recruitment, its somewhat covert flavor, and the focus on a target population of rather well-to-do, educated, and alienated youth.

Hooking took place after the initial successful contact with a potential recruit. It involved promotional techniques such as lectures or dinners with Moonies and other recruits, with a heavy emphasis on the emotional level. Recruits were assigned a "buddy," who was always with them. The buddy and other Moonies would attempt to find out what the recruit was interested in as a way of showing interest and of "hooking" them into conversions. This technique was something like a "rush" at a college sorority. At the dinners or other meetings there was usually a lecture or talk presenting some of the general principles of Unification theology, often in such an obscure fashion as to make it difficult to know the group was the Moonies. Although there was some effort to appeal to the potential recruit's cognitive or intellectual side, the emphasis in the recruitment process was on the emotional level. People visiting the dinner or lecture would be made to feel that everyone there cared for them and that the entire atmosphere of the group was one of love and caring. Most people rejected this appeal, but it worked with some to the extent that they were willing to move on to the next stage—*encapsulating.*

During lectures and dinners with potential recruits, an invitation was usually offered to participate in a weekend workshop at one of the organization's rural facilities. The most well-known (notorious?) of the Unification rural retreats was Camp K, operated in a beautiful northern California setting with redwoods and other natural beauty.

Eileen Barker visited Camp K and offers a good description of procedures used there.[14] At these weekend retreats, recruits were encapsulated totally in the Moonie recruitment experience. This allowed the promotion of affective ties as well as the continued presentation of Unification theology. Some have claimed that even during these weekend experiences they were not told that the group was the Moonies, but most apparently knew and participated anyway.

Lofland notes that the encapsulation process involves a total absorption of attention, with every waking hour programmed with group activities, thus offering a completely collective focus. There is an exclusive input to recruits. Television and radio are discouraged, and all the members (who make up about half those present) are continually talking about the topics the Moonies desire to discuss. Fatigue plays a role, according to Lofland, because of the intensity of the experience. All this enhances the likelihood of gaining acceptance for the theological principles.

The encapsulating process was carried to an extreme by a further sifting process; those handling the weekend experience well were often invited to participate in longer sessions of from one to three weeks at the rural retreat centers. A small proportion of those initially contacted agreed to go into this last phase. For those who went, there was an increasing dose of Moonie theology. The focus of efforts was to develop the affective ties and furnish more exposure to Moonie ideas.

Lofland included as a separate analytical element the idea of *loving*. The entire situation at the retreat was designed to make the person feel loved. The phrase "love-bombing" has been used by the Moonies and gained usage in scholarly literature as well. Recruits were welcomed into what was a loving commune, and they were encouraged to stay and participate in the group on a permanent basis.

Commitment was developed by getting recruits to participate in Moonie activities, such as street-witnessing (picking-up), selling flowers, or other money-raising activities. They were encouraged to practice their new-found beliefs, and they were discouraged from maintaining ties with outsiders. The process was gradual, and throughout it encapsulation of the recruit was maintained.

The process described by Lofland seems thorough, as if the Moonies were sparing no effort to gain new recruits. The organization was dependent on new recruits to do a number of important group functions (such as fundraising and recruitment), and thus they had to have a relatively large number of people flowing through the organization, if only to maintain these key activities.

There is little doubt that the elaborate process described could be effective. The reader should not be misled into thinking, however, that it worked with everyone who went through it. This was far from the case. Galanter notes that less than 10 percent of those participating in a several-week-long retreat actually stayed in the organization when the retreat was over.[15] Barker makes similar claims and adds that of those who did stay, over half were no longer members two years later.[16] Thus it appears that, like other religions, the Moonies' recruitment efforts were relatively ineffectual. The overall size of the Unification Church in America evidences this as well, with scholars such as Lofland and Bromley and Shupe estimating that there are only a few thousand full-time members in the country.

Hare Krishna

Rochford's book on the Hare Krishna contains a thorough treatment of the evolution of their recruitment practices.[17] His careful work reveals that during the time of the Krishnas' most rapid growth in America about half of the recruits were obtained by initial contact in public places; the rest were obtained by friendship ties with devotees or others. Rochford also points out some interesting differences by sex, with females more prone to have joined through personal ties and males more prone to have been approached at a public location. It is important to note that a sizeable proportion of new members were obtained through interpersonal networks, which is, of course, the "normal" way that traditional religious organizations gain most new members. Some important differences were found in the way in which recruitment was carried on at the various Krishna locations. This Rochford sees as an important indication that, even in such a strongly ideological movement as the Krishna, local conditions could dictate that recruitment would take place in different ways.

Because of its importance to the movement, the public-recruitment practices of the Krishna will be examined in more detail.[18] Recruitment of new members was originally a major aim of the second Krishna practice of *sankirtana* (devotional singing). This involved going into public places dressed in very obvious saffron robes and with shaved heads to chant, distribute literature, recruit new members, and solicit funds for the organization's support. Groups of devotees would go out to streetcorners and shopping centers, where some would chant and march around while others "worked the crowd" by asking for donations, handing out literature, and talking to people about participating. This very public practice tended to focus on target populations of young people in certain parts of the country. Rochford points out that originally the target group in New York was composed of older, more ordinary citizens; however, it was quickly discovered that they were uninterested, and the target group shifted.

During the Krishnas' salad days of the early 1970s, most recruits were gained through this public kind of effort. People would be approached directly through *sankirtana,* or they would take the literature and read it, which quickened the interest of some, especially if they were what is called in the literature on conversion "seekers." Anyone expressing interest in participating was immediately drawn into temple activities that included a heavy regime of meditation, chanting, change of diet to vegetarianism, acceptance of celibacy, and avoidance of stimulants. A great deal of self-selection took place, of course, as some found that the requirements of membership were too rigorous, while others responded favorably.[19] For the really dedicated, communal living in a temple center was possible, and this was the major thrust of recruitment. Full-time committed members were sought, and for a time relatively large numbers were obtained.

The halcyon days did not last, however, as Rochford amply describes. Pressure developed to take advantage of the fact that *sankirtana* was able to collect considerable money, and there was a discernible shift away from using the sacred practice to recruit and spread literature toward a focus on fundraising. This shift is quite similar to that noted with another well-known group, the Children of God, whose "litnessing" was first a recruitment device, but quickly evolved into a fundraising method.[20] The place of *sankirtana* activity shifted for the Krishna from streetcorners, where there were many people, to airports and other places where the general public gathered. This led to several major changes in the Hare Krishna. The number of recruits dropped off and has been declining since, and a very negative public reaction developed against the Krishna because of the way they engaged in public solicitation. The methods themselves became more duplicitous and covert, with many charges of various kinds of petty fraud, such as short-changing people who had agreed to pay for a book. Also, Krishna members began concealing their true identity by wearing ordinary clothing and wigs, or even Santa Claus suits. Thus, the practice of *sankirtana* was dramatically changed.

Since public street recruitment is not now being practiced as frequently, where do the Krishna get new members? The first response is that they are not gaining as many new members and their overall membership is declining. There are a number of reasons for this decline that are not germane here but are detailed by Rochford. He notes, however, that out of necessity the Krishna, like many other newer religions, are accepting more part-time, less-committed members.[21] They are developing into something of a denomination with a congregational lifestyle, which means that ordinary people in the neighborhood may participate on a part-time basis, as do most churchgoers in America. Also, and very importantly, the Hare Krishna organization is attracting new participants out of the Indian communities in areas where there are Krishna temples. Some Indians have attained leadership positions in Hare Krishna temples, and Hare Krishna temples have become centers of Indian community life in some areas. Thus we see a remarkable change taking place in this organization's recruiting, with a marked decline in the public recruiting of the relatively well-to-do white youth that had characterized Krishna recruitment earlier and which targeted the Krishna for so much animus from the public.

A Jesus Movement Organization

Several detailed analyses of one of the major Jesus Movement organizations that were so much in the news in the 1970s focused on the elaborate recruitment and resocialization processes developed by Christ Communal Organization (a pseudonym).[22] Like many other new religions developing out of the turmoil of the late 1960s and early 1970s, this group gained its members from street-witnessing, which is a public form of proselytizing among the disaffected youth so available in our society at that time. Members of their first communes went out into areas where large numbers of young people collected and openly sought to convince the youth that they should try their beliefs and lifestyles. Thus their recruitment was both overt and embodied, to use Lofland's terms. New communes were deliberately established close to major areas of congregating youth or to highways where there were many hitch-hikers. Sometimes members even moved into drug-oriented communes in an effort to convince users to give up drugs and "try Jesus."

The group offered friendship, a place to sleep, food, and other necessities to hundreds of young people. Many accepted the offer and moved into a commune, whereby they were agreeing to adopt the other members' ascetic and spartan lifestyle. This meant no drugs, no alcohol, no sex outside of marriage, and much hard work. The latter was especially the case, because the Christ Communal Organization chose not to solicit money on the street and not to beg for sustenance, but instead worked for funds at all kinds of tasks. The full history of this work-oriented development has been recounted elsewhere,[23] but for our purposes here, suffice it to say that the work regime taught useful skills, kept the converts very busy, earned money for the organization, and served as a kind of "work therapy" for those with personal difficulties. It was important to the resocialization process for the members, most of whom had used drugs regularly and were engaged in other sorts of deviant lifestyles.

As the group matured, other organizational arrangements were made to develop new members' commitment. A nation-wide headquarters was established which had as its major function the further training of new converts so that they could, in turn, go out and win more converts. Called "The Land," this headquarters was in a beautiful rural setting several miles outside of Eugene, Oregon. Although the group bought The Land without any facilities, within a few years they had built a number of buildings, including classrooms, dormitories, and various enterprises where the young people were taught useful skills such as animal husbandry, auto mechanics, and other needed tasks. Two separate schools were established that operated for several years. One was called Lamb's School, for newer members, and the other was called Team's School, for more long-term members who were preparing to go out as evangelism teams.

Lamb's School usually lasted for three months, with daily teaching of

Bible and related courses, and half of the day was devoted to teaching useful skills needed in the organization. After graduating from Lamb's School, members usually worked somewhere in the organization, which at that time was nation-wide with communities in about thirty states. Many of the members were placed on future evangelism teams and brought back to The Land within a year for further training. After three months of additional training, which focused on evangelism methods and a deeper understanding of group theology, the teams would be sent out to start the process anew—bringing in new members (see figure 1).

The organization was also developing many other methods of recruitment and changed rapidly, becoming much more differentiated. Figure 2 shows some of the ways in which the evangelism methods developed and demonstrates the elaborate and sophisticated nature of Christ Communal Organization's efforts to win others to its point of view. As with other newer religions, even more changes were to occur, particularly after the demise of such a large target population of itinerant youth and the establishment of so many family units, as members married and started families within this group. Toward the end of its illustrious history as a separate organization, Christ Communal Organization became much more congregationally oriented, resembling a regular denomination in many ways.

Conclusion

We have used three major new religious groups that developed in the 1960s and 1970s to show some typical ways in which newer religions have tried to gain converts. Virtually all new religions, even those of Eastern origins, were proselytizing organizations. They were forced to proselytize or die an early death. These three are representative of some of the larger, more sophisticated groups. Many other groups were much more haphazard in their recruitment efforts and were usually less effective in gaining members.

It is easy to discern a typical, nonmysterious pattern for the groups described. Each group initially spent considerable time and resources with public forms of street-witnessing through which most of their members were gained. As they became established, more recruitment was done through friendship and kinship networks. Mainly because of the social and demographic changes that resulted in fewer street people being available, the groups diversified their recruitment methods, or they began to see a drop-off in membership numbers because of such groups' high turnover. As families developed within the organizations, a "domestication effect" was felt, leading to a tendency toward congregational (as opposed to communal) lifestyle and more recruitment among friendship networks. Thus the groups that manage to survive become more "normal" as time passes.

<u>FIGURE 1</u>

Flow of a New Member through the "Schools" for Resocialization, with Approximate Time Spent in Each

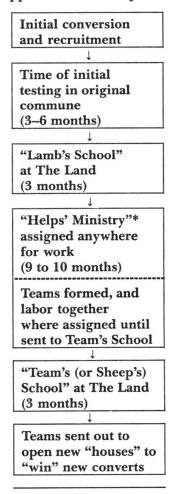

*"Helps' ministry," phased out in 1976, and Lamb's School and Team's School juxtaposed in time and renamed "Bible Survey" and "Bible Analysis," respectively. Also, those in Bible Analysis will not automatically be sent out as a missionary, as was the case with Team's School graduates.

FIGURE 2

Evolution* and Differentiation of Evangelism and Resocialization Methods

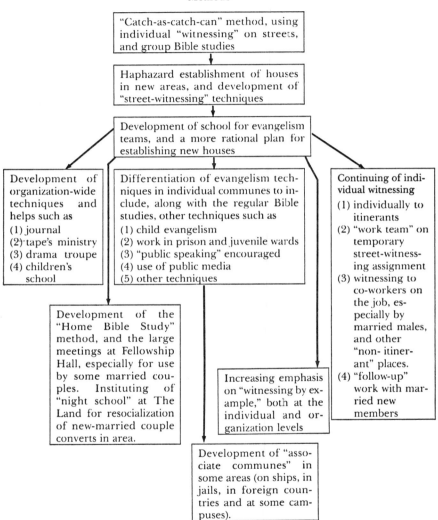

---

*The establishment of an exact pattern of evolution of evangelism methods is impossible, and unnecessary for our purposes. This figure should be treated as more a presentation of the differentiation itself, rather than a statement about exactly when the differentiation occurred, although some chronology is represented in movement from top to bottom of the figure.

Conclusion:
Proselytism in a Pluralistic World

MARTIN E. MARTY

"Why doesn't everybody leave everybody else the hell alone?" The late Jimmy Durante probably voiced that question as a signal of impatience, perhaps after having been approached too often by proselytizers for too many causes. What was for him a *cri de coeur* is for the authors in this book a matter of substantive inquiry. Why do people approach others in a spirit of proselytization? What in their faith and world view impels them to interfere with the lives of others? What keeps them from leaving "everybody else the hell alone?"

When people proselytize, they represent not just an impulse or an emotion but a world. Through their agency, one world advances and encroaches upon another. An embodiment of one world invites or urges others to become part of it, to see things in a new way, to be uprooted from old communities and contexts and to find new ones. The time and space that one invades usually represent a delicate and hard-won spiritual location, so the act of proselytization is aggressive. The risks are high. The subject, as the reader will have had good reason to agree, merits scholarly investigation. At the end of this pioneering inquiry, it is worthwhile assessing what has occurred, what has not been a part of the probe, and what individuals and groups might do to carry on the work.

What has become clear is that there is no neutral place to stand for observing both aggressive and passive worlds and world views in our culture. This is most obvious if we take apart some of the assumptions of the world represented on these pages, a world we usually code as "academic." The academic world in the present context seems "polite," to borrow a major theme. It is not always so. Try challenging its own sacred times and places and themes: tenure, academic freedom, the turf of a threatened department. Politeness disappears. It just happens that the academy in the modern pluralistic world does not find itself hospitable to overt religious aggression. That choice about themes and occasions for hospitality illustrates that the academy also represents a world of values, intentions, and projects. This means that a kind of ideology about conversion attaches itself to the apparently neutral, nonproselytizing academy.

One can see that there is a world by reviewing terms that keep appearing on these pages. A sectarian from some remote church would have to learn the liturgical rules and canonical terms used here: what we call proselytizing they might call "winning the world for Christ," "reaching out in love," "evangelizing," "witnessing," or "sharing." What these authors call "exclusivity" is to many of them simply patent truth. Debates over "particular" and "universal" certainly come up, but not in the present way. "Triumphalism," "avoidance," and "pluralism" itself are terms of the academic sanctuary, not of the ecclesial proselytizer.

The test for all this comes if we picture who is not on these pages. We can point to a few. First, the overt, frank proselytizer. If a "Jew for Jesus" crashed onto this scene, she would really be crashing. What is necessarily missing, then, is what anthropologists like to call "agent's description." The scholars here can reproduce such description, but the authors generally do not embody or exemplify it. Agents would call much of the scholarly work "reductionism," if by some other name. They do not want their efforts to convert seen as "nothing but" some sociopsychological expression.

Second, none of these authors is a willing coconspirator with a proselytizer; that is, we have no satisfied proselytes in this company. It may be that hidden in the *vitae* of one or more is an autobiographical reference to a conversion, and probably all have it in their grand-parenthood somewhere on a family tree. But in these chapters no one says, "I found it!" or, "He reached me, and let me tell you about it!" No one here, therefore, in the present constellation gives an agent's description of the sort a satisfied customer, not a broker or appraiser, would give.

No one is impolite. There might be aggressive contention for ideas, but there is nothing here of what Gabriel Marcel described as serving a "God of prey whose goal is to annex and enslave."[1] There is little intellectually machoismic enjoyment of others' proselytizing energies: "By God, at least they really believe something while we academics are, at best, half-believers." The interest is, throughout, academic in Spinoza's sense. The authors appear not to laugh or to cry—but to understand. Yet laughing and crying are also appropriate means for approaching the subject of proselytization.

An observer who comes with distance would notice some relative homogeneities in the inquiry group. They generally represent an ethos shaped by Judaism and Christianity, as may be appropriate when the sponsor is a Center for Judaic Studies at a university founded by Christians in a culture shaped by the Bible, not the Qur'an or some other holy book. Negatively, this means an absence of non-Western voices, of Shi'ites or African indigenous churches or Buddhism. That colors the inquiry. And all authors are heirs of the Western Enlightenment, who accept the terms of life not just in tribes but in the republic of faiths and world views.

Such an aegis further colors the question. One participant asked about the occasion: did we all feel that proselytization was a social menace? In Durante's terms, are we reacting because, in fact, everyone is refusing to let everyone else alone? I think of Yale Professor Paul Holmer, who toured Lutheran churches. There he heard preachers decrying efforts to earn salvation, merit heaven, try to win God's favor. He looked at smug and somnolent congregations and asked, "Who's trying?" Do we misfire by concentrating on overproselytization if most of us are untouched?

Recalling the cultural moment is helpful. American Jews *do* feel the presence and pressure of Christian proselytizers who intrude on their communities. There are not many Jews left in the world, so aggression against them is threatening, and even Distant Early Warning Systems demand response. Some of the "New Religions" invaded campus and home and family and, at least fifteen years ago, were a menacing presence to families that did not welcome disruption. Assertive fundamentalism uses airwaves for organizing, combining proselytizing with belligerent political organizing, against many conventional norms of life in a pluralist republic. It seems a good moment to do some appraising, since the phenomenon is sufficiently present to warrant examination but not so encroaching that it disrupts clear thinking.

It is in an academic spirit that one seeks to contribute by making some polite efforts, if not to say a good word for proselytizing, at least to try to understand why many say good words. A beginning response could be: What if no one ever did proselytize? What if everyone had always let everyone alone? Who'd be where? We all became situated in our traditions and historic communities because someone somewhere tried to convert others. The lucky ones met the proselytizer; the unlucky majorities acquiesced to the sword. The king, be he Clovis or Olaf or anyone else, would convert, and the ruled had to comply. The converter who appealed to volition was, on that scale, benign and mild, not menacing and growling.

Second, proselytizing, for all its impoliteness and perhaps because of it, represents an intercultural jostling that contributes to historical dynamics. It would be a more comfortable but probably soon comatose world if everyone left everyone else alone all the time. Georg Simmel wrote perceptively about "the sociology of the stranger" and what she or he brings.[2] One could write on the sociology of the proselytizers and find in their challenge great stimulus for communities to define themselves, for new ideas to revitalize stagnant cultures.

One asks, third, is it possible not to be a proselytizer of some sort or on some scale if one has deep convictions? The phenomenologists talk constantly about "intentionality" as being basic to consciousness. Does not intentionality project one into a world of others, inevitably with accompanying at least implicit efforts to commend one's own belief, way of life, and social construct to others? We do this even esthetically. We Chicagoans, for instance, are always pleased when a New Yorker, after acclimatization, "likes it here." We commend to others our choice of brand in the world of commercial products and take some delight (mixed with fear lest things go wrong) when a friend, on our recommendation, drives in an auto of the brand we witnessed to. Such acceptance ratifies our own choice, confirms us in our beliefs, adds dignity to our status as commending individuals of integrity and taste. Having been a pastor who was committed not to "sheep-stealing," I have to recall what must be a universal impulse. I took delight when "he" or "she" chose our church after a religiously "mixed marriage." The bride or groom who switched after our most subtle beckonings was as appreciatively received as a prodigal son returning, a lost sheep found.

If there is something thus to be said for the transactions of proselytization, it is likely that in the *oikoumene* of world religions and our Republic there can be no absolute avoidance of the activity. Numbers of the preceding chapters show that we are dealing instead with a spectrum and that real life is lived along it. At one end is "aggression," marked by intentional and imperial proselytization. At the other end is "avoidance/apathy," marked not by nothing, but by accidental or empathic engagements with others. Finding places and legitimacies along that spectrum is what this book has been about.

The authors of a number of these papers produce evidences or make contentions of what strike me as a remarkable character, and I will point to a few of these as a contribution to the "finding" project mentioned a few lines ago.

It becomes clear that there has been less clarified theological impetus behind proselytizing movements than one might expect. "One might expect" is a very subjective phrase, but it refers to the general notion that proselytizers work out of elaborate networks of meaning, bases rooted in the charter documents of their traditions. Thus, in the West, Christians have acted as if Jesus elaborately impelled them into evangelizing. Yet, as John Gager and others point out, the impulses are few. The "great commission" in the end of Matthew's Gospel is one, but it seems startling against the background of Gospels where Jesus shows little impulse to "go out." He often contributes to secrecy, to distance; he would not himself engage in proselytization and often seemed to keep possible converts at a distance. The Fourth Gospel has no note impelling proselytizing at all. On balance, despite the great-commission passage, the Gospels sound almost antievangelistic beyond one's own tribal circle.

Roman Catholicism gives evidence that it would build on more than this and in the Vatican Council and since has tried to locate the impulse for mission in the Divine Trinity, but this has been a rarely voiced rationale in the past and, as Robert Schreiter has shown, since Vatican II (1962–65) Catholicism has had some confusion of directives and resulting anomie with respect to missionizing. Did Jews, on the other hand, have a clear theological basis for their general withdrawal from proselytizing activity? Do modern mainstream Protestants have a theology for cessation of aggressive converting efforts? All such questions suggest an agenda.

It is remarkable to see how episodic proselytizing has been. As an activity it comes and goes in Judaism (as Robert Seltzer has also shown) and, of course, in Christianity. The Jew turns out not to be consistently non- or antimissionary. Christians for centuries converted chiefly or only with the sword. The Protestant reformers showed little interest in such activities. Suddenly in the 1790s the Euro-American world undertook Protestant efforts, half of which diminished late in the twentieth century—while the evangelistic half of Protestantism redoubled its own efforts. It would be valuable to use proselytizing or nonproselytizing endeavors as measures of other aspects of cultural and religious life in various epochs and locales.

From these papers, as they demonstrate the episodic character of efforts, one can move on to suggest how revisable policies have been and can be. William Hutchison describes efforts like the novel

"Laymen's Inquiry" of 1934 and shows other adjustments in the twentieth century.[3] Robert Schreiter shows dramatic instances in and after the Council. There were references to the ways Eastern religions change character as they move, say, from the remote and inaccessible Himalayas to the jumble of no-one-leaving-anyone-else-alone at Berkeley or Boulder or Boston. Jews turn to proselytization when survival of the community is at stake and the aggressives "move in on" the secular and uncommitted Jew. Protestants experience regular "revitalizations" on this front. Change comes when Protestants and Catholics no longer "target" each other, or when fundamentalists "target" Jews for special mission. All this suggests that the end of the story is not here, and that as a result of power shifts or dialogue, policies can change—for better or for worse, also depending upon one's point of view.

Another notable feature that strikes the reader of these pages and helps provide future agenda is this: Power and proselytization are ambiguously connected. In a recently discovered letter to an American Jew, Thomas Jefferson remarked that as power shifts from community to community, those in power seek more, and those once out of power but now in power also seek more.[4] Thus John Gager has shown how proselytization occurred as an expression of episcopal power in the early church, when agents of the "tall towers of total Christendom" forayed forth. Yet the activity also arises among weak and wan losers who suffer "cognitive dissonance" when prophecy fails. Then they must go out to recapture lost ground and power, or to confirm their faith and ways when these are challenged by a sense of defeat. The East may be nonproselytizing, but when its agents come to the West they enter a new market situation and must adjust. Hutchison has shown how proselytization has been part of the "rise of the West," but it can also belong to the decline of the West. Power corrupts and the absence of power corrupts; power inspires and the absence of power inspires.

A fifth remarkable or remark-worthy feature of these chapters is a rather consistent signal that modernity occasions ambiguity about proselytization. On the one hand, modernization in communities has meant a "diffusion" of what had been consolidated. Judaism had meant a bond between ethnicity and religion; Catholicism was a "thing," demanding a polity and a space in the world. Now people could "choose to be a Jew" or "happen to be a Catholic." With modernity came pluralism, and thus the politeness necessary among jostling groups. All these factors militated against proselytization. Yet, compensatorily and as just hinted, modernity also implies choice and the necessity to choose. Thus the market was opened for more proselytizing than ever.

As we move into various kinds of "post-modern" situations, the outlook for proselytization is strong in the tribal world; for resistance to it is likely to have to be a compensatorily strenuous endeavor lest there be conversionist wars of each against all, with the historically passive and tolerant groups jeopardized.

A sixth probe, one that relates to a puzzlement of several paragraphs ago, would connect proselytization with groups *in statu nascendi*, "on the rise." Those who sense that they are moving into winning situations engage more readily in conversionist efforts than those who are over-adapted to specific environments. One may, in other words, experience "cognitive dissonance" in the face of failed prophecy and compensatorily reinforce dedication to a prophecy still to be fulfilled, a prophecy of which one's group is agent. Belief in the inevitable spread of a righteous cause withers in the face of more aggressive righteous causes. Thomas Jefferson thought that in fifty years from his writing the country would turn toward Unitarianism, but he and Unitarians took few pains to propagate it. Therefore they and the Enlightenment in general were eclipsed by frontier revivalists whose movements were "on the rise" early in the nineteenth century. "On-the-riseness" lived off proselytization and inspired it.

Still another remarkable feature of these chapters are the signs they give that proselytizing styles are multiplex, rich in competing signals. For some, Catholic theologian Karl Rahner's mere terminology for "the anonymous Christian" looked as aggressive as, to historic missionaries, it looked passive. That is, humanists and Jews and Buddhists thought that to apply a particular Christian term, even if the application comes with politeness and good intentions, was an imperial act. In the eyes of some critics, engaging in dialogue—which always means openness to change—is a crypto-proselytizing program.

Pioneer sociologist E. A. Ross thought that America was saved from terrible conflict because instead of having but one cleavage or fissure through it, the society had many cross-fissures, thus protecting it from a single traumatizing possibility.[5] Walter Lippmann described what I call a pluralist personality, someone who with his or her spouse has multiple commitments and exposures: to lodge, church, club, alumni association, party, etc.[6] Again, crisscrossing was an asset. In these contexts one might say that "everybody not leaving anybody else alone" is a form of proselytization that cancels itself out or minimizes potential trauma. If all were passive but one large group that set out to "win America," citizens would be worse off than in the myriad claims and contentions that serve to blunt one another.

One should also note the clues in these chapters that depict side effects of proselytization. The act of setting out to cajole or convince others has much to do with "group-binding." Some church bodies fought over theology of missions before they had a missionary on the scene, while others used mission exposure to sharpen or settle debates on the home front. Christians who set out to win Jews make a theological statement about their identity that shapes them in a certain way, whether or not they ever convert a single Jew. Major pioneering Christian proselytizers spent a whole lifetime among Muslims without converting a single one. Yet their reports back home did much to solidify the Christian group. Portrayals of the to-be-converted heathen or pagan helped the missionizing group define itself, whether or not there were converts. Such group-binding or defining, such stimulation of conflict, may be dangerous and have detrimental effects. Here the point is not to condemn or to endorse but to observe: it is possible to "talk a good line" about proselytizing and have effects, entirely apart from the success of the mission.

This is a book, then, that deals much more easily with pluralism and politeness than with proselytization, even in this concluding chapter where I try to lift out some themes relating to potential positives connected with proselytization. This is not a book that must settle society's problems or promote religious groups and understandings. It is itself an effort in understanding, a kind of pioneering effort in an emergent cultural situation. It helps set an academic agenda; its results or those that issue from consequent studies can then be used in various ways in the society.

What becomes clear to many of us is the need for inquiry into the assumptions of "pluralism" itself. Does it rely on and promote a kind of religion-of-pluralism, a metaphysics of group understanding, an ontology about human nature and truth, one that is itself a kind of proselytizing agent? If so, what are the rules of *its* game? Should it be privileged, is it legally endorsed, does it work to the disadvantage of antipluralist would-be theocratic endeavors?

Is it possible that in this unfolding of human history there will be significant groups who can, without a sense of superiority, still project their truths and values among others, without manipulating them? Is that not what "we pluralists" try to do? Is "politeness" a style that has issued in rites and ceremonies that crowd out equally licit aggressivenesses in a Republic? One ends with more questions than answers, which is how a project like this should conclude.

If I may be permitted a personal word: In a crowded, weapon-filled, terrorist-preoccupied world, the concept of pluralism with politeness may be more urgent, delicate, and threatened than ever before in its two-century-old history in its little corners of the world. So far as I know, nowhere does this polity and its implicit world view prosper in open competition with antitolerant proselytizing groups. The proselytizers get credit for having the conviction and commitment. If pluralism is to survive—and it is modern pluralism that assures freedom for proselytization itself—it is likely to demand conviction and commitment and, with them, more reflective philosophical supports than we have seen since it was invented about two centuries ago.

Why doesn't everybody leave everybody else the hell alone? We have addressed but not completely answered this question about the proselytizers of the world. I think the contributors to this book have, again, at least implicitly, shown that people don't leave everybody alone because they don't have to do so. They prosper within polities that give them license to propagate. They often scorn the propluralists as people lacking all conviction and commitment. Now and then it would be nice if they would send a card of thanks to the heirs and custodians of a tradition that demands reflection and courage, the pluralist tradition that created the climate in which we are free to deal with each other in many ways. If sometimes these ways mean encroaching instead of mere approaching, that is not a high price to pay. Consider the alternatives.

Notes

Introduction

1. Isaiah 10:5 and 45:1; the word used is the Hebrew form of "messiah."

2. Isaiah 2:2.

3. Isaiah 44:6.

4. Rabbi Eliezer is quoted in *Tosefta Sanhedrin* 13:2 and Cyprian of Carthage in his letter to Jubaianus 21 (*PL* 3:1123). Neither statement can be considered normative for its tradition. Judaism has more commonly followed the view of Rabbi Joshua (*T. Sanh.* 13:2), as digested by Maimonides: "The righteous of all nations have a portion in the world to come" (*Mishneh Torah, Hilchot Teshuvah* 3:5), while the Christian formula has been subject to a variety of interpretations (see, for example, M. Eminyan, "Extra Ecclesiam Nulla Salus," *New Catholic Encyclopedia* [New York: McGraw-Hill, 1967] 5: 768).

5. For the link between monotheism and violence, see Paul C. Ciholas, "Monothéisme et violence," *Recherches de Science Religieuse* 69 (1981) 326.

6. Matthew 23:15 and 28:19.

7. Wilfred Cantwell Smith observes that, until recent times, proselytizing activities have rarely succeeded in winning converts away from one "great religion" to another, except for Islam, which did prove attractive to many Christians ("Muslim-Christian Relations: Questions of a Comparative Religionist," presented at the University of Toronto, October 1986; p. 2).

8. Jean-Jacques Rousseau, *The Social Contract* (New York: Penguin Books, 1968) 187.

9. Walter Lippmann, *A Preface to Morals* (New York: Macmillan, 1929) 75.

10. The phrase is from Peter J. Gomes, "Saints and Strangers: The Problem of Pluralism in American Life," presented at the University of Denver, February 1984; p. 18.

11. Christian imperialism is described by Rosemary Ruether, *Faith and Fratricide: The Theological Roots of Anti-Semitism* (New York: Seabury, 1974) 234, 238.

12. See Peter Berger, "Converting the Gentiles," *Commentary* 67 (May 1979) 35, and also note 19 below. For a broader view of Jewish proselytizing, see Frederick E. Greenspahn, "But Jews Are Proselytizing," *Sh'ma* 11:219 (October 16, 1981) 151–52.

13. Wilfred Cantwell Smith lists "five great missionary movements in world history," viz., Buddhism, Christianity, Islam, Marxism, and Western secularism ("Philosophia as One of the Religious Traditions of Humankind: The Greek Legacy in Western Civilisation. Viewed by a Comparativist," in *Differences, valeurs, hiérarchie, textes offerts à Louis Dumont*, ed. Jean-Claude Galey [Paris: Editions de l'Ecole des Hautes Etudes en Sciences Sociales, 1984] 262).

14. Cf. Gustav Mensching, "Folk and Universal Religion," in *Religion, Culture, and Society: A Reader in the Sociology of Religion*, ed. Louis Schneider (New York: John Wiley & Sons, 1964) 254–61.

15. Jean de Brébeuf in *The Jesuit Relations and Allied Documents; Travels and Explorations of the Jesuit Missionaries in New France, 1610–1791*, ed. Reuben Gold Thwaites (Cleveland: Burrows Brothers, 1897; reprinted New York: Pageant Book Co., 1959) 8.119.

16. Such is the implication of the editorial "Jewry and Democracy" in *The Christian Century* 54 (June 9, 1937) 734–35; the quotation is from Emil Brunner, *The Word and the World* (New York: Charles Scribner's Sons, 1931) 108.

17. Updated pamphlet (from the mid-'80s) for Beth Shifra in Brooklyn, New York.

18. J. Pohle, "Toleration," in *The Catholic Encyclopedia* (New York: Robert Appleton, 1912) 14: 766.

19. See Alexander Schindler's 1978 presidential address to the Union of American Hebrew Congregations' Board of Trustees (delivered in Houston on December 2, 1978): "Nor do I suggest that we strive to wean people from religions of their choice and with the boast that ours is the only true and valid faith engage in eager rivalry with all established churches. . . . Millions of Americans are searching for something . . . we Jews possess the water which can slake the thirst, the bread which can sate the Great Hunger" (pp. 6–8).

20. See Sigmund Freud, *Moses and Monotheism* (New York: Vintage Books, 1939) 111 and 175. The magnitude of this obsession can be seen in post-Holocaust church statements about the Jews, such as that made in 1946 by the Council of the Synod of the Hungarian Reformed Church that "After the terrible and unprecedented persecution of the Jews and in view of disturbing signs of a growing antisemitism, the Council feels all the more strongly its great responsibility which our Lord Jesus Christ has laid upon the church to win for Him all peoples and especially the people of Israel" (quoted in John S. Conway, "Protestant Missions to the Jews," *Holocaust and Genocide Studies* 1 [1986] 138).

21. The relative size of the Jewish and Christian communities in America is also a likely factor; however, it cannot account for some Jews' concern over the prospect of Mormon (or, earlier, fundamentalist) missionizing in Israel; see Thomas L. Friedman, "Mormons in Israel Alarm Orthodox," *New York Times*, August 13, 1985, A3.

22. Cf. Josephus, *The Jewish War* 2.8.2, and Pliny, *Natural History* II 5.15.73.

23. Felix A. Levy, "The Uniqueness of Israel," in the *Yearbook* of the Central Conference of American Rabbis 33 (1923) 120–21.

24. See *Uncivil Religion: Interreligious Hostility in America*, ed. Robert N. Bellah and Frederick E. Greenspahn (New York: Crossroad, 1987).

25. Martin E. Marty, "Religious Power in America: A Contemporary Map," *Criterion* 21:1 (Winter 1982) 31.

Chapter 1 / Religions, Worlds, and Order:
The Search for Utopian Unities

1. See Mircea Eliade, *The Myth of the Eternal Return* (Princeton, NJ: Princeton University Press, 1971) especially chapter one. Paul Wheatley, *The Pivot of the Four Quarters: A Preliminary Enquiry into the Origins and Character of the Ancient Chinese City* (Chicago: Aldine Publishing Co., 1970), and Joseph Rykwert, *The Idea of a Town: The Anthropology of Urban Form in Rome, Italy, and the Ancient World* (Princeton, NJ: Princeton University Press, 1976).

2. Lionel Rothkrug, *Religious Practises and Collective Perceptions: Hidden Homologies in the Renaissance and Reformation* (Historical Reflections 7; Waterloo, Ontario: Historical Reflections Press, 1980); one of his essays dealing with the same issue is "Popular Religion and Holy Shrines" in *Religion and the People, 1000–1700: Studies in the History of Popular Religious Beliefs and Practices*, ed. James Obelkevich (Chapel Hill: University of North Carolina Press, 1979) 20–86. Rothkrug's analysis is very clear in the Roman form of Christianity; however, his extension of this into the Lutheran Reformation is new.

3. Benjamin Nelson, *The Idea of Usury: Tribal Brotherhood to Universal Otherhood*, 2nd ed. enlarged (Chicago: University of Chicago Press, 1969).

4. Cf. Norbert Elias, *The Civilizing Process: The History of Manners* (New York: Urizen Books, 1978).

5. John Murray Cuddihy, *The Ordeal of Civility: Freud, Marx, Lévi-Strauss, and the Jewish Struggle with Modernity* (New York: Basic Books, 1974).

6. Catherine Albanese, "On Reconsidering Protestant, Catholic, and Jew: Thoughts on American Religion and American Dreams," delivered at Drew University (1982); cf. Will Herberg, *Protestant, Catholic, Jew* (Garden City, NY: Doubleday, 1955).

7. See Charles H. Long, *Significations, Signs, Symbols and Languages in the Interpretation of Religion* (Philadelphia: Fortress Press, 1986).

Chapter 2 / Modernity and Pluralism

1. Peter Berger, Brigitte Berger, and Hansfried Keller, *The Homeless Mind: Modernization and Consciousness* (New York: Random House, 1973).

2. Talcott Parsons, "Some Considerations on the Theory of Social Change," *Rural Sociology* 26 (September 1961) 219–39, and *Societies: Evolutionary and Comparative Perspectives* (Englewood Cliffs, NJ: Prentice-Hall, 1966) 20–24.

3. Jürgen Habermas, *Reason and the Rationalization of Society* (vol. 1 of *The Theory of Communicative Action*), trans. with an introduction by Thomas McCarthy (Boston: Beacon, 1985), and Niklas Luhmann, *The Differentiation of Society*, ed. and trans. with an introduction by Stephen Holmes and Charles Larmore (New York: Columbia University Press, 1982).

4. Richard J. Bernstein, "Introduction," in *Habermas and Modernity*, ed. Richard J. Bernstein (Cambridge, MA: MIT Press, 1985) 24.

5. Harry Braverman, *Labor and Monopoly Capitalism: The Degradation of Work in the Twentieth Century* (New York: Monthly Review Press, 1974) 77–80.

6. N. Luhmann, *The Differentiation of Society*, 236.

7. Emile Durkheim, *The Division of Labor in Society*, trans. by W. D. Halls and introduction by Lewis Coser (New York: Free Press, 1984).

8. E. Durkheim, *The Division of Labor in Society*.

9. N. Luhmann, *The Differentiation of Society*.

10. John Murray Cuddihy, *The Ordeal of Civility: Freud, Marx, Lévi-Strauss, and the Jewish Struggle with Modernity* (New York: Basic Books, 1974) 12.

11. Michael Novak, *The American Vision: Essays on the Future of Democratic Capitalism* (Washington, D.C.: American Enterprise Institute, 1978) 20–22.

12. Reginald W. Bibby and Merlin B. Brinkerhoff, "The Circulation of the Saints: A Study of People Who Join Conservative Churches," *Journal for the Scientific Study of Religion* 12 (September 1973) 273–83.

13. T. Parsons, "Polarization of the World and International Order," *Sociological Theory and Modern Society* (New York: Free Press, 1967) 482.

14. J. M. Cuddihy, *The Ordeal of Civility*, 9.

15. P. Berger et al., *The Homeless Mind*, and J. Habermas, *Reason and Rationalization*.

16. T. Parsons, *Societies: Evolutionary and Comparative*, 22.

17. Robert N. Bellah, Richard Madsen, William M. Sullivan, Ann Swidler, and Steven M. Tipton, *Habits of the Heart: Individualism and Commitment in American Life* (Berkeley: University of California Press, 1985).

18. J. M. Cuddihy, *The Ordeal of Civility*, 10.

19. T. Parsons, "Some Sociological Aspects of the Fascist Movements," in *Essays in Sociological Theory* rev. ed. (Glencoe, IL: Free Press, 1954) 124–41; see also Frank J. Lechner, "Modernity and Its Discontent" in *Neofunctionalism*, ed. Jeffrey C. Alexander (Beverly Hills, CA: Sage, 1988) 157–76.

20. James Davison Hunter, "Religion and Political Civility: The Coming Generation of American Evangelicals," *Journal for the Scientific Study of Religion* 23 (December 1984) 364–80.

21. N. Luhmann, *The Differentiation of Society*, xvii–xxxii.

22. T. Parsons, "Polarization of the World and International Order," 484.

23. R. N. Bellah, *The Broken Covenant: American Civil Religion in Time of Trial* (New York: Seabury, 1975).

24. "Neoconservative Culture Criticism in the United States and West Germany: An Intellectual Movement in Two Political Cultures," in R. J. Bernstein, ed., *Habermas and Modernity*, 78–94.

Chapter 3 / The Place of Other Religions in Ancient Jewish Thought, with Particular Reference to Early Rabbinic Judaism

1. This matter hardly requires documentation, but *loci classici* include the two Decalogues (Exod. 20:3 and Deut. 5:7), Deuteronomy 7:25–26 and 13:7–17, and Isaiah 44:6–20. The story of Elijah at Mt. Carmel (1 Kings 18) suggests

this intense hostility was very old. All scriptural citations in these notes follow the Masoretic text and the divisions of the Hebrew Bible.

2. The best-known cases of foreigners renouncing the worship of their native gods include the Syrian Naaman (2 Kings 5:15), the Moabitess Ruth (Ruth 1:16), and Rahab, the two spies' hostess in Jericho (Josh. 2:11). It should be noted that Ruth, unlike Naaman, has undergone a change in national allegiance, not what we might call a religious conversion, and that Rahab recognizes the sovereign power of the God of Israel but is not led by this recognition to abjure her own ancestral cults.

3. See Deuteronomy 4:19 and 19:25, also Jeremiah 10:16.

4. Certain particular pagan deities are of course named from time to time (e.g., Bel in Isa. 46:1), but these are treated as localized examples of an essentially unvarying phenomenon. The widespread prophetic denunciation of "the Baals" reflects a similar view. Saul Lieberman says rabbinic polemics resembled the Bible in that they were directed against idolatry in general, while Hellenistic Jewish polemics aimed more specifically at Greek and Egyptian targets (*Hellenism in Jewish Palestine* [New York: Jewish Theological Seminary of America, 1962] 118), but texts like the Wisdom of Solomon (quoted on p. 29) do not support this distinction.

5. See the large number of passages cited by H. A. Wolfson, *Philo* (Cambridge, MA: Harvard University Press, 1947) 1:22–23.

6. *B. Shabbat* 116a.

7. See, for example, the citations from Theophrastus, Hecataeus, and Megasthenes in Menahem Stern, *Greek and Latin Authors on Jews and Judaism* (Jerusalem: Israel Academy of Arts and Sciences, 1976 et seqq.) 1:10, 28, and 46 respectively. Examples could be multiplied, but these are of particular interest because they are the earliest known, and thus suggest the initial Greek reaction to the distinctive features of the Jews' religion.

8. There is no monographic study of Aristobulus, whom Hengel calls "the first known Jewish philosopher of religion" (*Judaism and Hellenism* [Philadelphia: Fortress, 1974] 1:163–69).

9. See Hengel, *Judaism and Hellenism*, 1:90–92, 165, and 2:61, note 259.

10. Psalm 9:18.

11. *M. Sanhedrin* 10:1.

12. Such discussion was never elaborate; see *b. Sanhedrin* 105a and Maimonides, *Code*, Laws of Repentance 3:5. Whereas the earlier source in the Tosefta speaks of a "righteous" gentile (*ṣaddiq*), Maimonides speaks of a "pious" gentile (*ḥasid*). It is difficult to know how much to make of this change.

13. See the general discussion in S. W. Baron, *A Social and Religious History of the Jews* 2d ed. (Philadelphia; Jewish Publication Society, 1952 et seqq.) 1:171–79; Bernard J. Bamberger, *Proselytism in the Talmudic Period* repr. (New York: KTAV, 1968) 16–24. This topic is also treated in this volume by Robert Seltzer, 41–63.

14. See G. F. Moore, *Judaism in the First Centuries of the Christian Era* (Cambridge, MA: Harvard University Press, 1927) 1:324, but compare pp. 228–29.

15. At *Sifre Deuteronomy* 354 it is claimed that gentiles are so impressed when they encounter Jewish unity and Jewish piety that they convert "at once."

16. Much Greek religious thought had arrived by now at an essentially monotheist conception of deity; see the summary comments of W. W. Tarn, *Hellenistic Civilisation* (Cleveland and New York: Meridian Books, 1952) 339, 348, 360. The philosophical tendency toward monotheism, and the philosophical critique of anthropomorphic idolatry, both congenial to Judaism, can be traced back to Xenophanes, long before the first contacts between Greeks and Jews; see Hengel, *Judaism and Hellenism*, 1:261–67, and Wolfson, *Philo*, 1:19.

17. *Code*, Laws of Idolatry, beginning.

18. See, for example, Josephus, *C. Ap.* 2.236–49; Philo, *Immut.* 59, *de Spec. Leg.* 1.28, *de Decal.* 156. All this goes back to Plato, *Republic* 2, 378D.

19. See Josephus, *C. Ap.* 2.282–86; Philo, *de Vit. Mos.* 2.18-21.

20. See, for example, the *Manual of Discipline* (1QS) 2:4–18.

21. It should be observed (following Baron, *A Social and Religious History of the Jews,* 1:197–98) that most ancient Jewish literature had a Jewish audience; Josephus and in some measure Philo are the important exceptions here. See Wolfson, *Philo,* 1:26.

22. The long eschatological *aggadah* at *b. Avodah Zarah* 2b–3a is revealing in this respect. It begins by considering which nations have oppressed Israel and which have come to her aid, and goes on to imply that no gentile nations would have the patience and discipline to live according to the Torah. Both these themes, however, reflect national conflict and rivalry more than rejection of gentile religious traditions; in fact, the latter theme gets in the way of the call for conversion that is the implied subtext of all religious condemnation of gentiles. It is noteworthy as well that the only emperor of Rome who is frequently reviled in rabbinic texts is Hadrian, also the only emperor who ever carried out a sustained persecution of Judaism.

23. Both Philo and Josephus cite a traditional exegesis of Exodus 22:27 ("You shall not revile *elohim*") as referring to the gods of the gentiles: "You shall not mock the religions of other peoples"; see Josephus, *C. Ap.* 2.237, *Ant.* 4.207, Philo, *de Vit. Mos.* 2.205, *de Spec. Leq.* 1.53. The explanation given is that nothing called a "god" should be reviled. Rabbinic literature seems unaware of this exegesis (in fact *b. Megillah* 25b suggests that obscene language is permitted only for the purpose of mocking idols), and presents the idea that "a Jew should be a Jew; a gentile should be a gentile" (*j. Shevi'it* 4:2 35ab) as the view of a gentile. See Saul Lieberman, *Greek in Jewish Palestine* (New York: Philipp Feldheim, 1965) 86; rabbinic teachers could learn to accept pious gentiles, but not to encourage them.

24. Jewish readiness to think along these lines was encouraged by the fact that the prophets had long ago predicted such a development; see Isaiah 14:1, 56:6–7, Jeremiah 16:19–20, Micah 4:2 (= Isa. 2:3), Zephaniah 3:9, Zechariah 8:21–23, Psalm 67:3.

25. Moore, *Judaism in the First Centuries of the Christian Era,* 1:233. Converts joined not the Jewish religion but the Jewish people.

26. See Victor Tcherikover, *Hellenistic Civilization and the Jews* (Philadelphia and Jerusalem: Jewish Publication Society and Magnes Press, 1961) 296–332 and 409–15, for a convenient summary.

27. Rabbinic tradition ascribed to R. Yohanan b. Zakkai a warning that destroying pagan altars could lead only to unfortunate consequences. Saul Lieberman connects this tradition to an incident reported by Philo, *Legat. ad Ga.*, 201–3 ("Palestine in the Third and Fourth Centuries," *Jewish Quarterly Review* n.s. 36 [1942] 366, n. 263), see also E. E. Urbach, "The Rabbinic Laws of Idolatry in the Second and Third Centuries in the Light of Archeological and Historical Facts," *Israel Exploration Journal* 9 (1959–60) 156.

28. A somewhat uncertain Talmudic text (*b. Berakhot* 16b) ascribes to a second-century teacher the opinion that gentiles (more particularly slaves) can properly be eulogized with the words, "a good man, a faithful man, a man supported by his own labor." For some, even this mild acknowledgment of gentile virtue was too radical a departure from previous norms ("They said to him, 'In that case, what have you left for the truly worthy?' "); see Saul Lieberman, *Greek in Jewish Palestine*, 76–77. *J. Rosh Hashanah* 1:3 57a quotes the Babylonian sage Samuel: "The One who judges Israel is the One who judges the nations . . . according to the worthy among them," that is, by their own highest standard. The text is uncertain, but this seems the best reading, the marginal comment of Ettinger and Nathansohn *(gilyon ha-Shas)* notwithstanding. (Lieberman's further comments seem to contradict themselves; *Greek in Jewish Palestine*, 84 bottom; see also Kaufmann Kohler, *Jewish Theology* [New York: Macmillan, 1918] 399.)

29. Lieberman, *Greek in Jewish Palestine*, 77.

30. This vengeful expectation—not in itself surprising—was in some tension with the attitude identified in note 19 above.

31. The most radical expression of the centrality of law to rabbinic spirituality is a *midrash* on Jeremiah 16:11 to the effect that even abandoning the Lord would be acceptable as long as the people continued to obey his Torah; see *j. Ḥagigah* 1:7 76c.

32. *B. Qiddushin* 31a, *Bava Qama* 87a, and elsewhere.

33. Under cover of this renunciation, this idea also preserves the universal Jewish conviction that the life of Judaism—the life of the commanded—is better than any other.

34. Maimonides (*Code*, Laws of Kings 8:11) makes the remarkable claim that gentiles who observe the seven Noahide laws must do so because the Torah commands them. Anyone who observes such rules simply because he has found merit in them is not to be counted among the "pious of the gentiles"; see note 12 above and note 40 below.

35. There was, however, one interesting change: As part of the general individualization and denationalization of piety that characterized Christianity from its earliest days, the threat shifted from a divine punishment at the end of this-worldly history, which seems to have been the older Jewish idea, to the notion of other-worldly eternal punishment in hell.

36. Hadrian forbade circumcision throughout the empire, an act that either

provoked or responded to (an important difference that need not be resolved here) the disastrous rebellion of Bar Kokhba. His successor Antoninus Pius exempted the Jews from this prohibition, but only with respect to their own sons. See E. M. Smallwood, "The Legislation of Hadrian and Antoninus Pius against Circumcision," *Latomus* 18 (1959) 334–47 and 20 (1961) 93–96.

37. Nonrabbinic evidence for Jewish attitudes becomes very hard to uncover as one moves into the final centuries of antiquity, but John Gager has commented that two bodies of such evidence are indeed available: the magical texts and large numbers of inscriptions. He is right, of course; space permits here only the brief reply that neither of these bodies of data offers much explicit discussion of the matter now being considered. The magical texts reflect considerable exchange of ideas and practices between Jews and others, but shed little light on the attitudes and relationships that lay behind such exchanges. Epigraphic evidence again reveals much about movement into and out of Jewish communities, but always in a fragmentary manner and rarely with much extended description of the views being studied here. Nevertheless, Gager has quite correctly indicated an important extension of the questions raised in this paper.

38. See Jeremiah 44.

39. See above, note 13.

40. For a convenient summary, see Saul Berman and Steven S. Schwarzschild, "Noachide Laws" in *Encyclopedia Judaica* (Jerusalem: Keter, 1972) 12:1189–91.

41. See *b. Yevamot* 47a.

42. A "new-born child," *b. Yevamot* 22a; no heirs, *m. Bava Batra* 3:3, 4:9; no right of inheritance, *b. Qiddushin* 17b; no obligation to mourn, Maimonides, *Code,* Laws of Mourning, 2:3.

43. *M. Oholot* 2:3, 18:6; *b. Shabbat* 15a.

44. At *b. Sanhedrin* 63b, Rav Judah is said to have quoted Rav to the effect that the Israelites at Baal Peor in the desert (Num. 25) knew perfectly well that idols have no reality, but seized on idolatry nevertheless as an excuse for acting lewdly in public. Texts such as Judith 8:18, *b. Yoma* 69b or *b. Arakhin* 32b are cited by numerous modern writers to support the view that by late antiquity idolatry had lost all attraction for Jews, but other texts, such as 2 Maccabees 12:40 or the continuation of the text just cited from *b. Sanhedrin,* suggest that exceptions to this generalization must still have caused concern; see E. Urbach, "The Rabbinic Laws of Idolatry," 154, 236–37, and 243; Mireille Hadas-Lebel, "Le paganisme à travers les sources rabbiniques des IIe et IIIe siècles", in *Aufstieg und Niedergang der Römischen Welt* II:19/2 (Berlin and New York: de Gruyter, 1979) 400; and S. Lieberman, *Hellenism in Jewish Palestine,* 116–20. Lieberman's claim that tractate *Avodah Zarah* "only records and discusses laws and precepts, but does not engage in refutations of the principles of idol worship" cannot be supported from the texts cited by him in note 8. Urbach explains that "vacillations between severity and leniency [concerning the avoidance of idolatry] . . . can only be explained by the different ways in which different [rabbis] estimated the danger to Judaism presented by any given

situation" (op. cit., 158). This is not implausible, but again it suggests that generalizations about Jews in rabbinic times being attracted to idol-worship must be offered with great caution.

45. This principle, apparently first enunciated by Cyprian of Carthage in 256 C.E. (*Epistle* 73.21), has had more application to heretics and schismatics than Jews, but it is not without implications for them as well; see the remarks of Adolf Harnack, *History of Dogma*, trans. Neil Buchanan (New York: Dover, 1961) 2:113.

46. M. Hengel, *Judaism and Hellenism*, 1:307 and 313. The voluntary self-isolation of the Jews is an important theme in Hengel's book and clearly provokes his distaste; see also pp. 152, 161, 168–69, 261, and 300. The same phenomenon receives a dramatically different evaluation from E. Urbach, "The Rabbinic Laws of Idolatry," 241–42.

47. These are my formulations, not Professor Hengel's.

Chapter 4 / Joining the Jewish People from Biblical to Modern Times

1. Ruth 1:16. The book's provenance is discussed by Edward F. Campbell, Jr. (*Ruth: A New Translation* [Anchor Bible 7: Garden City, New York: Doubleday, 1975], 23–28), who prefers a date early in the period 950 to 700 B.C.E.

2. Most recently by J. Maxwell Miller and John H. Hayes, *A History of Ancient Israel and Judah* (Philadelphia: Westminster Press, 1986) 92.

3. Some of the difficulties in reconstructing the history of Israel in the settlement period are summarized by George W. Ramsey, *The Quest for the Historical Israel* (Atlanta: John Knox Press, 1981) chapter 4. George E. Mendenhall was one of the first to argue that the formation of the people of Israel was tied to social upheavals within the Canaanite population; see for example, his *The Tenth Generation: The Origins of the Biblical Tradition* (Baltimore: Johns Hopkins University Press, 1973) 19–31. In a similar vein, but insisting on a strictly sociological as opposed to an idealistic religious revolution is Norman K. Gottwald's controversial *The Tribes of Yahweh: A Sociology of the Religion of Liberated Israel, 1250–1050* B.C.E. (Maryknoll, NY: Orbis Books, 1979), which discusses Canaanite "conversion" to Israel on pages 556–63. An apt critique of Mendenhall and Gottwald is Baruch Halpern, *The Emergence of Israel in Canaan* (Chico, CA: Scholars Press, 1983), especially chapters 5 and 12. In addition to Ruth the Moabitess, other prototypes of the social absorption of non-Israelites during this period are Rahab of Jericho (Josh. 2 and 6:22–25) and Uriah the Hittite (2 Sam. 11). The Gibeonites of Joshua 9:1–27 were not absorbed into the tribal structure of Israel but did provide religious functionaries (i.e., Temple slaves) for the worship of Israel's God. A valuable critique of Mendenhall's and Gottwald's argument that there was religious conversion in biblical times with a consideration of the related issues is Jacob Milgrom, "Religious Conversion and the Revolt Model for the Formation of Israel," *Journal of Biblical Literature* 101 (1982) 169–76; I wish to thank Rabbi Jack Bemporad for calling my attention to this study.

4. Roland de Vaux summarizes the status of the *ger* in Israelite society (*Ancient Israel* [New York: McGraw-Hill Book Company, 1961] 1:74–76), pointing out that in Judges 19:16 an Ephraimite is called a *ger* in the territory occupied by the tribe of Benjamin. He suggests that the influx of northern *gerim* into Judah toward the end of the monarchy must have hastened the assimilation of *gerim* of foreign birth and paved the way for the status of proselytes.

5. "Metics" in *The Oxford Classical Dictionary* (London: Oxford University Press, 1949) 563.

6. I Kings 8:41–43 and 2 Kings 5.

7. I Kings 18:39 is not a story of the conversion of Canaanites but the recognition by Israelites that "the Lord, He is God; the Lord, He is God."

8. E.g., Deuteronomy 29:14–15.

9. Deuteronomy 7:1–5.

10. Judges 1:19, 27–36.

11. In his magisterial study of this religious and intellectual reform, Moshe Weinfeld suggests that the Deuteronomic ban on all preexisting groups in Canaan, whether engaged in war or not, "could only have been created at the writing-desk and does not reflect any real circumstances" (*Deuteronomy and the Deuteronomic School* [London: Oxford University Press, 1972] 167). Elsewhere Weinfeld suggests that the Deuteronomic movement was responsible for a profound shift in the status of the *ger* away from that in the Priestly Code: the Priestly writers had wanted to ensure that the sanctity and purity of the holy land not be profaned by the *ger*, whereas the author of Deuteronomy did not impose any obligations of holiness on the *ger*, which was a peculiar obligation of the people of Israel (pp. 230–32). I suggest that sharpening the distinction between the Israelite and the *ger* contributed considerably to Ezra's insistence on divorcing non-Israelite wives.

12. Ezra 9:12.

13. Ezra 9:2.

14. That the attempt to force the Judahites to put away their foreign wives was not very successful is suggested by J. Maxwell Miller and John H. Hayes (*A History of Ancient Israel and Judah*, 472–74). A valuable essay on the absorption into Israel in biblical times and the emergence of formal conversion later is Shaye J. D. Cohen, "Conversion to Judaism in Historical Perspective: From Biblical History to Postbiblical Judaism," *Conservative Judaism* 36:4 (Summer 1983) 31–45.

15. Isaiah 56:3–7, cf. 19:19–24.

16. Zephaniah 3:9.

17. Note that Isaiah 56:7 assumes a plurality of national groups at the end of time: "My house shall be a house of prayer for all *peoples*."

18. On the eschatological nature of the conversion of the gentiles in biblical prophecy see Yehezkel Kaufmann, *The Babylonian Captivity and Deutero-Isaiah*, trans. Clarence W. Efroymson (New York: Union of American Hebrew Congregations, 1970) Appendix II: "Missionary Activity among the Gentiles."

19. Esther 8:17.

20. The large-scale expansion of the population of Jews in the Diaspora and Judea from the third century B.C.E. to the first century C.E. has been attributed as much to conversion as to natural increase; cf. Salo Wittmayer Baron, *A Social and Religious History of the Jews* 2d ed. (New York: Columbia University Press, 1952) 1:167–79.

21. *Jewish Antiquities,* trans. Ralph Marcus (LCL; Cambridge, MA: Harvard University Press, 1943) 7:357: "Hyrcanus also captured the Idumaean cities of Adora and Marisa, and after subduing all the Idumeans, permitted them to remain in their country so long as they had themselves circumcised and were willing to observe the laws of the Jews. And so, out of attachment to the land of their fathers, they submitted to circumcision and to making their manner of life conform in all other respects to that of the Jews. And from that time on they have continued to be Jews."

22. Josephus, *Jewish Antiquities,* 387: "In his reign of one year, with the title of Philhellene, he conferred many benefits on his country, for he made war on the Ituraeans and acquired a good part of their territory for Judaea and compelled the inhabitants, if they wished to remain in their country, to be circumcised and to live in accordance with the laws of the Jews."

23. Cf. Daniel 7:13–18, which is usually dated to the period of Antiochus IV's persecution of Judaism that triggered the uprising.

24. "On the Virtues," line 102, by F. H. Colson (LCL; Cambridge, MA: Harvard University Press, 1939) 8:225.

25. "On Rewards and Punishments," line 152 (LCL 8:409). For a discussion of Philo's view of the moral and legal status of proselytes, see Harry Austryn Wolfson, *Philo: Foundations of Religious Philosophy in Judaism, Christianity, and Islam* (Cambridge, MA: Harvard University Press, 1948) 2:355–64 and 369–74.

26. *B. Shabbat* 31a.

27. *M. Avot* 1:12.

28. Matthew 23:15. According to 10:6 and 15:24 it does not seem that Jesus and his circle were interested in making proselytes, contrary to subsequent Christian tradition represented by 28:18–20.

29. E.g., Josephus, *Against Apion,* II.281 (LCL 1:405–6.) Tacitus, *The Histories,* trans. Kenneth Wellesley (Baltimore: Penguin Books, 1964) 273–74. Remarks on Jewish proselytes in Greek and Latin sources are enumerated in the various encyclopedia articles on Jewish proselytism, such as the *Jewish Encyclopedia* (New York: Funk and Wagnalls, 1905) 10:221. On the much debated question of the social and legal status of the so-called "semi-converts" to Judaism in the Hellenistic and Roman Diaspora, see the references in note 45 below.

30. Lawrence H. Schiffman argues that these requirements were formulated while the Second Temple still stood (*Who Was a Jew? Rabbinic and Halakhic Perspectives on the Jewish-Christian Schism* [Hoboken, NJ: KTAV Publishing House, 1985]), especially chapter three. Shaye J. D. Cohen argues that only after 70 C.E. was a procedure standardized that had before been personal, spontaneous, and uncontrolled ("Conversion to Judaism," p. 41).

31. Among the most valuable works in English on proselytism are Bernard J. Bamberger, *Proselytism in the Talmudic Period* (New York: KTAV Publishing

House, 1968), part 2; William G. Braude, *Jewish Proselytizing in the First Five Centuries of the Common Era: The Age of the Tannaim and Amoraim* (Providence, RI: Brown University, 1940), chapters 5 through 10; Joseph R. Rosenbloom, *Conversion to Judaism: From the Biblical Period to the Present* (Cincinnati: Hebrew Union College Press, 1978), part 2; George Foot Moore, *Judaism in the First Centuries of the Christian Era: The Age of the Tannaim* (Cambridge, MA: Harvard University Press, 1927), vol. 1, chapter 7; Sidney B. Hoenig, "Conversion during the Talmudic Period," in *Conversion to Judaism: A History and Analysis,* ed. David Max Eichorn (New York: KTAV Publishing House, 1965). A fine overview is Samuel S. Cohon's essay, "Proselytism" in his *Essays in Jewish Theology* (Cincinnati: Hebrew Union College Press, 1987) 311–34. Included among the late, smaller tractates of the Talmud is *Masseket Gerim,* a manual of the laws relating to converts (*The Minor Tractates of the Talmud,* ed. A. Cohen [London: Soncino Press, 1965] 2.603–13).

32. David Novak proposes that before the era of the *tannaim* (70 C.E.–200 C.E.) the *ger toshav* was considered a gentile on the way to being gradually integrated into the Jewish community and that the concept of the *ger toshav* spurred the rabbis' development of the concept of the Noahide laws (*The Image of the Non-Jew in Judaism: An Historical and Constructive Study of the Noahide Laws* [New York and Toronto: Edwin Mellen Press, 1983] 14–35).

33. *B. Megillah* 17b.

34. *Genesis Rabbah* 39:14.

35. *Song of Songs Rabbah* 1:1, 10.

36. Tanhuma (Buber edition) *Lekh lekha* 6.

37. *Numbers Rabbah* 8:9; the priestly benediction is described in Numbers 6:22–27.

38. *B. Yebamot* 24b.

39. *B. Yebamot* 47a-b; cf. Ephraim E. Urbach, *The Sages: Their Concepts and Beliefs,* trans. Israel Abrahams (Jerusalem: Magnes Press, 1975) 1:547–49.

40. *B. Pesachim* 87b.

41. *B. Baba Metzia* 59b.

42. *B. Yebamot* 47b, 109b; *b. Qiddushin* 70b, *b. Niddah* 13b.

43. Bamberger, *Proselytism in the Talmudic Period,* 163–64; Braude, *Jewish Proselytizing,* 42–44.

44. Bamberger, *Proselytism in the Talmudic Period,* part 3; Braude, *Jewish Proselytizing,* chapters 2–4.

45. On the *sebomenoi* or God-fearers, who were said to have adopted some Jewish practices and beliefs without consummating a formal conversion, see Robert S. MacLennan and A. Thomas Kraabel, "The God-Fearers—A Literary and Theological Invention"; Robert F. Tannenbaum, "Jews and God-Fearers in the Holy city of Aphrodite"; and Louis H. Feldman, "The Omnipresence of the God-Fearers" in the *Biblical Archeological Review* 12:5 (September/October 1986).

46. The classic work on conversion in late antiquity is A. D. Nock, *Conversion: The Old and the New in Religion from Alexander the Great to Augustine of Hippo* (London: Oxford University Press, 1933), which occasionally touches on Jewish

proselytizing. Also see John G. Gager, *Kingdom and Community: The Social World of Early Christianity* (Englewood Cliffs, NJ: Prentice-Hall, 1975), especially his remarks on the institutional similarities between early Christianity and Diaspora Judaism (pp. 128–29) and the problem of Jewish proselytism in the Diaspora (pp. 135–40).

47. Jacob R. Marcus, *The Jew in the Medieval World: A Source Book: 315-1791* (New York: Harper and Row, 1965) 6; and Edward A. Synan, *The Popes and the Jews in the Middle Ages* (New York: Macmillan, 1965) 23–24.

48. For a Christian to convert to Judaism was apostasy, which was a form of heresy. Heresy was not only an error, but a crime for which the church could inflict its own penalties (excommunication) and for which it could invoke the power of the state to exact penalties that included torture and death; see *Encyclopedia Britannica,* 11th ed. (1910) 13:360–61. One of the most complete and influential medieval law codes, *La Siete Partidas* of Alfonso X of Castile (1260), specifies: "Where a Christian is so unfortunate as to become a Jew, we order that he shall be put to death just as if he had become a heretic. We decree that his property shall be disposed of in the same way that we stated should be done with that of heretics" (*Church, State and Jew in the Middle Ages,* ed. Robert Chazan [New York: Behrman House, 1980]) 194). That these were theoretical ideas which may not have always been enforced does not detract from their importance in determining the medieval context of conversion to Judaism.

49. That the death penalty is to be imposed for conversion from Islam to another faith is treated under the concept of apostasy (*irtidad* or *ridda*). Thus there is a *hadith* that Muhammad said, "Slay him who changes his religion" (see *"Murtadd"* in *The Shorter Encyclopedia of Islam,* ed. H.A.R. Gibb and J. H. Kramers [Leiden: E. J. Brill, 1961] 413); also Abdullah Ahmed An-Na'im, "The Islamic Law of Apostasy and Its Modern Applicability," in *Religion* 16 (1986) 210–13. I am grateful to Professor Stephen D. Ricks for calling my attention to this article.

50. On the Judaized Himyarite kingdom of southern Arabia about a century before Muhammad, see H. Z. Hirschberg, *Yisrael ba-Arav* ([The People of Israel in Arabia; Tel Aviv] Mossad Bialik, 1946) 50–72, and Bernard Lewis, *The Jews of Islam* (Princeton, NJ: Princeton University Press, 1984), note 15 on page 204.

51. The Arabic and Hebrew evidence for the conversion of the Khazars is treated in D. M. Dunlop, *The History of the Jewish Khazars* (New York: Schocken Books, 1967), chapters 5 and 6. Of value in this regard is Norman Golb and Omeljan Pritsak, *Khazarian Hebrew Documents of the Tenth Century* (Ithaca, NY: Cornell University Press, 1982).

52. Ben Zion Wacholder, "The Halakah and the Proselyting of Slaves During the Gaonic Era," *Historia Judaica* 18:2 (October 1956) 89–106, and Michael Panitz, "Conversion to Judaism in the Middle Ages: Historic Patterns and New Scenarios," *Conservative Judaism* 36:4 (Summer 1983) 48–49.

53. These clerical or aristocratic converts are described in Ben Zion Wacholder, "Attitudes toward Proselytizing in the Classical Halakah," *Historia Judaica* 20:2 (October 1958) 77–96; Ben Zion Wacholder, "Cases of Proselytizing in the Tosafist Responsa," *Jewish Quarterly Review* n.s. 51 (1961) 288–315;

Norman Golb, "A Proselyte Who Fled to Egypt," *Sefunot* 8 (1964/65) 85–104; Norman Golb, "Notes on the Conversion of European Christians to Judaism in the Eleventh Century," *Journal of Jewish Studies* 16 (1965) 69–74; J. Rosenbloom, *Conversion to Judaism*, 81; and David J. Seligson, "In the Post-Talmudic Period", in D. M. Eichorn, *Conversion to Judaism: A History and Analysis*. Histories of medieval Jewry in Christian lands usually mention one or more of these proselytes; for example, on Bodo the Deacon, see Synan, *The Popes and the Jews in the Middle Ages*, 63–64; on Bodo and also Wecilinus of Mainz, chaplain of a certain Duke Conrad, James Parkes, *The Jew in the Medieval Community* (New York: Hermon Press, 1976) 35, 39, and 55. A list of articles on these and other proselytes are contained in Johanan Arnon, *Abraham Ben Abraham: A Comprehensive Bibliography of Proselytes and Proselytism from the Ninth Century Up to Our Times* (Tel Aviv: 1969 [privately published]).

54. For a modern example of a born Christian who found his way, through visions and identification with biblical tales, to Judaism, and brought a whole community with him to Israel, see Elena Cassin, *San Nicandro: The Story of a Religious Phenomenon*, trans. Douglas West (Philadelphia: Dufour Editions, 1962).

55. *M. Bikkurim* 1:4.

56. Isadore Twersky, ed., *A Maimonides Reader* (New York: Behrman House, 1972) 475–76; Joshua Blau, *Teshuvot HaRambam* (Jerusalem: Meqitsei Nirdamin, 1960) 2:548-50 and 725-28. On Maimonides' spiritual conception of Judaism in connection with this letter, see Isadore Twersky, *Introduction to the Code of Maimonides (Mishneh Torah)* (New Haven: Yale University Press, 1980) 485–86. Maimonides' summary of the laws of conversion is found in the *Mishneh Torah, Issurei Bi'ah* (Forbidden Intercourse, in the Book of Holiness), chapters 12–14.

57. Judah Halevy, *The Kuzari: An Argument for the Faith of Israel*, trans. Hartwig Hirschfeld (New York: Schocken Books, 1964) 79.

58. Jochanan H. A. Wijnhoven, "The Zohar and the Proselyte", in *Texts and Responses, Presented to Nahum N. Glatzer on the Occasion of His Seventieth Birthday by his Students*, ed. Michael A. Fishbane and Paul R. Flohr (Leiden: E. J. Brill, 1975) 120–40.

59. Jacob Katz contrasts the positive medieval Jewish attitude to proselytism with the rather negative attitude toward it in the sixteenth and seventeenth centuries (*Exclusiveness and Tolerance: Jewish-Gentile Relations in Medieval and Modern Times* [New York: Schocken Books, 1962] 77–81 and 143–48); but Jonathan I. Israel discerns a clandestine Jewish proselytizing movement in West Europe in the sixteenth century (*European Jewry in the Age of Mercantilism, 1550–1750* [Oxford: Oxford University Press 1985] pp. 81–86).

60. In a recent study of European Jewry from the mid-sixteenth to the early eighteenth century, one scholar goes so far as to argue that Europe during this period produced "a more rounded, complete, and coherent Jewish culture" than ever before, and that a "Jewish society, indeed Jewish nationhood, as something distinct from Jewish religion, now emerged as much more definite realities than before" (Jonathan I. Israel, *European Jewry in the Age of Mercan-*

tilism, 1550–1750, 71). On the Marranos, see Michael Panitz, "Conversion to Judaism in the Middle Ages," 56 and the literature cited there.

61. On the "philo-Semitism" that manifested itself in the mid- and late seventeenth century, occasionally to the point of open conversion to Judaism, see J. Israel, *European Jewry in the Age of Mercantilism,* 224–29. On page 221 he points out that ideologies that rejected the divinity of Christ, along with other Christian religious beliefs, would be just as antagonistic to Jewish religious beliefs as the medieval church was.

62. Eva Jospe, ed., *Moses Mendelssohn: Selections from His Writings* (New York: Viking Press, 1975) 134. On Mendelssohn's view of Judaism as a religion of tolerance that does not mandate conversion of gentiles, see Alexander Altmann, *Moses Mendelssohn: A Biographical Study* (Philadelphia: Jewish Publication Society of America, 1973) 216–20, and Jacob Katz, *From Exclusiveness to Tolerance,* 172–73.

63. On the various seventeenth- to nineteenth-century converts (Johann Peter Spaeth/Moses Germanus, Alexander Voznitzin, Lord George Gordon, Warder Cresson and others), see J. Israel, *European Jewry in the Age of Mercantilism,* 227; J. Rosenbloom, *Conversion to Judaism,* 83; D. M. Eichhorn, *Conversion to Judaism,* 121–22, 126–35, 138–40; and the bibliography by Johanan Arnon in *Abraham Ben Abraham.*

64. We will not be dealing with the situation in Islamic lands of modern times.

65. Joseph Jacobs, of the Jewish Historical Society of England, was inclined, at the beginning of the twentieth century, to estimate that there were five hundred converts to Judaism a year compared to three thousand Jewish conversions to Christianity in Austria-Hungary, Russia, Germany, and the Anglo-Saxon world in the 1890s (*Jewish Encyclopedia* [New York: Funk and Wagnalls, 1905] 11:630). Reform discussions of the circumcision of proselytes can be found in the *Yearbook* of the Central Conference of American Rabbis, vol. 2 (1891–92), 66–128 and vol. 3 (1892–93), 15–19, 33–39. Efforts to found Jewish missionary societies are described in J. Rosenbloom, *Conversion to Judaism,* 132–34, and D. M. Eichhorn, *Conversion to Judaism,* 163–65.

66. The estimate of ten thousand conversions a year is from Harold I. Stern, "Gerut and the Conservative Movement: Introduction," *Conservative Judaism* 33:1 (1978) 29. In this issue of *Conservative Judaism,* Seymour Siegel treats the history of the concept of conversion to Judaism and discusses Orthodox authorities that have taken a rather positive view of it ("Gerut and the Conservative Movement: Halakhah"); Siegel calls for a sympathetic attitude to conversion and converts. Stephen C. Lerner sketches an outreach program similar to Schindler's speech of December 1978 to the Union of American Hebrew Congregations in "Gerut and the Conservative Movement: An Approach for Our Time."

67. For a recent sociological treatment, see Egon Mayer, *Love and Tradition: Marriage between Jews and Christians* (New York: Plenum Press, 1985) chapter 8 ("Your People Are My People"). On intermarriage-induced conversion, see also Steven M. Cohen, *American Modernity and Jewish Identity* (New York and

London: Tavistock Publications, 1983) 123–24. The volume *Conversion to Judaism: A History and Analysis* expresses the enthusiasm of its editor, David Max Eichhorn, for the value of conversion to Judaism and contains a number of accounts by contemporary converts, as does the issue of *Conservative Judaism* cited in the previous note.

68. David Ellenson, "The Development of Orthodox Attitudes to Conversion in the Modern Period," *Conservative Judaism* 36:4 (Summer 1983) 57–73; Robert N. Levine and David H. Ellenson, "Jewish Tradition, Contemporary Sensibilities, and Halacha: A Responsum by Rabbi David Zvi Hoffmann" in *Journal of Reform Judaism* 20:1 (Winter 1983) 49–56.

69. The Argentinian episode is described in Moshe Zemer, "The Rabbinic Ban on Conversion in Argentina," *Judaism* 37:1 (Winter 1988) 84–96. Of note are the legal fictions used by the Israeli and Argentinian rabbis to circumvent this ban. I appreciate Rabbi Zemer's providing me with an advance copy of his study.

70. See the panel discussion of Denver rabbis in the Central Conference of American Rabbis' Yearbook 96 (1986) 47–58. Dr. Stanley M. Wagner, Director of the University of Denver's Center for Judaic Studies and rabbi of Beth haMedrosh Hagodol Congregation kindly allowed me to see a preliminary draft of a responsum presenting an argument supporting the Denver conversion process with halakhic citations.

Chapter 5 / Proselytism and Exclusivity in Early Christianity

1. *Prescription against Heretics* 7.

2. *Die Mission und Ausbreitung des Christentums in den ersten Jahrhunderten* (Leipzig: J.C. Heinrichs, 1902).

3. Ramsey MacMullen, *Christianizing the Roman Empire* (New Haven: Yale University Press, 1984). Even more recently Robin Lane Fox has published a massive treatment of these issues, in part quite critical of MacMullen, in *Pagans and Christians* (New York: Knopf, 1987).

4. Cambridge: The University Press, 1965, p. 134.

5. R. L. Fox, *Pagans and Christians*, 16.

6. Rosemary Ruether, *Faith and Fratricide: The Theological Roots of Anti-Semitism* (New York: Seabury Press, 1979) 181.

7. E. P. Sanders (Philadelphia: Fortress Press, vol. 1 [1980]; vol. 2 [1981]; vol. 3 [1982]).

8. "Theological Norms and Social Perspectives in Ignatius of Antioch" (3: 30–56) and "The Problem of Self-Definition: From Sect to Church" (3: 1–15).

9. W. Schoedel, "Theological Norms," 36.

10. See in particular L. Festinger, H. W. Riecken, and S. Schachter, *When Prophecy Fails* (New York: Harper and Row, 1956), and L. Festinger, *A Theory of Cognitive Dissonance* (Stanford: Stanford University Press, 1957).

11. L. Festinger, *Theory*, 32ff.

12. L. Festinger et al., *When Prophecy Fails*, 28.

13. My own rather loose translation.

14. John Chrysostom was a Christian preacher in Antioch, the same city served earlier by Ignatius, in the 380s, under a Christian emperor. The passage appears in a series of sermons delivered against members of his own Christian congregation who were in the habit of observing the Jewish holidays and otherwise involving themselves in local synagogues. See W. A. Meeks and R. L. Wilken, *Jews and Christians in Antioch in the First Four Centuries of the Common Era* (Missoula, Montana: Scholars Press, 1978).

15. P. Berger and T. Luckmann, *The Social Construction of Reality* (New York· Anchor Books, 1967) 108.

16. Ibid., 159f.

17. R. Ruether, *Faith and Fratricide*, 181.

18. L. Coser, *The Functions of Social Conflict* (New York: Free Press, 1956) 67

Chapter 6 / Christianity, Culture, and Complications

1. William H. McNeill, *The Rise of the West: A History of the Human Community* (Chicago: University of Chicago Press, 1963).

2. Stephen Neill, *A History of Christian Missions* (Harmondsworth: Penguin Books, 1964) 220–23.

3. Philip Schaff, *America: A Sketch of its Political, Social and Religious Character* [1854] (Cambridge, Massachusetts: Harvard University Press, 1961) 94–95.

4. William R. Hutchison, *Errand to the World: American Protestant Thought and Foreign Missions* (Chicago: University of Chicago Press, 1987), chap. 5.

5. See Wilfred C. Smith, *The Meaning and Truth of Religion* (New York: Macmillan, 1962) 18–19.

6. W. Hutchison, *Errand*, especially chap. 2. Timothy L. Smith recapitulated the argument for the purity and transnational character of the missionaries' "religious" motivation in a paper on "Missions and Millennialism: The Ecumenical Vision in Evangelical Protestantism, 1800–1850," for the Evangelical Theological Society, March 11, 1985.

7. Arthur T. Pierson, *The Crisis of Missions; or, The Voice out of the Cloud* (New York: Robert Carter and Bros., 1886) 193–94.

8. Samuel Hopkins, *A Treatise on the Millennium* (Boston: Thomas and Andrews, 1793); C. C. Goen, "Jonathan Edwards: A New Departure in Eschatology," *Church History* 28 (March 1959) 25–40.

9. There is no adequate study of the resistance to missions, but see B. H. Carroll, *The Genesis of American Anti-Missionism* (Louisville: Baptist Book Concern, 1902), which chronicles a Baptist movement mainly opposed to centralization, and secondarily opposed to foreign missions.

10. W. Hutchison, *Errand*, 158–75.

11. Prudential Committee, ABCFM, "Instructions" appended to Heman Humphrey, *The Promised Land* (Boston: Samuel T. Armstrong, 1819) ix; Francis Wayland, *The Apostolic Ministry* (Rochester: Sage and Brother [sic], 1853) 19.

12. S. Neill, *Christian Missions*, 179.

13. John Tracy Ellis, *Documents of American Catholic History,* 2 vols., rev. ed (Chicago: Regnery, 1967) 1:75.

14. Ola E. Winslow, *John Eliot, Apostle to the Indians* (Boston: Houghton Mifflin, 1968) 171.

15. Rufus Anderson, "The Theory of Missions to the Heathen", in *To Advance the Gospel: Selections from the Writings of Rufus Anderson,* ed. R. Pierce Beaver (Grand Rapids: Eerdmans, 1967) 73–74.

16. R. Anderson, *Foreign Missions, Their Relations and Claims* (New York: Scribner, 1869) 97; W. Hutchison, *Errand,* 84–87.

17. Ibid., 87–90, 95–99.

18. Ralph Cooper Hutchison, "Islam and Christianity," *Atlantic Monthly* 138 (November 1926) 707–9.

19. "Christianity and Proselytism," *Atlantic Monthly* 140 (November 1927) 620–21. R. C. Hutchison, the author's father, returned to the United States in 1931 to serve as president first of Washington and Jefferson and then of Lafayette College.

20. Daniel Johnson Fleming, "If Buddhists Came to Our Town," *Christian Century* 46 (February 28, 1929) 293–94.

21. D. J. Fleming, *Whither Bound in Missions?* (New York: Association Press, 1925) 135, 122–44.

22. W. Hutchison, *Errand,* 158–75.

23. Rodger C. Bassham, *Mission Theology, 1948–1975* (South Pasadena: William Carey Library, 1979) 72–73.

24. "Notes on the Meaning of Mission(ary)," in *Planning for Mission,* ed. Thomas Wieser (New York: U.S. Conference for the World Council of Churches, 1966) 46–47.

25. W. Hutchison, *Errand,* 194–96.

26. R. Bassham, *Mission Theology,* 81.

27. Sydney E. Ahlstrom, *A Religious History of the American People* (New Haven: Yale University Press, 1972) 12.

Chapter 7 / Changes in Roman Catholic Attitudes toward Proselytism and Mission

1. *Acta Apostolicae Sedis* 11 (1919) 440–55.

2. *Rerum Ecclesiae,* ibid., 18 (1926) 65–83; *Evangelii Praecones,* ibid., 43 (1951) 497–528; *Fidei Donum,* ibid., 49 (1957) 225–48; *Princeps Pastorum,* ibid., 51 (1959) 833–64. For an overview of the contents of these encyclicals, see Rene-Pierre Millot, *Missions in the World Today* (New York: Hawthorn Books, 1961).

3. *Evangelii Praecones,* 55–60.

4. Josef Schmidlin, *Katholische Missionslehre im Grundriss* (Münster: Verlag der Aschendorffsche Bucchhandlung, 1919).

5. Freiburg: Erich Wewel Verlag, 1962.

6. The two best histories of the preparation of this document may be found in Suso Brechter, "Decree on the Church's Missionary Activity: Origin and

History of the Decree," *Commentary on the Documents of Vatican II,* ed. Herbert Vorgrimler (New York: Herder and Herder, 1969) IV: 87–111; Saverio Paventi, "Etapes de l'elaboration du texte," *L'Activité missionnaire de l'Eglise,* ed. Johannes Schuette (Paris: Editions du Cerf, 1967) 150–77.

7. The proceedings of this meeting were published as *Foundations of Mission Theology* (Maryknoll: Orbis Books, 1972).

8. Ibid., pp. 39–50.

9. Article 24; I am citing here from the edition issued by the United States Catholic Conference in 1976.

10. Ibid., art. 53.

11. The proceedings may be found in *Mission in Dialogue,* ed. Mary Motte and Joseph Lang (Maryknoll: Orbis, 1982).

12. "Study Outline on the Mission and Witness of the Church," *SIDIC* 11 (1978) no. 3.

13. To be found in the *Bulletin* of the Secretariat, no. 56 (1984) 126–41.

14. At a conference held at Union Theological Seminary in Richmond, Virginia, in 1979, the proceedings of which were published as *Christ's Lordship and Religious Pluralism* (Maryknoll: Orbis Books, 1981). The Anderson response is on pages 110–19.

15. Paul Knitter, "Roman Catholic Approaches to Other Religions: Developments and Tensions," *International Bulletin of Missionary Research* 8 (1984) 50–54; William Burrows, "Tensions in the Catholic Magisterium about Mission and Other Religions," ibid., 9 (1985) 2–4; "Mission in the Context of 'Conscientized Action' and Dialogue," *Missiology* 13 (1985) 473–86.

16. Cf. Omer Degrijze, *Going Forth: Missionary Consciousness in Third World Churches* (Maryknoll: Orbis Books, 1984).

Chapter 8 / Fundamentalists Proselytizing Jews: Incivility in Preparation for the Rapture

1. Among the best sources on the early history of fundamentalism are George M. Marsden, *Fundamentalism and American Culture* (New York: Oxford University Press, 1980); Ernest Sandeen, *The Roots of Fundamentalism* (Chicago: University of Chicago Press, 1970); and George W. Dollar, *A History of Fundamentalism in America* (Greenville, SC: Bob Jones University Press, 1973).

2. The essential doctrines are discussed at length by G. W. Dollar in *A History of Fundamentalism in America.*

3. Historians who concentrate on the 1920s controversy include Steward A. Cole, *The History of Fundamentalism* (New York: Smith, 1931), and Norman F. Furniss, *The Fundamentalist Controversy, 1918–1931* (New Haven: Yale University Press, 1954).

4. This organizational growth is documented in G. W. Dollar, *A History of Fundamentalism in America;* Joel A. Carpenter, "Fundamentalist Institutions and the Rise of Evangelical Protestantism, 1929–1942, "*Church History* 49 (1980) 62–75; and Martin E. Marty, *A Nation of Behavers* (Chicago: University of Chicago Press, 1976).

5. On the split between fundamentalists and evangelicals, see Jerry Falwell (with Ed Dobson and Ed Hindson), *The Fundamentalist Phenomenon* (Garden City, NY: Doubleday, 1981), and James D. Hunter, *American Evangelicalism: Conservative Religion and the Quandary of Modernity* (New Brunswick, NJ: Rutgers University Press, 1983).

6. J. D. Hunter, *American Evangelicalism.*

7. These issues of "boundary maintenance" in the fundamentalist community are explored more fully in Nancy T. Ammerman, *Bible Believers: Fundamentalists in the Modern World* (New Brunswick: Rutgers University Press, 1987), chapter 5.

8. Fundamentalism has often been linked with prejudice by means of a presumed "status discontent" that might produce both. For recent critiques of that connection, see John Simpson, "Moral Issues and Status Politics," in *The New Christian Right*, ed. R. Liebman and R. Wuthnow (New York: Aldine, 1983) 104–17, and M. Wood and M. Hughes, "The Moral Basis of Moral Reform: Status Discontent vs. Culture and Socialization as Explanations of Anti-pornography Social movement Adherence," *American Sociological Review* 49 (1984) 86–99.

9. This is how the organization lists itself in the *Encyclopedia of Associations* (Detroit: Gale Research Company, 1986).

10. There are, of course, many other Hebrew Christian groups. B. Z. Sobel, *Hebrew Christianity: The Thirteenth Tribe* (New York: Wiley, 1974) and Arnold G. Fruchtenbaum, *Hebrew Christianity: Its Theology, History, and Philosophy* (Washington: Canon, 1974) offer comprehensive descriptions of the range of groups that have existed in modern Christianity. Jacques Gutwirth describes a Jewish branch of the Open Door Community Church in Los Angeles ("Jews among Evangelists in Los Angeles," *Jewish Journal of Sociology* 24 [1982] 39–55). The Jews for Jesus are merely the most visible organization in this movement.

11. Steven M. Tipton, *Getting Saved from the Sixties* (Berkeley: University of California Press, 1982).

12. Will Herberg, *Protestant-Catholic-Jew* (New York: Anchor, 1960).

13. My description of the Jews for Jesus is heavily dependent on the excellent ethnography done by Juliene Gloria Lipson, "Jews for Jesus: An Anthropological Study," Ph.D. Dissertation, University of California (San Francisco: 1978).

14. Grand Rapids: Zondervan (1962). Fundamentalists are prolific writers and publishers, and each version of coming events varies a bit from the others. Among the most respected recent writers on the dispensations is Charles C. Ryrie, *Dispensationalism Today* (Chicago: Moody Press, 1965).

15. J. F. Walvoord, *Israel in Prophecy*, 115; see also Hal Lindsey (with C. C. Carlson), *The Late Great Planet Earth* (Grand Rapids: Zondervan, 1970).

16. J. Dwight Pentecost, *Things to Come* (Grand Rapids: Dunham, 1958).

17. Merrill Simon, *Jerry Falwell and the Jews* (Middle Village, NY: Jonathan David, 1984) 9.

18. M. Simon, *Jerry Falwell and the Jews*, 47.

19. For an extensive discussion of the tensions between passive waiting for

the Rapture (and thus toleration of anti-Semitism) and active support for Jews (and thus opposition to anti-Semitism), see William R. Glass, "Fundamentalism's Prophetic Vision of the Jews: The 1930s," *Jewish Social Studies* 47 (1985) 63–76.

20. James David Owen, "Premillennial Dispensationalists and the Great Depression, 1929–1939: An Analysis of Their Political, Economic and Social Thought and Action," M. A. Thesis, California State University, Dominquez Hills, 1979.

Chapter 9 / The Psychology of Proselytism

1. J. Fowler, *Stages of Faith: The Psychology of Human Development and the Quest for Meaning* (New York: Harper and Row, 1981).

2. D. F. Polish, "Contemporary Jewish Attitudes to Mission and Conversion", in *Christian Mission–Jewish Mission*, eds. M. A. Cohen and H. Croner (New York: Paulist Press, 1982) 161–62.

3. E. Erikson, *Identity: Youth and Crisis* (New York: Norton, 1968).

4. C. Stewart, *Adolescent Religion: A Developmental Study of the Religion of Youth* (New York: Abingdon, 1967).

5. R. J. Ofshe, Deposition taken in the case of Wallersheim versus Church of Scientology (October 15, 1985, document number c.332027, Superior Court of the State of California, for the County of Los Angeles). M. T. Singer, "Coming Out of the Cults," *Psychology Today* 12 (1979) 72–82.

6. See J. T. Richardson, R. B. Simmonds, and M. W. Harder, "Thought Reform and the Jewish Movement," *Youth and Society* 4 (1972) 185–200; T. Robbins and D. Anthony, "Cults, Brainwashing, and Counter-Subversion," *The Annals of the American Academy of Political and Sociological Science* (1979); and J. T. Ugerleider and K. K. Wellisch, "Coercive Persuasion (Brainwashing), Religious Cults and Deprogramming," *American Journal of Psychiatry* 136:3 (1979) 279–82.

7. H. N. Malony, "Conversion: The Sociodynamics of Change," *Theology News and Notes* 33:2 (1986) 16–19, 25.

8. B. Wilson, *Religion in Sociological Perspective* (New York: Oxford University Press, 1982) 61.

9. E. P. Bettinghaus, *Persuasive Communication* (New York: Holt, Rinehart and Winston, 1973); see pages 7 and following for this distinction between communication and persuasion.

10. D. F. Polish, "Contemporary Jewish Attitudes . . .," 166–68, for his discussion of "active" and "passive" witnessing. Polish believes that Christians and Jews can share with each other in a "passive manner" where they communicate their faiths for the sake of their own inner lives without any concern about their effect on others.

11. N. A. Bert, "Marxist Models for Christian Drama," *Religious Communication Today* 2:1 (1979) 5–9. Bert compares the "epic" and "documentary" theories of contemporary Marxist dramatists with traditional "dramatic" theater.

12. T. Scheidel, *Persuasive Speaking* (Glenview, IL: Scott, Foresman, 1967), quoted in E. P. Bettinghaus, *Persuasive Communication*, 10.

13. E. P. Bettinghaus, *Persuasive Communication*, 10.

14. W. James, *The Varieties of Religious Experience* (New York: New American Library [Mentor], 1958; originally published 1902).

15. J. F. Engel, *Contemporary Christian Communications: Its Theory and Practice* (Nashville, TN: Thomas Nelson, 1979). See pp. 15ff. for a discussion of whether all Christians should be evangelists.

16. M. E. Galper, "The Cult Phenomenon: Behavior Science Perspectives Applied to Therapy," in *Cults and the Family*, ed. F. Kaslow and M. B. Sussman (New York: Haworth Press, 1982) 142.

17. M. Yinger, *The Scientific Study of Religion* (New York: Macmillan, 1970).

18. W. Kraiss, "Fragmented Christianity," *The Vanguard* 8:2 (1986) 2.

19. E. Troeltsch, *The Social Teachings of the Christian Churches*, trans. Olive Wyon (New York: Harper and Row, 1960; originally published 1911).

20. I. Ibraham, *Black Gold and Holy War* (Nashville, TN: Thomas Nelson and Sons, 1983).

21. G. Cronkite, *Persuasion: Speech and Behavior Change* (New York: Bobbs-Merrill, 1969) 50–51.

22. Ibid., p. 5.

23. W. C. Minnich, *The Art of Persuasion* (Boston: Houghton-Mifflin, 1957) 3 (quoted in G. Cronkite, *Persuasion*, 5).

24. J. T. Richardson, "Conversion Careers," *Society* 17:3 (March–April, 1980) 47–50.

25. J. F. Engel, *Contemporary Christian Communications*, 203.

26. G. Marwell and D. R. Schmitt, "Dimensions of Compliance-Gaining Behavior: An Empirical Study," *Sociometry* 30:35 (1960) 364 (cited in G. R. Miller, "On Being Persuaded," in *Persuasion: New Directions in Theory and Research*, ed. M. E. Roloff and G. R. Miller [Beverly Hills, CA: Sage Publications, 1980] 13).

27. B. H. Raven and W. Kruglianski, "Conflict and Power," in *The Structure of Conflict*, ed. P. G. Swingle (New York: Academic Press, 1975) 177–219.

28. J. F. Engel, *Contemporary Christian Communications*, 192.

29. K. Barth and E. Brunner, *Natur und Gnade* (Zurich: Zwingli Verlag, 1935).

30. New York: Abingdon Press, 1961.

31. R. D. Winter, "The Highest Priority: Cross-Cultural Evangelism," in *Mission Trends No. 2: Evangelization*, ed. G. H. Anderson and T. F. Stransky (New York: Paulist Press, 1975) 110ff.

32. See S. Levine and N. E. Salter, "Youth and Contemporary Religious Movements: Psychological Findings," *Canadian Psychiatric Association Journal* 21 (1976) 411–20; L. L. Schwartz and F. W. Kaslow, "Religious Cults, the Individual and the Family," *Journal of Marital and Family Therapy* (April 1979) 15–26.

33. J. Lofland and R. Stark, "Becoming a World-Saver: A Theory of Conversion to a Deviant Perspective," *American Sociological Review* 30:6 (1965) 862–74.

34. R. Austin, "Empirical Adequacy of Lofland's Conversion Model," *Review of Religious Research* 18:3 (1977) 282–87.

35. J. T. Richardson, "Conversion Careers."

36. E. Erikson, *Identity.*

37. C. Stewart, *Adolescent Religion.*

38. W. Sargant, *Battle for the Mind: A Physiology of Conversion and Brainwashing* (New York: Doubleday, 1957).

39. H. N. Malony and A. A. Lovekin, *Glossolalia: Social and Psychological Perspectives on Speaking in Tongues* (New York: Oxford University Press, 1985). This volume includes a more extensive discussion of Sargant's hypothesis and reviews the literature that examines it.

40. H. N. Malony, "Conversion: The Sociodynamics of Change," 17.

Chapter 10 / Proselytizing Processes of the New Religions

1. Peter Berger, *The Sacred Canopy* (New York: Doubleday, 1967) 152.

2. See Thomas Pilarzyk, "Conversion and Alternation Processes in the Youth Culture: A Comparative Analysis of Religious Transformations," in *The Brainwashing/Deprogramming Controversy, Sociological, Psychological, Legal, and Historical Perspectives,* ed. D. Bromley and J. Richardson (New York: Edwin Mellen Press, 1950) 51–72.

3. Neil Smelser, *Theory of Collective Behavior* (Glencoe, IL: Free Press, 1963).

4. Neil Smelser, ibid.

5. See James T. Richardson, *Conversion Careers: In and Out of the New Religions* (Beverly Hills, CA: Sage Publications, 1978) and "The Active vs. Passive Convert: Paradigm for Conflict in Conversion/Recruitment Research," *Journal For the Scientific Study of Religion* 24 (1985) 163–79 for reviews of this literature.

6. See J. T. Richardson and Bruce Kilbourne, "Classical and Contemporary Applications of Brainwashing Models: A Comparison and Critique", in *The Brainwashing/Deprogramming Controversy,* 29–49, and "Psychotherapy and New Religions," *American Psychologist* 39 (1984) 243–44.

7. Frederick Bird and Bill Reimer, "Participation Rates in the New Religious Movements," *Journal for the Scientific Study of Religion* 21 (1982) 11–14; James T. Richardson, Jan Van der Lans, and Frans Derks, "Leaving and Labeling: Voluntary and Coerced Disaffiliation from New Religious Movements," in *Social Movements, Conflict and Change,* ed. K. Long and G. Lang (Greenwich, CT: JAI Press, 1986) vol. 8; and Eileen Barker, *The Making of a Moonie: Choice or Brainwashing?* (London: Basil Blackwell, 1984) 259.

8. John Clark, "Problems in Referral of Cult Members," *Journal of the National Association of Private Psychiatric Hospitals* 9 (1978) 19–21; Richard Delgado, "Religious Totalism as Slavery," *New York University Review of Law and Social Change* 9 (1979) 51–58; and Margaret Singer, "Coming Out of the Cults," *Psychology Today* 12:8 (January 1979) 72–82.

9. Eileen Barker, *The Making of a Moonie,* 94–103; David Bromley and Anson D. Shupe, Jr., *"Moonies" in America: Cult, Church, and Crusade* (Beverly Hills, CA: Sage, 1979) 169–92; Marc Galanter, "Psychological Induction into the Large-Group: Findings from a Modern Religious Sect," *American Journal of Psychiatry* 137 (1980) 1574–79: John Lofland, *Doomsday Cult* enlarged ed. (New York:

Irvington, 1977) 63–189, and "Becoming a World Saver Revisited", in *Conversion Careers*, 10–23.

10. John Lofland, *Doomsday Cult*, 66.

11. John Lofland, *Doomsday Cult*, 291–304. These efforts are also described in David Bromley and Anson D. Shupe, Jr., *"Moonies" in America*, 149–57.

12. Eileen Barker presents a more detailed and full discussion of the Moonies' methods in England and America (*The Making of a Moonie*, 94–120) and her treatment should be used to supplement this brief discussion.

13. John Lofland, "Becoming a World Saver Revisited," 10–11.

14. Eileen Barker, *The Making of a Moonie*, 112–15; M. Galanter also did research in this location.

15. M. Galanter, "Psychological Induction," 1575.

16. Eileen Barker, "Who'd Be a Moonie? A Comparative Study of Those Who Join the Unification Church in Britain," in *The Social Impact of New Religious Movements*, ed. Bryan Wilson (New York: Rose of Sharon Press, 1981) 64.

17. E. Burke Rochford, Jr., *Hare Krishna in America* (New Brunswick, NJ: Rutgers University Press, 1985) 151–52.

18. Gregory Johnson, "The Hare Krishna in San Francisco," in *The New Religious Consciousness*, ed. C. Glock and R. Bellah (Berkeley: University of California Press, 1976) 37–39; and E. Burke Rochford, Jr., *Hare Krishna in America*, 149–69.

19. See Gregory Johnson, "The Hare Krishna in San Francisco," 38, for a good analysis of the importance of involvement in temple life for eventual conversion into the group.

20. James T. Richardson and Rex Davis, "Experiential Fundamentalism: Revisions of Orthodoxy in the Jesus Movement," *Journal of the American Academy of Religion* 51 (1983) 406; and Rex Davis and J. T. Richardson, "The Organization and Functioning of the Children of God," *Sociological Analysis* 37 (1976) 334–46.

21. Eileen Barker says this about the Moonies (*The Making of a Moonie*, 259).

22. Mary W. Harder, James T. Richardson, and Robert B. Simmonds, "Jesus People," *Psychology Today* 6:7 (December, 1972) 45–50, 110–13; J. T. Richardson, Mary Stewart, and Robert Simmonds, *Organized Miracles: A Study of a Contemporary Youth, Communal, Fundamentalist Organization* (New Brunswick, NJ: Transaction Books, 1979); and J. T. Richardson and Mary Stewart, "Conversion Process Models and the Jesus Movement," in *Conversion Careers*, 24–42.

23. James T. Richardson, Mary Stewart, and Robert B. Simmonds, *Organized Miracles*, 57–58.

Conclusion: Proselytism in a Pluralistic World

1. Gabriel Marcel, *Creative Fidelity*, trans. Robert Rosthal (New York: Crossroad, 1982) 219. Marcel concludes that such service imposes "on the person I claim to convert a loathsome image of the God whose interpreter I say I am."

2. Cf. Kurt H. Wolff, ed., *The Sociology of Georg Simmel* (New York: Free Press, 1950) 402–8.

3. Cf. William Ernest Hocking, ed., *Re-Thinking Missions: A Laymen's Inquiry After One Hundred Years* (New York: Harper and Brothers, 1932).

4. Cf. *New York Times,* October 17, 1986, C17.

5. Edward A. Ross, *The Principles of Sociology* (New York: The Century Co., 1920) 164–65.

6. Walter Lippmann, *A Preface to Morals* (New York: Macmillan, 1929) 268.

Contributors

Nancy T. Ammerman is Assistant Professor of the Sociology of Religion at Emory University's Candler School of Theology and author of *Bible Believers: Fundamentalists in the Modern World*.

John G. Gager is Professor of Religion at Princeton University and author of *Moses in Greco-Roman Paganism, Kingdom and Community: The Social World of Early Christianity*, and *The Origins of Anti-Semitism: Attitudes toward Judaism in Pagan and Christian Antiquity*.

Robert Goldenberg is Associate Professor and Director of Judaic Studies and Chair of the Department of Comparative Studies at the State University of New York, Stony Brook, and author of *The Sabbath Law of Rabbi Meir*.

Frederick E. Greenspahn is Associate Professor of Judaic Studies at the University of Denver. He is the author of *Hapax Legomena in Biblical Hebrew* and has edited several books dealing with interfaith relations, including most recently *Uncivil Religion: Interreligious Hostility in America* (with Robert N. Bellah).

William R. Hutchison is Charles Warren Professor of the History of Religion in America at Harvard University. His books include *The Transcendentalist Ministers: Church Reform in the New England Renaissance, The Modernist Impulse in American Protestantism*, and *Errand to the World: American Protestant Thought and Foreign Missions*.

Benton Johnson is Professor of Sociology at the University of Oregon and author of *Functionalism in Modern Sociology: Understanding Talcott Parsons*, co-editor of *American Mosaic*, and the author of numerous articles on the sociology of religion, in particular the sociology of American religion.

Charles H. Long is Jeanette K. Watson Professor of Religion at Syracuse University. He is the author of *Alpha: The Myths of Creation* and

Significations, Signs, Symbols and Languages in the Interpretation of Religion.

H. Newton Malony, Jr., is Professor of Psychology at Fuller Theological Seminary. His most recent books include *Glossolalia: Social and Psychological Perspectives, Psychology and Religion: A Bibliography of Historical Bases for Psycho-Theological Integration,* and *Speak Up: Assertiveness for Christians.*

Martin E. Marty is the Fairfax M. Cone Distinguished Service Professor of the History of Modern Christianity at the University of Chicago and the author of many books, including most recently *Modern American Religion,* vol. 1 *The Irony of It All,* 1893–1919, and *Religion and Republic: The American Circumstance.*

James T. Richardson is Professor of Sociology at the Unviersity of Nevada, Reno. He is the co-author of *Organized Miracles: A Sociological Study of the Jesus Movement* and has edited *Conversion Careers: In and Out of the New Religions, The Brainwashing/De-Programming Controversy: Sociological, Psychological, Legal and Historical Perspectives* (with David Bromley), and *Money and Power in the New Religions.*

Robert J. Schreiter is Professor of Theology at the Catholic Theological Union in Chicago and author of *Constructing Local Theologies.* He has also edited *The Schillebeeckx Reader.*

Robert M. Seltzer is Professor of Jewish History at Hunter College and the Graduate School of City University of New York and author of *Jewish People, Jewish Thought.*